# Old English

*Old English* provides a clear linguistic introduction to English between the fifth century and the Norman invasion in 1066. Tailored to suit the needs of individual course modules, it assumes no prior knowledge of the subject, and presents the basic facts in a straightforward manner, making it the ideal beginners' text. Students are guided step-by-step through the main characteristics and developments of English during that period, aided by concise chapter summaries, suggestions for further reading, and a comprehensive glossary. Each chapter is accompanied by an engaging set of exercises and discussion questions based on authentic Anglo-Saxon texts, encouraging students to consolidate their learning, and providing essential self-study material. The book is accompanied by a companion website (www.cambridge.org/Smith), featuring solutions to the exercises and useful additional resources. Providing essential knowledge and skills for those embarking on the study of Old English, it is set to become the leading introduction to the subject.

JEREMY J. SMITH is Professor of English Philology in the Department of English Language at the University of Glasgow. His recent publications include *Sound Change and the History of English* (2007), *Essentials of Early English* (second edition, 2005) and *An Introduction to Middle English* (with S. Horobin, 2002).

# Cambridge Introductions to the English Language

*Cambridge Introductions to the English Language* is a series of accessible undergraduate textbooks on the key topics encountered in the study of the English language. Tailored to suit the needs of individual taught course modules, each book is written by an author with extensive experience of teaching the topic to undergraduates. The books assume no prior subject knowledge, and present the basic facts in a clear and straightforward manner, making them ideal for beginners. They are designed to be maximally reader-friendly, with chapter summaries, glossaries and suggestions for further reading. Extensive exercises and discussion questions are included, encouraging students to consolidate and develop their learning, and providing essential homework material. A website accompanies each book, featuring solutions to the exercises and useful additional resources. Set to become the leading introductions to the field, books in this series provide the essential knowledge and skills for those embarking on English Language studies.

### Books in the series

*The Sound Structure of English* Chris McCully

*Old English* Jeremy J. Smith

# Old English

## A Linguistic Introduction

Jeremy J. Smith

 CAMBRIDGE
UNIVERSITY PRESS

CAMBRIDGE UNIVERSITY PRESS
Cambridge, New York, Melbourne, Madrid, Cape Town, Singapore,
São Paulo, Delhi

Cambridge University Press
The Edinburgh Building, Cambridge CB2 8RU, UK

Published in the United States of America by Cambridge University Press,
New York

www.cambridge.org
Information on this title: www.cambridge.org/9780521685696

First published 2009

Printed in the United Kingdom at the University Press, Cambridge

*A catalogue record for this publication is available from the British Library*

*Library of Congress Cataloguing in Publication data*
Smith, J. J. (Jeremy J.)
Old English : a linguistic introduction / Jeremy J. Smith.
    p.   cm. – (Cambridge introductions to the English language)
Includes bibliographical references.
ISBN 978-0-521-86677-4
1. English language – Old English, ca. 450-1100.   I. Title.   II. Series.
PE123.S65   2009
429–dc22

                                                          2008053265

ISBN 978-0-521-86677-4 hardback
ISBN 978-0-521-68569-6 paperback

For Amy

# Contents

# Figures

# Preface

This book is designed for the use of undergraduate and postgraduate students who wish to understand the linguistic structure of Old English. It is designed as a bridge between elementary primers (e.g. Hough and Corbett 2006, Hogg 2002, the OE sections of Smith 2005, and classic and still useful outlines such as Sweet/Davis 1953) and more advanced discursive works (e.g. Lass 1994) and OE grammars (e.g. Campbell 1959, Hogg 1992). I envisage the book being used, at a fairly early stage, as part of a general programme in English historical linguistics or (it is hoped) wider Germanic philology.

This book was commissioned some time ago, and since I undertook it other publications have appeared which cover some of the same ground. Perhaps the most important of these, and certainly the best, is McCully and Hilles 2005, which is designed with a similar audience in mind. However, I see my book as complementary to such works; it derives its orientation from 'traditional' philology (though drawing, of course, on more recent scholarship), and it is laid out as a resource rather than in units. Although, happily, old antagonisms between traditional approaches and more 'modern' linguistics are now receding, there is maybe a place for an approach which tries to synthesise long-established and more recent scholarship, accessible to scholars of both backgrounds.

Materials in this book derive from courses I have taught in English historical linguistics over the last twenty years, and I am most grateful to undergraduate and postgraduate students and colleagues who have used and commented on them. In particular, I am grateful to Simon Horobin, who read through the first draft of the book and made many suggestions for improvements. I am also very grateful to Helen Barton of Cambridge University Press, for her tolerance and understanding in putting up with a dilatory and distracted author, to Rosina Di Marzo, to Jill Lake for her skilful and tactful copy-editing, and to Philip Riley for his meticulous proofreading.

Jeremy Smith

# Notations and Conventions

EModE    Early Modern English
EWS      Early West Saxon
IPA      International Phonetic Association
LWS      Late West Saxon
ME       Middle English
ModE     Modern English
OE       Old English
PDE      Present-Day English

<..>     graphemic transcription
<<..>>   allographic/graphetic transcription
/../     phonemic transcription
[..]     allophonic/phonetic transcription

>        goes to, becomes, is realised as
<        comes from
$        syllable boundary
#        morpheme boundary
Ø        zero
/        in the environment: X > Y/A_B = 'X becomes Y in the environment
         of a preceding A and a following B, i.e. AXB becomes AYB.'

V        vowel
C        consonant
:        indicates full length of preceding vowel (i.e. long vowel)
ˈ        main accentual stress or pitch prominence on following syllable

In the following list of phonetic symbols, based on those used by the International Phonetic Association, pronunciations are as in 'Received Pronunciation' (RP), the prestigious accent used in England, 'General American' (GenAm), the reference accent commonly used for US English, or sometimes 'Standard Scottish English' (SSE), the prestigious accent used in Scotland. Occasionally reference is made to other languages, e.g. French, German. For a full account of IPA usage, see the *Handbook of the International Phonetic Association* (Cambridge: Cambridge University Press, 1999).

| | |
|---|---|
| a | front open unrounded vowel, as in CAT (RP, GenAm, SSE) |
| æ | front unrounded vowel between open and mid-open, as in some RP pronunciations of CAT |
| ɑ | back unrounded vowel, as in BATH (RP), PALM (GenAm) |
| ɒ | back rounded vowel, as in CLOTH (RP) |
| b | voiced bilabial plosive, as in BEE |
| β | voiceless bilabial fricative, as in BLAVA 'blue' (Catalan) |
| ç | voiceless palatal fricative, as in ICH 'I' (German) |
| ɔ | back mid-open rounded vowel, as in THOUGHT (RP, GenAm) |
| d | voiced alveolar plosive, as in DEEP |
| ð | voiced dental fricative, as in THOSE |
| e | front mid-close unrounded vowel, as in FACE (SSE) |
| ɜ | unrounded central vowel, as in NURSE (RP), NURSE (GenAm) |
| ɛ | front mid-open unrounded vowel, as in DRESS (GenAm), PÈRE (French) |
| f | voiceless labio-dental fricative, as in FEE |
| g | voiced velar plosive, as in GOAT |
| h | voiceless glottal fricative, as in HOT |
| i | front close unrounded vowel, as in FLEECE (RP, GenAm) |
| ɪ | centralised unrounded mid-close vowel, as in KIT (RP, GenAm) |
| j | palatal unrounded semi-vowel, as in YACHT |
| k | voiceless velar plosive, as in CLOTH |
| l | voiced alveolar lateral continuant, as in LOT |
| ł | voiced alveolar lateral continuant with velarisation, as in ILL (RP) |
| m | voiced bilabial nasal, as in MOUTH |
| n | voiced alveolar nasal, as in NURSE |
| ŋ | voiced velar nasal, and in THING (RP) |
| o | back mid-close rounded vowel, as in GOAT (GenAm, SSE) |
| ø | front mid-close rounded vowel, as in PEU 'few' (French) |
| œ | front mid-open rounded vowel, as in PEUR 'fear' (French) |
| θ | voiceless dental fricative, as in THING |
| p | voiceless bilabial plosive, as in PALM |
| r | voiced alveolar trill, as in RED (SSE) |
| s | voiceless alveolar fricative, as in SING |
| ʃ | voiceless palato-alveolar fricative, as in SHIP |
| t | voiceless alveolar plosive, as in TAP |
| u | back close rounded vowel, as in GOOSE |
| ʊ | centralised rounded mid-close vowel, as in FOOT (RP, GenAm) |
| v | voiced labio-dental fricative, as in VIEW |
| ʌ | back mid-open unrounded vowel, as in STRUT (RP, GenAm) |
| w | labial-velar semi-vowel, as in WEATHER |
| ʍ | voiceless labial-velar fricative, as in WHETHER (SSE) |

x    voiceless velar fricative, as in LO<u>CH</u> (SSE)

y    front close rounded vowel, as in <u>TU</u> 'you (sg)' (French)

ʏ    centralised rounded mid-close vowel, as in F<u>OO</u>T (SSE)

ɣ    voiced velar fricative, as in AU<u>GE</u> 'eye' (German)

3    voiced palato-alveolar fricative, as in MEA<u>S</u>URE

z    voiced alveolar plosive, as in <u>Z</u>OO

# CHAPTER 1

# About Old English

## In this chapter …

This chapter explains the purpose of this book, and how to use it. We look at the origins of Old English and how it developed from its ancestor, Proto-Germanic. We also look at the evidence for Old English, which derives for the most part from Anglo-Saxon manuscripts.

### Contents

## 1.1 **The purpose of this book**

This book is intended for undergraduate students, and some postgraduates, who are working on the history of the English language and/or Old English literature and who wish to develop a comprehensive understanding of the language of the Anglo-Saxons, i.e. *Old English* (hence OE), enabling them to proceed to more advanced study in English historical linguistics.

There are many excellent modern introductory books on OE, but most focus on the material needed for a basic literary understanding of the poetry and prose of the period, or have other limited goals. This book is rather different, and is designed to complement such approaches: it is designed to equip students with a secure grasp of OE linguistic structure. It is hoped that students who work through this book will not only have acquired an understanding of the basic features of OE but also will be able to engage with some of the fascinating textual and linguistic problems with which this form of English presents us.

1

## 1.2 **How to use this book**

There is no single correct way to use this book. Most readers will probably be studying with teachers, all of whom will have their own ideas about what is appropriate for their own institution. However, some readers will be working on their own, and for them suggestions for further reading are offered as part of *Appendix 2*, at the back of the book.

It is envisaged that most students will be using the book alongside a collection of OE texts, moving between text and discussion; it is important that anyone seeking to understand how OE works linguistically should spend a good deal of time reading OE. A small collection of illustrative texts, many of them not often printed in standard readers, has been included as *Appendix 1*.

This book is organised as follows. In chapter 1 I give a broad-brush account of OE: its historical setting and how we know about it. Chapter 2 provides an outline of linguistic terminology used generally in the book, applicable both to OE and to Present-Day English (PDE), and chapter 3 gives a detailed linguistic analysis of a series of short OE texts. The student who has worked through these three chapters will have acquired a basic understanding of OE structure.

From chapter 4 onwards these linguistic characteristics are studied in much greater depth, in terms of *levels of language*, namely *meaning (semantics)*, *lexicon*, *grammar*, and *transmission (speech* and *writing)*. These levels of language are related as follows: meaning is expressed through the lexicon and grammar of a language; the lexicon (vocabulary) of a language is made up of the words it uses; the grammar of a language is to do with how words are put together (its *morphology*) or relate to one another (its *syntax*). In turn, the grammar and lexicon of a language are transmitted from speaker to speaker primarily through speech, and secondarily – a comparatively recent development – through writing. Chapter 4 deals with spellings and sounds, chapter 5 with the lexicon, chapter 6 with syntax, and chapter 7 with inflexional morphology.

The various levels of language are presented in two ways in these four chapters. First, they are described *synchronically*; that is, the systemic features (or *rules*) of the language are described with reference to a particular point in time and space. The form of OE which is described in this way is that which is traditionally dated to the time of Alfred, King of Wessex, i.e. Early West Saxon (EWS) of the ninth century AD; this form of the language is adopted as a convenient reference-point for later use. Second, this EWS usage is placed in relation to two contexts: *diachronic* ('through time'), in which it is compared to earlier and later states of the language, including earlier varieties of Germanic, and *diatopic* ('through space'), that is, in relation to forms of OE from other parts of the country.

It is important to realise that the adoption of EWS as a reference-point is a matter of convenience for modern readers. As we shall see, OE has come down to us in many forms; indeed most material survives in that variety known as Late West Saxon (LWS), whose relationship with EWS is not straightforward. However, the adoption of EWS as a point of departure for description gives a reference-point for further study. The student who has worked through these chapters should have a broader grasp of OE, sufficient to engage with advanced topics in English historical linguistics.

The book finishes with a number of resources to support the reader's learning. *Appendix 1* offers a selection of texts, some of which are discussed in the course of the book, but all of which will repay close study. *Appendix 2* poses some general discussion questions to work on, and a substantial 'further reading' section to enhance all areas of study covered in the book. A *Glossary of Old English–Present-Day English*, a *Glossary of Key Terms*, *References* and a thematic *Index* complete this section.

## 1.3 The origins of English

The English language belongs to a large family of related languages whose native speakers now occupy wide swathes of the world, notably Europe, the Indian sub-continent and the Americas: the *Indo-European language-family*. Other modern Indo-European languages include, for example, Russian, Hindi, Albanian, French, German and Scottish Gaelic. All Indo-European languages descend from a common ancestor, *Proto-Indo-European*, which – some scholars argue, controversially – was spoken in what are now the steppes of southern Russia and the Ukraine, perhaps in the fourth or third millennium BC.

One group of Indo-European languages, the *Germanic* languages, emerged in the first millennium BC in northern Europe. The speakers of what were to become the Germanic languages seem to have originated, possibly in the fifth and fourth centuries BC, in what has been referred to as 'that bottleneck of the Baltic which is constituted by present-day Denmark and southern Sweden' (Haugen 1976: 100). In the sixth century AD, the writer Jordanes, probably himself of Germanic origin, though writing in Latin, referred to Scandinavia as *vagina gentium*, 'a womb of peoples', and this description – if extended to the north of Germany between the rivers Weser and Oder – seems to be an accurate one, even though it should be recognised that Jordanes was referring to events which took place perhaps a thousand years before he was born.

From this area of origin the Germanic peoples spread south and east; their migration to the west was constrained by resistance from first the Celtic peoples and subsequently the Roman Empire. Antagonism between the Germanic peoples and the other groups they encountered was not consistent, warfare alternating with more peaceful contacts through trade and other forms of cultural exchange. Towards the end of the imperial period, the Romans took to hiring large numbers of Germanic mercenaries as auxiliary troops; many of the great generals of the late Roman period, such as Stilicho, were of Germanic origin.

The language spoken by the first identifiable Germanic peoples was *Proto-Germanic*, which is the presumed common ancestor of all the modern Germanic languages. Proto-Germanic, like all natural languages, cannot have been homogeneous, and it is likely that the differences between its dialects – which subsequently developed into distinct languages – were present from the outset. Records of Proto-Germanic do not survive. This proto-variety itself eventually split into three further groups, commonly referred to as *East*, *North* and *West Germanic*. Most modern scholars are of the opinion that an initial split led to the emergence of two proto-languages, *Proto-East Germanic* on the one hand, and *Proto-North-West Germanic* on the other. Subsequently, it is held that two further proto-languages emerged from the latter: *Proto-North Germanic*, the common ancestor of Present-Day Norwegian, Danish, Swedish, Icelandic and Faroese, and *Proto-West Germanic*, the common ancestor of Present-Day German, Dutch, Frisian, Afrikaans and English.

It is usually held that English emerged from the other Germanic usages in the first three centuries AD, deriving from a group of dialects on the shores of the North Sea with common characteristics distinct from the other West Germanic usages. It is usual to refer to this group of dialects either as *North Sea Germanic* or as *Ingvaeonic*, the latter being derived from the Roman term for the tribes who lived along the North Sea coasts. There is considerable controversy about what is meant by an Ingvaeonic language; most scholars hold that core Ingvaeonic languages are English and Frisian, with Old Saxon as another possible – if peripheral – member of the group.

A diagram illustrating the relationship between the principal varieties of Indo-European, and of the Germanic languages in relation to those varieties, appears as Figure 1.1. The lines which connect the various nodes summarise periods of considerable complexity, representing times when different languages were in the process of divergence; whereas the nodes represent *proto-languages*, the lines represent *pre-languages*. Thus, for instance, we might refer to Proto-Germanic (a node) as a common ancestor of the Germanic languages, but we might refer to *pre-English* when we wish to

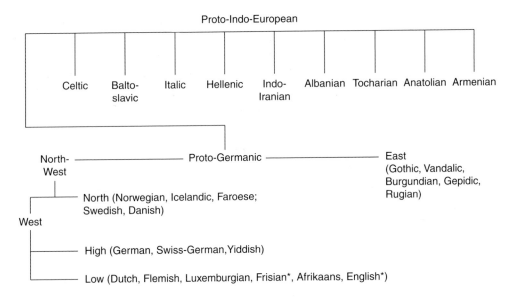

Proto-Indo-European

Celtic    Balto-slavic    Italic    Hellenic    Indo-Iranian    Albanian    Tocharian    Anatolian    Armenian

North-West —— Proto-Germanic —— East (Gothic, Vandalic, Burgundian, Gepidic, Rugian)

North (Norwegian, Icelandic, Faroese; Swedish, Danish)

West

High (German, Swiss-German, Yiddish)

Low (Dutch, Flemish, Luxemburgian, Frisian*, Afrikaans, English*)

\* Member of Ingvaeonic group of languages

Figure 1.1 The Indo-European family of languages, with special reference to Germanic

refer to the period of divergence which resulted in the appearance of what may reasonably be considered a language distinct from other varieties of Germanic.

Varieties of West Germanic were brought to Britain in the fifth century AD by the Angles and Saxons, invaders from what are now northern Germany and southern Denmark. These tribes took over from the retreating Roman Empire; the varieties they spoke combined to create a new language, OE. OE was eventually used over much of the old Roman province, from the English Channel into what are now the Lowlands of Scotland.

The Anglo-Saxons displaced the earlier inhabitants of Britain, the Romano-Britons. These people, who formed the bulk of the population of Roman Britain, spoke British, a variety of another Indo-European language-family known as Celtic; a descendant of British, Welsh, is now spoken only in the western part of the British mainland. Other varieties of Celtic, such as Scottish Gaelic, developed in the northern parts of Britain; Irish Gaelic emerged in Ireland.

The English of the period between the invasion of the Angles and Saxons (sometimes known as the *Adventus Saxonum*) and the Norman Conquest of 1066 AD is generally referred to as *Old English* (OE). OE is also sometimes referred to as *Anglo-Saxon* after the peoples who used it, though this term is used comparatively rarely by modern scholars.

OE is the earliest form of English. It may be distinguished from *Middle English* (ME), the form of the language spoken and written after *c.* 1100, and from *Modern English* (ModE), which is the term used to refer to English after *c.*1500, including *Present-Day English* (PDE). The OE period thus corresponds roughly to the period between the arrival of Germanic tribes in Britain in the middle of the fifth century AD and the Norman Conquest of 1066, though OE texts continued to be copied after 1066.

Since OE is closer in date to Proto-West Germanic than is PDE, it is, as we shall see, rather more like other West Germanic varieties. Contact with other languages from the end of the OE period onwards, notably with Old Norse (the language of the Viking invaders, early varieties of Norwegian and Danish) and with varieties of French, affected the history of English in a profound way, and caused it to diverge markedly from the other West Germanic languages.

Of course, it is important to realise that these transitions were gradual ones. OE gradually emerged, in Britain, through the interaction of West Germanic varieties spoken by the invaders. And OE did not become ME on the day that William the Conqueror landed; Anglo-Saxon texts continued to be copied, in a form of English which is recognisably OE, for at least a century after 1066. But it is generally accepted that there are certain common characteristics of OE which distinguish it from other language-states. The purpose of this book is to equip readers with an understanding of these common characteristics, enabling them to engage with more advanced work in English historical linguistics in general and in OE studies in particular.

## 1.4 Evidence for Old English

How has this material come down to us? Primarily, we depend on the (comparatively) fragmentary written records which have survived. A small amount of written OE survives in inscriptions carved on stone, metal and bone. This material includes some of the oldest texts known to us, for example, the phrases and short poem carved on the tiny *Franks Casket*, dating from the eighth century AD, which may be seen in the British Museum, or the poem carved on the massive stone *Ruthwell Cross*, which may still be seen near where it was erected, probably in the seventh/eighth century AD, overlooking the Solway Firth in what are now the Scottish Borders. Both the Ruthwell Cross and Franks Casket inscriptions were made in *runes*, an alternative to the Latin alphabet which was used for both ritual and more mundane communication in several varieties of Germanic.

However, most OE has come down to us in manuscripts, written by scribes on pieces of prepared skin known as parchment (see Ker 1957 for details, and Roberts 2005 for lavish illustrations). Some of these manuscripts, such as charters and other documents, consist of single sheets of parchment; other manuscripts form *codices*, or manuscript books. OE *prose* is fairly well attested, though many texts were copied at the very end of the period and in the two centuries immediately after the Norman Conquest. Major texts include *The Anglo-Saxon Chronicle,* which seems to have been begun in the ninth century and which survives in several copies, including a famous version made after the Conquest (the *Peterborough Chronicle*), and the prose sermons of Ælfric and Wulfstan, which date from the end of the Anglo-Saxon period and which continued to be copied and plagiarised by scribes well into the twelfth century. Almost all OE *poetry*, however, survives in just four major manuscripts dating from the end of the tenth century: *The Exeter Book* (which has been at Exeter Cathedral since Anglo-Saxon times), *The Vercelli Book* (which was left at a north Italian monastery, probably by an Anglo-Saxon pilgrim travelling to Rome, some time in the eleventh century), *The Junius Manuscript*, now in the Bodleian Library in Oxford, and *The Beowulf Manuscript*, now in the British Library in London.

It will be clear from this account that the direct evidence for OE is partial. The texts are few in comparison with those which survive from later in the history of the language, illustrating the usages of a few regional centres at a few points during the six centuries of the Anglo-Saxon period. Moreover – of course – no direct evidence exists for a whole level of language: speech. There are, obviously, no sound-recordings from the OE period, and scholars can only reconstruct the speech-patterns of the Anglo-Saxon period by the forensic analysis of these writings – the commonly used term is *witnesses*, an apt analogy – and by means of the method known as *linguistic reconstruction*, drawing upon the evidence of later states of the language and making comparisons with other languages.

Linguistic reconstruction was developed in the eighteenth and nineteenth centuries for the purposes of recovering the prehistory of languages. Sir William Jones (1746–1794) and others noticed the similarities between languages such as Sanskrit, Latin and English, and deduced that these similarities came from a common ancestor which had not been recorded in written form. Reconstruction of this common ancestor depends on the analysis of such similarities. Reconstruction also enables scholars to go beyond the evidence supplied by the (frequently) fragmentary pieces of primary sources of old languages or of older forms of languages to offer more comprehensive descriptions.

Linguistic reconstruction involves two procedures: *comparative* and *internal* reconstruction. Comparative reconstruction involves, as its name suggests, comparing distinct languages, or varieties of the same language, in order to work out the structure of the common ancestor language or variety. Internal reconstruction involves analysing what is termed *paradigmatic variation* within a single language or variety.

The two procedures are complementary, and can be illustrated from the history of English and related Germanic dialects. In OE, the verb **cēosan** 'choose' (infinitive) has the following 'principal parts', from which all other parts of the *'paradigm'* of the verb can be generated: **cēas** (3rd person preterite singular), **curon** (preterite plural), **(ge)coren** (past participle). As is suggested by the PDE pronunciation, **c** in **cēosan** was pronounced [tʃ] in OE; however, the evidence also suggests that **c** was pronounced as [k] in **curon**, **(ge)coren**. Internal reconstruction would suggest that [k] and [tʃ] in these words go back to a common ancestor. The evidence of other items in OE suggests that this common ancestor was [k].

This suggestion is supported if the complementary approach, comparative reconstruction, is used. In comparative terms, OE is closely related to other Germanic languages for which written records survive, such as Old Norse and Gothic, which are regarded as *cognate* languages (the word 'cognate' derives from Latin **cognātus**, literally 'born together'); thus OE, Old Norse and Gothic are seen as deriving from a common ancestor, and closely related. The Old Norse cognate form for **cēosan** is **kjōsa**, and the Gothic cognate is **kiusan**, and in both cases the evidence suggests that **k** was pronounced [k]. It seems likely, therefore, that [tʃ] in **cēosan** is an innovation in OE, derived from an earlier *[k] (it is conventional to flag reconstructed forms with an asterisk, *).[1]

Linguistic reconstruction was one of the great intellectual advances of the nineteenth century, relating to similar developments in, for example, textual criticism of the Bible and (most spectacularly) the Darwinian insights as to the origin of species, and it has shown its value for historians of the language on numerous occasions. But it is important to be aware of its limitations. The reconstructed form *[k] is of course an abstraction; we have no historically attested information as to how precisely it was pronounced, as we have for present-day languages using the equipment of a modern phonetics laboratory. Thus it is not possible, using reconstruction, to be absolutely certain as to what this reconstructed form sounded like. A pronunciation [k] is therefore a 'reasonable hypothesis' rather than an absolutely proven fact.

Moreover, the whole process of reconstruction depends on the adoption of a particular model of linguistic evolution: the so-called *tree-model*, whereby cognate languages and forms descend from a common ancestor. Such diagrams are useful, but their limitations need to be recognised. The tree-model is a nineteenth-century invention, clearly relating to the phylogenetic tree of biological evolution. However, linguistic evolution differs from biological evolution in that languages and varieties can acquire characteristics through contact with other languages and varieties, e.g. so-called *borrowing* of vocabulary; and this fact makes the tree-model problematic.

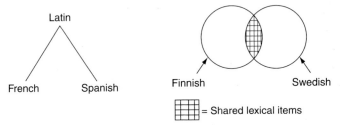

= Shared lexical items

French and Spanish are both descended from Latin. Finnish and Swedish are genetically unrelated – Finnish is a non-Indo-European language – but there are loanwords in Finnish from Swedish deriving from contact between geographical neighbours.

Figure 1.2 Trees and waves

Nineteenth-century scholars were of course well aware of this difficulty, and developed a supplementary *wave-model* to accommodate the phenomenon of contact. (See Figure 1.2 for a simplified comparison between a tree-model and a wave-model of language relationships.)

Despite these limitations, it remains clear that reconstruction takes on a primary role in historical linguistics when dealing with the more distant past, when the sources of evidence become scarcer and more alien as time-distance increases. In later chapters, reconstructive techniques will underpin a good deal of the discussion.

At this point, given that some technical terms have already been used, it is perhaps worth raising the question of *descriptive terminology*. Without using descriptive terms, any discussion about language is impossible. Chapter 2 offers an outline of the terminology used in this book, and applies it to both OE and PDE.

## Note

1. It should be observed that although Gothic and Old Norse are cognate with OE, their records are not contemporary. The major Gothic text, the Biblical translation of Bishop Ulfilas (*c.*311–383 AD), survives only in manuscripts dating from *c.* 500 AD and thus predates OE written records by several centuries, while the bulk of Old Norse materials, notably those written in Old Icelandic, date from the twelfth and thirteenth centuries, and are thus contemporary with early ME. Gothic therefore provides us with information about a comparatively archaic form of Germanic, while Old Norse is in some ways more 'advanced'. For this reason, Gothic in particular is frequently cited for comparative purposes in this book, especially in the last four chapters.

## Key terms introduced in this chapter
Old English
Middle English
Modern English
Present-Day English

Early West Saxon
Late West Saxon
Germanic (Proto-Germanic, East/North/West Germanic, North Sea Germanic)
semantics (meaning)
lexicon (vocabulary)
grammar (morphology, syntax)
transmission (speech, writing)
proto-language
pre-language
synchronic
diachronic
diatopic
linguistic reconstruction (comparative, internal)

# CHAPTER 2

# Describing Language

## In this chapter...

This chapter equips the reader with the terms needed to describe Old English sounds, writing-systems, grammar and vocabulary. We look at how these terms can be used in the description of some example words and sentences.

**Contents**

## 2.1 Introduction

Linguistics, the academic discipline which seeks to understand language, has developed its own descriptive and technical terminology, and this terminology has already been used at points in chapter 1. This chapter is designed to give students an outline of the terminology needed for the description and discussion of OE. The terminology used is that which is in very common agreed use. Students may also wish to consult the *Glossary of Key Terms*, where definitions of notions and concepts are collected.

## 2.2 Spellings and sounds: basic terminology

English has been transmitted for the last 1500 years in two ways: by speech, which – until mechanical and electronic recording was invented – was not recorded directly and was thus transient, and through writing, which is comparatively permanent. Speech and writing are both methods of transmission, and in that sense they map onto the 'same' grammatical and lexical structures, but the distinction between transience and permanence means that the two modes of transmission are likely to diverge in important ways. The mapping of sound onto symbol is not after all a natural one: for instance, the letter (or *graph*) <w> maps onto the sound [w] for an English speaker, but onto the sound [v] for a German. There is, in short, nothing intrinsically sound-symbolic about a letter; communities have simply agreed, as they do when assigning values to money (coins, paper), to assign sound-values to particular symbols.

In classical times, writers such as Donatus (fourth century AD) and Priscian (sixth century AD) developed the 'doctrine of *littera*' to express the relationship between spellings and sounds, and this doctrine still underpins traditional ways of teaching children to read. According to this doctrine, distinctions were made between *figura* (symbol), *potestas* (sound-equivalent) and *nomen* (name of the letter), with *littera* (letter) as the term to describe the combination of the three.

More recently, linguists have developed more sophisticated notions and approaches. First, a special alphabet for representing sounds with greater delicacy than the standard English alphabet has been developed: the International Phonetic Alphabet or IPA. Secondly, linguists have developed a four-fold system of definition which allows for distinctions between underlying form and contextual realisation: *phonemes* and *allophones*, *graphemes* and *allographs*. These terms may be defined as follows:

*phoneme*: either the smallest speech-unit that distinguishes one word from another in terms of meaning, or the prototypical sound being aimed at by speakers within a speech community. Replacement of one phoneme by another changes the meaning of the word in which it occurs; thus /a/ and /ɔ/ are distinct phonemes, illustrated by the pair /pat, pɔt/ 'pat, pot'. It is conventional to place phonemes in slash brackets: /../.

*allophone*: the realisation of the phoneme in speech. Replacement of one allophone with another realisation of the same phoneme does not change the meaning of the word in which it occurs; thus [l] and [ł] are allophones of the phoneme /l/. It is conventional to place allophones in square brackets: [..].

*grapheme*: the written language equivalent of the phoneme, i.e. the symbolic unit being aimed at by the scribe. Replacement of one grapheme by another changes the meaning of the word in which it occurs; thus <a> and <o> are distinct graphemes, illustrated by the pair <pat>, <pot>. It is conventional to place graphemes in angle brackets: <..>.

*allograph*: the realisation of the grapheme in writing. Replacement of one allograph by another realisation of the same grapheme does not change the meaning of the word; thus <<a, *a*, a, **a**>> are all allographs of the grapheme <a>. There seems to be no accepted notation, distinct from that used for the grapheme, for signalling allographs. Although allographic distinctions will not often be referred to in this book, I propose to use double angle-brackets to represent them: <<..>>.

Broadly speaking, written languages are either *phonographic*, where there is a mapping (however conventional) between grapheme and phoneme, or *logographic*, where there is a mapping between a conventional symbol and a word. The boundary between these different systems is of course not clear-cut. Towards the logographic end of the scale is Chinese, whose conventionalised characters derive ultimately from pictorial representations of certain key concrete concepts, though this practice was rapidly modified to deal with more abstract notions. PDE, even with its various conventionalisations, is in comparison broadly phonographic; OE writing systems were – in origin at least – even more so.

In an ideal phonographic system, phonemes map onto graphemes; allophonic representation in a writing-system would be uneconomical and communicatively inefficient. Of course, as in all human institutions, ideal phonographic systems do not exist; since they are designed to give permanence to something as dynamic and ever-changing as human language, historical residualisms and conventionalisations are to be expected.

Languages and varieties have *inventories* of phonemes; distinctions between vowel inventories are matters of *accent*. A *phonemic inventory* for varieties of PDE, using the symbols of the IPA accompanied by a list of keywords, appears in the *Notations and Conventions* section at the front of this book.

The phonemic inventory for PDE distinguishes between *vowels* and *consonants*. Vowels may be defined as those segments of sound where the airstream from the lungs does not give rise to audible friction, or is not prevented from escaping through the mouth; all other sound-segments are consonants. Groups of sound-segments may be formed into *syllables*.

*Vowels* may be defined as either *monophthongs* or *diphthongs*. Diphthongs are vowel-clusters with a glide from one vowel to another, as in most PDE pronunciations of **doubt**; monophthongs are so-called 'pure' vowels without any change in that vowel's quality in its duration, as in most PDE pronunciations of **soup**. Different vowels are made by a combination of the following procedures: raising and lowering the tongue; pushing the tongue forward or dragging it back; opening the mouth or making it less open; rounding or unrounding the lips. It is usual to define a vowel

13

with reference to the positioning of the highest point of the tongue combined with the presence or absence of lip-rounding. Vowels can thus be classified as follows:

as *close, mid (mid-close* and *mid-open), open* (with reference to the height of the tongue and the degree of openness of the mouth);

as *front, centre* or *back* (with reference to the positioning of the highest point of the tongue in relation to the front, centre or back of the mouth);

as *rounded* or *unrounded* (with reference to whether or not the lips are rounded).

Thus, in most PDE accents, the vowel in **feel** is close front unrounded, symbolised in the IPA by [i]; the vowel in **fat** is open front unrounded, symbolised by [a]; and the vowel in **more** is back mid-open rounded, symbolised by [ɔ]. For a list of PDE vowels, with corresponding IPA symbols, see *Notations and Conventions* at the beginning of this book.

*Consonants* are made by a combination of the following procedures: bringing one of the organs of the vocal tract (for example, the teeth, lips, tongue) into contact or very near proximity with another; varying the nature of the contact between the organs of the vocal tract, such as allowing a small explosion of air to escape as the organs part (*plosive*, e.g. **b** in **bat**) or allowing a small quantity of air to pass between them, producing a hissing sound (*fricative*, e.g. **s** in **sat**); vibrating or opening the *vocal folds* or (an older term) *vocal cords*, a pair of membranes housed in the larynx, an organ in the windpipe (*trachea*) through which air passes on its way from the lungs to the mouth. Consonants can thus be classified with reference to:

*the place of articulation*, with reference to the lips, teeth, alveolar ridge (the ridge of cartilage behind the top teeth), the hard palate ('roof of the mouth'), and the soft palate or velum: for example, dentals such as **t, d,** palatals such as **g, y,** bilabials such as **b, p;**

*the manner of articulation*, such as fricative or plosive, but also including *nasals*, where the airstream is diverted to emerge through the nostrils (e.g. **m** in **mat**), *laterals*, where a partial closure is made in the mouth but air is allowed to escape around it (e.g. **l** in **lap**), and *approximants, trills* and *taps. Affricates* may be defined as units which begin with plosives and end as fricatives (e.g. **ch** in **chat**);

*the state of the vocal folds*; if the vocal folds are vibrating then a sound is referred to as *voiced* (e.g. **z** in **zoo**), but if the vocal folds are relaxed a sound is *voiceless* (e.g. **s** in **sue**).

Thus, in most accents of PDE, the consonant **p** in **pat** is a voiceless bilabial plosive, symbolised in the IPA by [p]. For a list of PDE consonants, with corresponding IPA symbols, see *Notations and Conventions* at the beginning of this book.

*Syllables* are made up of groups of vowels and consonants. A syllable in English prototypically consists of a vowel, sometimes referred to as the *peak* of the syllable, which may be preceded and/or followed by consonants; a consonant which precedes the vowel is known as the *onset*, while a following consonant is the *coda*. Thus, in a PDE word such as **meat, m** is the onset, **ea** is the peak, and **t** is the coda. The combination of peak and coda is known as the *rhyme*. Syllables may be *light* (with rhymes consisting of V, VV or VC), or *heavy* (with rhymes consisting of VVC, VCC), or *superheavy* (with rhymes consisting of VVCC), where V = any vowel and C = any consonant. Many handbooks refer to light syllables as *short* syllables and heavy syllables as *long* syllables.

Scholars commonly discuss the short/long distinction in OE in terms of *morae* 'beats' (singular *mora*). A short consonant consists of a single mora, C; a long consonant consists of two morae, CC. A short vowel consists of a single mora, V, while diphthongs and long vowels consist of two morae, VV, as do sequences such as VC, CV etc.

Syllables may be *stressed* or *unstressed*. Stress is to do with the assignment of prominence to a particular syllable. A prominent, or stressed, syllable, may be louder, or more heavy, or distinct in pitch, or may manifest any combination of these features; this is the case in many varieties of English, where a stressed syllable is louder, heavier and higher in pitch than an unstressed syllable. In the word **booklet**, the syllable represented in writing as **book** is more prominent than the syllable represented by **let**: **book-** is stressed, **-let** is unstressed. Syllables and stress are phenomena at a 'higher' analytic level than segments such as individual phonemes; the standard handbooks therefore refer to them as *supra-segmental* features.

## 2.3 The OE system of sounds and spellings

The notions and categories exemplified from PDE can also be applied to OE. Thus writing and speech in OE, as in PDE, can be discussed in terms of phonemes and graphemes.

It is usually stated that OE had no 'silent' graphemes, and that every grapheme therefore mapped onto a phoneme; thus the <c> in **cnoll** 'summit' (cf. PDE **knoll**), the <w> in **wrecan** 'avenge' (cf. PDE **wreak**) and the final <e> in **mete** 'food' (cf. PDE **meat**) were all, it seems, pronounced. Varieties of OE seem to have been 'rhotic', in the same way as PD Scottish or many PD American accents, and thus <r> was pronounced in words such as **māra** 'more', **scīr** 'shire, county'. There are exceptions; the <e> (underlined) in **sceolde** 'should' and **hycgean** 'think', common spellings in Late West Saxon alongside **scolde, hycgan**, seems to be a kind of diacritic indicating the quality of the preceding consonant clusters <sc, cg> respectively.

Many consonant-graphemes mapped onto the same sounds as their PDE equivalents, e.g. <b> in **bindan** 'bind', <p> in **prēost** 'priest', <t> in **tunge** 'tongue', <d> in **dēofol** 'devil', <m> in **macian** 'make', <n> in **nama** 'name', <w> in **wīd** 'wide'. The PDE distinctions between <v> and <f> and between <s> and <z> were not reflected in the OE writing-system, thus **feld** 'field', **ceorfan** 'cut, carve', **hūs** 'house', **āmasian** 'amaze'. Two graphemes, <þ> and <ð>, were used interchangeably to represent both voiced and voiceless dental fricatives, thus **þancian** 'thank', **tīð** 'grant, share' (cf. PDE **tithe**), **wrāð** 'angry', **norþ** 'northern', **sēoþan** 'boil' (cf. PDE **seethe**).

OE distinguished long and short consonants – thus the double <nn> in **sunne** 'sun' was distinct from the single <n> in **sunu** 'son' – and also between long and short vowels; long vowels are conventionally marked in modern editions by a length-mark or *macron*, e.g. **hām** 'home', **fōt** 'foot', **cū** 'cow'. Length distinctions were important in OE, as witnessed by such pairs as **God** 'God', **gōd** 'good', **wendon** 'turned' and **wēndon** 'believed', **āwacian** 'awaken', **āwācian** 'grow weak'.

As in PDE, some consonant-graphemes mapped onto several phonemes and/or allophones. The grapheme <c> mapped onto [k] in **cyning** 'king' but [tʃ] in **cild** 'child'. The distribution of [k] and [tʃ] commonly relates to whether or not the grapheme <c> precedes a front vowel (when [tʃ] is usual) or precedes or follows a back vowel or precedes a consonant (when [k] is common): thus **cēosan** 'choose', **micel** 'great', **sprǣc** 'speech' (all with [tʃ]), and **cuman** 'come', **cōl** 'cool', **bōc** 'book', **cnāwan** 'know' (all with [k]). However, there are many exceptions which can often be worked out from a knowledge of the word which descends from it in PDE, i.e. its *reflex*, for example, **cēne** 'bold' (cf. PDE **keen**).

The grapheme <g> was pronounced as [j] initially and medially before **i/ī, e/ē**, as in **gīet** 'yet', **gē** 'you' (cf. EModE **ye**), **þegen** 'thane', and also after **i/ī, e/ē, æ/ǣ**, as in **weg** 'way', **hālig** 'holy', **dæg** 'day', **sægde** 'said'. The pronunciation [g] is usual elsewhere, as in **gān** 'go', **gylden** 'golden', **glæd** 'glad', **frogga** 'frog'; thus [j], [g] were allophones. However, the grapheme <g> was pronounced as [ɣ] between back vowels, between <l, r>, and back vowels, and after back vowels, as in **dagas** 'days', **hālga** 'saint', **genōg** 'enough', **burg** 'city'. In final position, forms with <h> often appear in place of those with <g>, thus **genōh, burh**, and the grapheme <h> also has a range of sound-values. Initially it was pronounced for the most part as [h], as in PDE, e.g. **hūs** 'house'. It was also used in the clusters <hw, hl, hn, hr>, as in **hwīl** 'while', **hlāf** 'loaf', **hnesce** 'soft, delicate' (cf. PDE dialectal **nesh**), **hræfn** 'raven'. In final position, as in **seah** 'saw' (verb), it seems to have mapped onto [x].

The grapheme <g> could be pronounced as [dʒ] after n, e.g. **engel** 'angel', though [dʒ] was usually represented by the cluster <cg>, as in **ecg** 'edge'. The cluster <sc> was usually pronounced [ʃ], as in **scip** 'ship', **fisc** 'fish', but there are exceptions, for example **āscian** 'ask', **Scottas** 'Scots'.

The graphemes for monophthong vowels in OE were <y, i, e, æ, a, o, u>; all could be pronounced long and short. It is usual to state that there was no qualitative distinction between long and short vowels in OE, in contrast to the PDE difference in quality between the vowels in **pit, peat**; the distinction seems to have arisen during the ME period.

The phoneme/grapheme mappings for monophthongs largely correspond with those of the IPA, except that the grapheme <a> was probably pronounced /ɑ, ɑ:/. Two graphemes, <æ> and <y>, were used differently in OE in comparison with PDE: <y> was used to reflect the front close rounded vowel /y/, while <æ> was used to reflect a front open unrounded vowel, rather like PDE /a/. The phonemic vowel inventory of OE therefore consisted of something like /y(:), i(:), e(:), æ(:), ɑ(:), o(:), u(:)/, a 'three-height' system where /æ(:)/ was an open front vowel and /e(:), o(:)/ were mid-vowels; many scholars believe that OE did not have a distinction between mid-close and mid-open vowels. There were also in OE three sets of grapheme-clusters which are usually interpreted as diphthongs: <ea, eo, ie>.

OE, like PDE, distinguished between stressed and unstressed syllables; vowels in unstressed syllables were generally pronounced, at least during the EWS period, more distinctively than they are in varieties of PDE.

## 2.4 Grammar and lexicon: basic terminology

For some scholars, the term *grammar* is used to refer to all linguistic categories other than the lexicon, but in this book a more restricted definition has been adopted: grammar is taken to refer to *syntax* and *morphology*. Syntax is concerned with the ways in which words combine to form phrases, clauses and sentences, i.e. *constructions*. For example, the relationship between words in such constructions as **Amy loves ponies** and **We love ponies**, where the choice of **loves** or **love** is determined by the relationship between this word and other words in the construction. Morphology is concerned with word-form, such as the kinds of ending which the form **love** can adopt, for example **loves** as opposed to **loved**; it is also concerned with how words can be put together from other words, such as **blackbird** (from **black + bird**) or **undo** (from **un + do**). Morphology dealing with alternations of the **love–loves** kind is known as *inflexional morphology*. Morphology dealing with such forms as **blackbird** or **undo** is known as *lexical morphology* or *word-formation*.

Syntactic categories can be formed into a *hierarchy of grammatical units*. *Sentences* are composed of one or more *clauses*; *clauses* are composed of one or more *phrases*; *phrases* are composed of one or more *words*; *words* are made up of one or more *morphemes*.

The morpheme is often defined as the minimal unit of grammatical analysis. It is probably easiest to demonstrate what a morpheme is by example. Thus, in the sentence:

(1) **The kind girls have given sweets to all their friends.**

there are ten words but fourteen morphemes. This can be demonstrated if we separate each morpheme with a hyphen (-):

(1a) **The-kind-girl-s-have-give-n-sweet-s-to-all-their-friend-s**

These morphemes cannot be placed in *any* order to produce acceptable English sentences. Some permutations are acceptable (*well-formed*) in PDE, for example:

(1b) **The-sweet-s-were-give-n-by-the-kind-girl-s-to-all-their-friend-s**

but other combinations are not:

(1c) **\*Sweet-the-s-give-were-n-by-kind-the-s-girl-their-to-s-all-friend**

Thus **sweet, girl, friend** and so on are potentially mobile or *free*, and can be employed in many positions within a construction, whereas **s** and **n** are immobile or *bound* morphemes, that is, they must be attached to some other element to produce a 'block' in a construction. Moreover, this ordering of elements within the block is *stable*, in the sense that **s** and **n** have to follow, not precede, the element to which they are attached: thus **girl-s** and **giv(e)-n** are acceptable, but not **\*s-girl** or **\*n-giv(e)**. These stable, uninterruptible blocks, made up from a free morpheme and (optional) bound morphemes, may be termed *words*.[1]

Bound morphemes are sometimes used to express syntactic relationships; thus, in the sentence:

(2) **The girl loves her pony.**

the bound morpheme **-s** in **loves** indicates that the verb **loves** is 'governed' by the subject-noun phrase **The girl**. Such bound morphemes are often referred to as *inflexions*. Students may also encounter another term in word-studies: the *lexeme*. A lexeme is the overall term for words which are related in terms of *paradigms*, that is, which vary inflexionally; thus **love, loves, loved** are members of one lexeme, **pony, ponies** are members of another, and so on.

The definition of the notion *word* offered above is a formal one, in that it relates to the grammatical role of the category in question and its structural characteristics. However, another older definition is that words map onto *concepts*. There are several theoretical problems with this definition, but it has its uses. The practice of *lexicography* (i.e. dictionary-making) would be very difficult without the ability to map a word onto a definition, and children's language-learning would be impossible, since children build up their lexicons by isolating individual words and attaching them to individual concepts. Most readers are able to recognise words in PDE since they are clearly marked in our writing-system. The set of words found in a particular language makes up its *vocabulary* or *lexicon*.

Words are traditionally classified into *parts of speech*. Parts of speech fall into two classes: *open* and *closed*. Open-class words are:

*nouns* (for example **table, thing, idea, James**)
*lexical verbs* (for example **sing, drive, go, love, dance**)
*adjectives* (for example **good, bad, friendly, sociable**)
*adverbs* (for example **now, then, calmly, actually, today**)
*interjections* (for example **oh!, argh!**).

Open-class words can be joined readily by new coinages, for example **scooter** (noun), **jive** (verb), **hip** (adjective), **groovily** (adverb), or by *borrowings* from other languages.

Closed-class words are:

*determiners* (for example **the, a, this, that, some, any, all**)
*pronouns* (for example **I, me, she, you, they**)
*prepositions* (for example **in, by, with, from, to, for**)
*conjunctions* (for example **and, but, if, when, because, although**)
*auxiliary verbs* (for example **can, may, will, shall, be, have**)
*numerals* (for example **one, two, first, second**).

Closed-class words cannot be joined readily by new coinages; they form a restricted set of forms which play important *cohesive* roles in discourse. They are therefore sometimes known as 'grammar words', a rather confusing description which will be generally avoided here.

All these words function within the next element in the grammatical hierarchy, the *phrase*. Prototypically, nouns function as the *headwords* (principal elements) of *noun phrases* (**girl, good girls, the good girl**) and lexical verbs function as the headwords of *verb phrases* (**sings, was singing**). Adjectives prototypically function as *modifiers* of nouns within noun phrases (**the good girl**), although they can also function as the headword of an adjective phrase (**good, very good** in **The girls were very good**). Adverbs can function as the headwords or modifiers of *adverb phrases* (**carefully, very carefully**), or as modifiers of adjectives within *adjective phrases* (**very good**).

Determiners always act as modifiers to nouns within a noun phrase (**the girl**). Auxiliary verbs act as modifiers to lexical verbs (**was singing**). Prepositions can be linked to noun phrases to produce *prepositional phrases* (**in the room**). Conjunctions prototypically link phrases or clauses together: **the girl and the boy** (linked phrases); **If you eat that, you will be sick** and **The girl was singing a song, and the boy was eating a banana** (linked clauses). Pronouns function in place of nouns within noun phrases (**She was singing a song**). Numerals prototypically act as modifiers within noun phrases (**two bananas**).

Phrases may be classified as follows: *noun phrases* (including *genitive* and *prepositional phrases*), *verb phrases*, *adjective phrases* and *adverb phrases*. In PDE, the noun phrase prototypically consists of a headword with optional modifiers, the latter being determiners, adjectives and numerals; thus the phrases **girls, good girls, the good girls, two girls** are all noun phrases. In prepositional and genitive phrases, nouns are prototypically headwords accompanied by prepositions and marked by special possessive endings respectively. Thus, **with the girls** is a prepositional phrase, while, within the phrase **the girl's book**, the phrase modifying **book** (**the girl's**) is a genitive phrase. Noun phrases prototypically function as *subjects* and *objects*; thus, in a clause such as **The girl read the book**, the noun phrase **The girl** is the subject whereas **the book** is the object. Noun phrases can also be *complements*, as in the phrase **a good boy** in the clause **John is a good boy**. Adjective phrases also function as complements, as in **The girl was very good**. Adverb phrases function as *adverbials*, as in **The girl rode the pony very carefully**. Verb phrases function prototypically as *predicators* within a clause, as in **The girl was reading the book**.

Finally, clauses can be classified as *main* or *subordinate*; main clauses can stand as sentences on their own, while subordinate clauses function within a main clause. Thus, in the sentence **If you eat that, you will be sick**, **If you eat that** is a subordinate clause while **you will be sick** is a main clause. Subordinate clauses often have *non-finite verb phrases*: **Having crossed the Rubicon, Caesar marched on Rome**.

## 2.5 The OE lexicon

Many 'core' lexemes in OE, i.e. those words dealing with very basic notions, such as **stān** 'stone', **nama** 'name', **bindan** '(to) bind', **lufian** '(to) love', **gōd** 'good', **cwic** 'alive', have reflexes in PDE, although the spelling and/or pronunciation may have changed. Some of these PDE reflexes do not have quite the same meaning as their ancestors had in OE; thus OE **cwic** is the ancestor of PDE 'quick', but it has a distinct meaning.

Regular sound-correspondences in relating OE lexemes to their PDE reflexes can be distinguished, and are useful for vocabulary-building. The correspondence between OE <cw> and PDE <qu> in **cwic, quick** has just been noted; compare also **cwacian** 'quake', **cwellan** 'kill' (the PDE reflex is **quell**). Other forms, such as **scip** 'ship', **biscop** 'bishop', **fisc** 'fish', for instance, reflect the distinct ways in which OE and PDE represent the phoneme /ʃ/ in their writing-systems, i.e. <sc> and <sh> respectively, while the regular correspondence between OE **ā** /ɑ:/ and PDE /o:/ (in its various realisations) is exemplified not only by **stān** 'stone' but also by forms such as **hām** 'home', **bāt** 'boat', **āc** 'oak', **hlāf** 'loaf', **hāl** 'whole' etc.

Like the other Germanic languages, OE had in addition other strategies for adding to its wordstock: *affixation, compounding* and *borrowing. Affixation* at its simplest made it possible to produce derived forms in other word-classes (*conversion*) through the addition of affixes (bound morphemes). Thus **dōm** 'judgement' is clearly related to **dēman** 'judge', and **lȳtel** 'little' is related to **lȳtlian** '(to) diminish'. Here the transfer is carried out by the addition of an inflexional ending to the stem with (in the case of **dēman**) subsequent sound-changes. Other productive affixes include **-ig** added to the noun **blōd** 'blood' to yield the adjective **blōdig** 'bloody', while the addition of **-līce** to the adjective **sōþ** 'true' yielded the adverb **sōþlīce** 'truly'. Another important method of adding vocabulary was by *compounding,* that is placing two free morphemes together, as in **sciprāp** 'cable', derived from **scip** 'ship' and **rāp** 'rope'. A range of such compounds is conventionally distinguished, for example noun + noun combinations, such as **sciprāp**, or adjective + noun combinations, such as **blīþemōd** 'happy'. Of course, compounding and affix-ation remain a productive method of adding words in PDE, with additional elements available through post-OE contact with French, for example the addition of **-able** as in **doable** 'possible', or **-ity** as in **textuality**. Good examples of new PDE compounds include **webcam** and **cellphone**.

In PDE, however, *borrowing* from other languages is common, and this openness to borrowing has been the case in the history of English since the ME period, encouraged by the nature of the contacts between English and other languages, notably varieties of French, which has given PDE words such as **action, courtesy, grief, honour, noise, people, reason** etc. Latin learning, some-times mediated through French, has given PDE words such as **arbiter, junior, vertigo**, while contact with the world beyond western Europe has given most of the European languages such words as **harem** (from Arabic), **taboo** (from Tongan) and **chocolate** (from Nahuatl/Aztec); imperial expansion in India gave English such items as **thug, pyjama, gymkhana, mulligatawny**.

In OE, borrowing was less common, and largely restricted to particular registers of language where available native words for modification through conversion, affixation or compounding were few. Thus many *borrowings* (sometimes referred to as *loanwords*) found in OE are derived from Latin and transferred to OE as a result of Christian beliefs or practices, as was the case with **abbod** 'abbot' (Latin **abbātem**), **sealm** 'psalm' (Latin **psalma**), **sanct** 'saint' (Latin **sanctus**), **alter** 'altar' (Latin **altāre**).

## 2.6 OE grammar

OE differs from PDE most obviously in its grammatical structure, through its widespread use of *inflexions* to relate words to each other. To put it another way, word-form and word-function are closely related in OE. Inflexions are significant at every level within the grammatical hierarchy: they relate *words* to each other within *phrases*, they relate phrases to each other within *clauses*, and they relate clauses to each other within *sentences*.

To demonstrate these points, a simple test sentence is useful:

(1) **Sēo cwēn lufode þone gōdan cnapan.**
    'The queen loved the good servant.'

Within this sentence, there are two noun phrases:

(1a) **Sēo cwēn**

(1b) **þone gōdan cnapan**

(1a) and (1b) mean 'the queen' and 'the good servant' respectively, and it will be observed that the OE words equivalent to the PDE determiner 'the' are different (**sēo, þone**). They differ firstly because the words **cwēn** and **cnapan** belong to different *genders*: **cwēn** is *feminine* while **cnapan** is *masculine*, and different forms of the determiner, *agreeing* with the nouns they modify, are used accordingly. They are both, moreover, *singular* in *number* (as opposed to *plural*), and number is also a factor in the choice of determiners.

(1a) and (1b) also differ in form because of the functions of the two noun phrases. (1a) is the subject of the sentence, while (1b) is the object, and this difference constrains the forms of both determiners and nouns, in accordance with the grammatical category known as *case*. In OE, subjects are marked for *nominative case*, while objects are marked for *accusative case*.

It is now possible to offer a grammatical description of (1a) and (1b) in terms of gender and case. (1a) consists of a determiner functioning as a modifier and a noun functioning as a headword. The determiner is in the nominative case, **sēo**, marked for feminine gender and singular number because it modifies (and thus agrees with) a feminine singular noun, **cwēn**, which is also in the nominative case. The choice of nominative case is made because (1a) is the subject of the sentence. It is also singular (as opposed to plural) in *number*. (1b) also consists of a determiner (followed by an adjective) and a noun, but in this instance functioning as an object. Thus **þone** is a masculine accusative singular determiner modifying a masculine accusative singular noun **cnapan**. It should further be noted that the adjective **gōdan**, also modifying **cnapan**, is also in the masculine accusative singular.

We might now turn to the verb, **lufode** 'loved', which forms a simple (i.e. single-word) verb phrase. The ending -**ode** is equivalent to PDE -**ed**, and it indicates that the verb is in the past (or *preterite*) *tense*. As in PDE, the form of the verb is determined by its relationship to the subject, i.e. it *agrees*; the verb phrase is thus singular in number, a grammatical category common to noun and verb phrases, because the subject which governs it is also singular, and it thus adopts a singular form. Of course, in PDE the preterite ending -**ed** is shared by both singular and plural forms of the verb; this was not the case in OE, where singular and plural verbs were distinguished by different inflexions. The sets of forms which nouns, determiners and verbs can adopt are known as *paradigms*; more details of these paradigms, and their functions, are given in chapters 5 and 6.

Since the functions of noun phrases were indicated inflexionally, in principle OE word-order was much more flexible than that of PDE, i.e. the core meaning of a sentence did not change when phrases were moved around. Thus the sentence:

(1) **Sēo cwēn lufode þone gōdan cnapan.**

means the same as:

(2) **Þone gōdan cnapan lufode sēo cwēn.**

since the relationship between **sēo cwēn** and **þone gōdan cnapan** is expressed primarily by inflexional means and not through element order. This practice contrasts with PDE, where element order is the primary method for expressing relationships between subject and object; in PDE:

(3) **The queen loved the good servant.**

does not mean the same as PDE

(4) **The good servant loved the queen.**

## Note
1. The distinction between a word and a phrase is exemplified by a word such as **blackbird** (i.e. a particular kind of bird, *turdus merula*), made up from two free morphemes, compared with a phrase such as **black bird** (i.e. a bird which is black, such as a crow, a raven, a chough or indeed a blackbird).

## Key terms introduced in this chapter
phoneme
allophone
grapheme

allograph
phonographic vs. logographic
accent
vowel (monophthong, diphthong)
consonant
place and manner of articulation
stress
syllable
syntax
construction
phrase
clause (main, subordinate)
headword
modifier
morphology
morpheme
inflexion
lexeme
word
lexicography
parts of speech (open-class, closed-class)
paradigm

# CHAPTER 3

# The Structure of Old English

## In this chapter...

This chapter uses the terms discussed in chapter 2 to analyse some longer Old English texts, both prose and poetry. Some comparisons are made with texts in related languages, and the structure of OE poetry is briefly discussed.

### Contents

## 3.1 **What did OE look like?**

So far, examples of OE have been limited to individual lexemes and short test sentences. We need now to look at some more extended OE. Here is a text of *The Lord's Prayer* in OE, with ME, Early ModE (hence EModE) and PDE versions supplied for comparative purposes.[1]

OE (Early West Saxon dialect, late ninth century)
Þū ūre fæder, þe eart on heofonum, sīe þīn nama gehālgod. Cume þīn rīce. Sīe þīn wylla on eorþan swā swā on heofonum. Syle ūs tōdæg ūrne dæghwāmlican hlāf. And forgief ūs ūre gyltas swā swā þē forgiefaþ þǣm þe wiþ ūs āgyltaþ. And ne lǣd þū nū ūs on costnunge, ac ālīes ūs fram yfele.

ME (Central Midlands, *c.*1380)
Oure fadir, þat art in heuenys, halewid be þi name. Þi kingdom come to. Be þi wile don ase in heuene and in erþe. ȝiue to us þis day oure breed ouer

oþer substaunse. And forȝiue to us oure dettes, as and we forȝiuen to oure dettouris. And leede us not into temptaciouns, but delyuere vs from yuel.

### EModE (*Book of Common Prayer*, 1549)

**Our Father, which art in heaven, Hallowed be thy Name. Thy kingdom come. Thy will be done, in earth as it is in heaven. Give us this day our daily bread. And forgive us our trespasses, As we forgive them that trespass against us. And lead us not into temptation; But deliver us from evil.**

### PDE (*Alternative Service Book* of the Church of England, 1980)

**Our Father in heaven, your name be hallowed; your kingdom come, your will be done, on earth as in heaven. Give us today our daily bread. Forgive us our sins, as we have forgiven those who have sinned against us. And do not bring us to the time of trial, but save us from evil.**

Analysis of these texts quickly reveals major differences between each language-state. OE uses some letters we no longer use, such as **p** 'wynn', **þ** 'thorn', **ð** 'edh' and **æ** 'ash', and a special form ('insular **g**', i.e. ȝ) in place both of 'g' and of 'y' in **gyltas** 'trespasses', 'sins' (lit. 'guilts'), **dæg** 'day'. It is, however, a scholarly convention, followed in this book, to use <w> in place of wynn, and <g> in place of insular **g**. 'Long' vowels are usually marked with a macron, as in **ē**, though this convention was not used by Anglo-Saxon scribes.

More importantly, as we have already noted in chapter 2, OE differs from PDE in its use of *inflexions*, special endings on words which are used to indicate their grammatical relationships. Examples in the OE passage include -**um**, -**an**, -**e** and -**as** on **heofon-um, eorþ-an, yfel-e** and **gylt-as**. PDE has such endings (e.g. -**s** to indicate plural number in **sins**), but many fewer. In the lexicon, OE differs from later forms of the language in having fewer *loanwords* or *borrowings*; words from French, e.g. **dettes, temptaciouns**, do not appear before ME.

Although this passage from *The Lord's Prayer* may be short, therefore, it is possible to find in it several linguistic features which mark OE off from later forms of the language. The set of distinctions 'Old – Middle – Modern' with reference to English, which was established in the second half of the nineteenth century, has its limitations, but it does capture the differences between each stage. 'Prototypical' OE differs from ME in all levels of language traditionally distinguished. Thus, in vocabulary, there are few loanwords in OE in comparison with ME, when large numbers of words enter English from French, and when Norse loanwords brought over by the Viking settlers start to be recorded in written texts. In grammar, OE had, in comparison with ME and ModE, a large number of inflexional markers flagging categories such as *case, number* and *gender*, allowing a greater degree of flexibility in word-order than was possible at later stages of the language. During the course of the ME period, these markers were significantly reduced, and other discourse-tracking mechanisms were introduced to compensate for the reduction and to sustain grammatical cohesion, such as a more fixed word-order, greater use of prepositions, and a more distinctive system of pronouns. In transmission, the distinctive phonologies of OE varieties were obscured by the existence of a 'standardised' set of spellings.

The OE text of *The Lord's Prayer* captures something of the otherness of OE; and the question therefore arises: how far is OE 'English'? Certainly, there are resemblances between OE and its cognate languages which might seem in some ways stronger than those with later stages of English. We might compare the OE version of *The Lord's Prayer* already cited with versions in Old High German, a variety of German contemporary with OE, and Gothic, an East Germanic variety whose written records date from several centuries before those for OE. The OE version is repeated to make comparison easy.

> Gothic (from the Bible of Bishop Ulfilas, fourth century AD)
> Atta unsar þu in himinam, weihnai namo þein. Qimai þiudinassus þeins. Wairþai wilja þeins, swe in himina jah ana airþai. Hlaif unsarana þana sinteinan gif uns himma daga. Jah aflet uns þatei skulans sijaima, swaswe jah weis afletam þaim skulam unsaraim. Jah ni briggais uns in fraistubnjai, ak lausei uns af þamma ubilin.

> Old High German (from the translation of *Tatian's Gospel Harmony*, *c*.830)
> Fater unser thu thar bist in himile, si giheilagot thin namo. Queme thin rihhi. Si thin uuillo, so her in himile ist, so si her in erdu. Unsar brot tagalihhaz gib uns hiutu. Inti furlaz uns unsara sculdi, so uuir furlazemes unsaran sculdigon. Inti ni gileitest unsih in costunga, uzouh arlosi unsih fon ubile.

> OE (West Saxon dialect, late ninth century)
> Þū ūre fæder, þe eart on heofonum, sīe þīn nama gehālgod. Cume þīn rīce. Sīe þīn wylla on eorþan swā swā on heofonum. Syle ūs tōdæg ūrne dæghwāmlican hlāf. And forgief ūs ūre gyltas swā swā þē forgiefaþ þǣm þe wiþ ūs agyltaþ. And ne lǣd þū nū ūs on costnunge, ac ālīes ūs fram yfele.

There are obvious differences between OE and the cognate languages, but there are also many similarities, especially (as might be expected) with Old High German; the word-order is a little different between the texts, but much of the vocabulary is very similar; for example, compare 'hallowed be thy name', which appears in Old High German as **si giheilagot thin namo**, and in OE as **sīe þīn nama gehālgod**.

But the 'foreign-ness' of OE can be overstated, for there are also very clear continuities between OE and PDE. Almost all the core vocabulary of PDE, i.e. those words commonly used in everyday discourse, is derived from OE, even though many of the pronunciations and some of the meanings of that vocabulary have changed. Mitchell and Robinson (1992: 171–2) give a long list of 'made-up' sentences where changes between OE and PDE have been minimal, including **Harold is swift. His hand is strong and his word grim. Late in līfe hē went tō his wīfe in Rōme.** And though many other words appear a little unusual they can be understood once a few rules about pronunciation are grasped. For instance, take the following sentence (Mitchell and Robinson 1992: 171):

> **Se fisc swam under þæt scip and ofer þone sciellfisc.**
> 'The fish swam under the ship and over the shellfish.'

OE <sc> seems to have been pronounced [ʃ]; we have already met <þ>, which was pronounced as a *dental fricative* ([θ] or [ð], depending on context); <æ> was pronounced as a *low front vowel* (somewhat like [a], though this pronunciation will be discussed further in chapter 4, section 3). Once these rules are grasped, the sentence becomes comprehensible for a modern reader, the only remaining confusion being that OE has three words equivalent to PDE 'the' (se, þaet, þone).

Moreover, it is worth recalling that some varieties of PDE are more like OE than others. We might take the words **cū, hū, nū, hūs, ūt,** which were all pronounced in OE with [u:]. These words are, in most PDE varieties, now pronounced with a *diphthong*: **cow, how, now, house, out.** This diphthongisation was a historical development in English, which took place in the fifteenth and sixteenth centuries; it is part of something called *the Great Vowel Shift*.

However, there are varieties which have not had this particular diphthongisation, notably Scots, the traditional Germanic variety spoken in Lowland Scotland; many speakers of Scots even now pronounce these words with a *monophthong*, and this has given rise to the habit of representing Scots in writing with such spellings as **coo, hoo, noo, hoose, oot.** It could reasonably be argued, therefore, that Scots is closer to OE than other varieties for this particular item.

In short, the continuities between OE and PDE are much stronger than the discontinuities, and this fact means that anyone seriously interested in the history of English has to have a sound grasp of the structure of OE.

The rest of this chapter is designed to demonstrate the range of differences between OE and later stages of the language through analyses of longer passages. The first passage comes from an OE prose text, a homily from the late OE period. The second passage is from an OE poem, *The Dream of the Rood*.

# 3.2  A passage of OE prose

The distinctive characteristics of OE which we have already seen in the OE version of *The Lord's Prayer* may be further illustrated by a short passage from one of the best-known and most frequently anthologised OE texts: Ælfric's *Life of King Edmund*.

Ælfric was a monk, born in the second half of the tenth century AD. He lived first in Winchester, where he was educated at the monastic school, and where he was taught by Æþelwold, Bishop of Winchester and one of the leading educators of his time. He then moved to the monastery at Cerne Abbas in Dorset, where he wrote the works for which he is best known: a *Grammar* (designed to teach Latin through the medium of OE), translations from the Bible, and sets of homilies and saints' lives; these last were dedicated to a pious member of the West Saxon royal house, Æþelweard, and thus reflect the taste of the late Anglo-Saxon nobility. Ælfric ended his career as an abbot of the monastery of Eynsham, where he moved in 1005.

*The Life of King Edmund*, one of the saints' lives dedicated to Æþelweard, describes events which took place in the ninth century. Edmund was king of the East Angles, killed by invading Scandinavian raiders led by Ivarr the Boneless, whose odd name is usually taken to indicate that he was double-jointed. (Ivarr's name is here Englished as **Hinguar**.) Edmund was subsequently sanctified. The short passage given here describes the moment of Edmund's martyrdom at Ivarr's command. A fairly literal translation is given underneath.

> Þā geseah Hinguar, se ārlēasa flotmann, þæt se æþela cyning nolde Crīste wiþsacan, ac mid ānrǣdum gelēafan hine ǣfre clipode. Hēt hine þā behēafdian, and þā hæþnan swā dydon. Betwix þǣm þe hē clipode tō Crīste þā gīet, þā tugon þā hæþnan þone hālgan tō slege, and mid ānum swenge slōgon him of þæt hēafod, and his sāwol sīþode gesǣlig tō Crīste.
>
> *(Sweet/Davis 1953:83–4)*

[Translation: 'Then Hinguar, the cruel sailor, saw that the noble king would not forsake Christ, but with single-minded faith called continually upon him. (Hinguar) commanded him then to be beheaded, and the heathens did so. While he cried out to Christ then still, then the heathens took the holy (one) for killing, and with one blow struck the head from him, and his soul travelled blessed to Christ.']

This passage demonstrates many features which we have already noted as characteristic of OE. For instance, the opening clause:

Þā geseah Hinguar
'Then Hinguar saw'

may be parsed as follows:

A(Þā) P(geseah) S(Hinguar)

Flexible element order in OE means that the predicator (P=verb phrase) can precede the subject (S) of a clause, and this regularly happens in OE when the clause starts, as here, with an adverbial (A). The same pattern is found in PD German.

The noun **Hinguar** is the subject of its clause, and thus (according to OE inflexional practice) is in the nominative case. Thus any element modifying **Hinguar** is also going to be in the nominative case, and thus the phrase **se ārlēasa flotmann** 'the cruel sailor', which is a modifier in what is known as *apposition* to **Hinguar**, is also in the nominative. This noun phrase consists of three elements: the determiner **se**, an adjective **ārlēasa**, and a noun **flotmann**.

The next element in the sentence is the subordinate clause

þæt se æþela cyning nolde Crīste wiþsacan
'that the noble king would not forsake Christ'

**Pæt** is a subordinating conjunction (= PDE 'that' ). The noun phrase **se æþela cyning** 'the noble king' is the subject of the subordinate clause, and is therefore in the nominative case, with determiner and adjective agreeing with the noun. There are two verbs, **nolde** 'would not' and **wiþsacan** 'forsake'; in PDE, such elements would not be split up around the object (**Crīste**) of the clause and would be parsed as a complex verb phrase consisting of an auxiliary verb and a main verb. OE characteristically splits them. Direct objects in OE are prototypically in the accusative case, as we have seen; however, this example (**Crīste**) is an exception, being in the *dative* case. The dative case is used prototypically in OE where in PDE we would use certain prepositions (**to** Tom, **with** the book) or to express the *indirect object* function, as in Tom gave **him** the book; it is also used, as here, to signal direct object function after certain verbs. **Crīste** is thus in the dative case, marked by the inflexional ending -e (cf. nominative **Crīst**).

The next clause:

ac mid ānrǣdum gelēafan hine ǣfre clipode
'but with single-minded faith called continually upon him'

is coordinated with the preceding subordinate clause, and is linked to it by the coordinating conjunction **ac** 'but'. No subject is expressed; the simple verb phrase **clipode** 'called' is governed by the noun phrase in the preceding clause, **se æþela cyning**. It will be noted that the verb is left to the end of the clause, a characteristic feature of subordinate clauses in OE. The phrase **mid ānrǣdum gelēafan** 'with single-minded faith' includes a preposition **mid**, and the adjective and noun which follow it, forming a prepositional phrase, are in the dative case. The adjective **ānrǣdum** consists of three components: an inflexional ending -**um**, marking the word as dative, and two stems, **ān** 'one' and **rǣd** 'advice', 'resolution'; the adjective **ānrǣd** is therefore a good example of a compound word, meaning literally 'one-resolution'. The word **hine** is a pronoun in the accusative case, 'him', functioning as the direct object of the verb, while **ǣfre** is an adverb, 'ever', 'continually'.

The form **hine** 'him' (accusative) also occurs in the next clause:

**Hēt hine þā behēafdian**
'(Hinguar) commanded him then to be beheaded'.

The subject of the clause is not expressed, and has to be understood from the context of the passage. **Hēt** 'commanded' is a verb in the *third person* and *preterite* (i.e. past) *tense*, while **behēafdian** 'to be beheaded' is an *infinitive* form of the verb; **þā**, a common word in OE, is in this case an adverb meaning 'then'.

Another meaning of **þā** is exemplified in the next clause:

**and þā hǣþnan swā dydon**
'and the heathens did so'

The clause begins with the coordinating conjunction **and** 'and'. The noun phrase **þā hǣþnan** 'the heathens' consists of a determiner, in this case **þā**, and an adjective *converted* into a noun – a common usage in OE. The verb **dydon** 'did' is in the preterite plural, governed by **þā hǣþnan**. The adverb **swā** 'so' exemplifies a common sound-correspondence between OE and PDE, in that OE **ā** is reflected in PDE with /oː/ (generally with diphthongal variants).

The clause:

**Betwix þǣm þe hē clipode tō Crīste þā gīet**
'While he called then still to Christ'

is a subordinate clause, flagged by the subordinating conjunction **betwix þǣm þe** 'while'. The subject of the clause (and thus in the nominative case) is the pronoun **hē** 'he', while the preterite verb governed by **hē**, **clipode** 'called', rather unusually – for a subordinate clause – follows immediately after. The prepositional phrase **tō Crīste** 'to Christ' consists of a preposition **tō** and a noun in the dative case, **Crīste** (nominative **Crīst**). The clause concludes with two adverbs: **þā** 'then' and **gīet** 'still'. The form **gīet** is the ancestor of PDE **yet**, but its range of meanings is somewhat different.

The clause:

**þā tugon þā hǣþnan þone hālgan tō slege**
'Then the heathens took the holy (one) for slaying'

is a main clause, introduced by an adverb **þā**; the element order, with the verb **tugon** immediately following the adverb, is characteristic of OE main clauses where an adverbial is clause-initial, and we have seen a simpler example already, **Þā geseah Hinguar** 'Then Hinguar saw'. The verb **tugon** is marked for preterite plural by the ending **-on**, and is followed by the plural noun phrase **þā hǣþnan**, which is the subject of the clause. The object of the clause is the noun phrase **þone hālgan** 'the holy (one)', where the headword is the adjective **hālgan**. The clause concludes with a prepositional phrase **tō slege**, with the noun in the dative case.

The next clause:

> **and mid ānum swenge slōgon him of þæt hēafod**
> 'and with a single blow struck the head from him'

is a coordinated main clause, introduced by a coordinating conjunction **and**. The prepositional phrase **mid ānum swenge** 'with a single blow' includes a preposition **mid** 'with' followed by a modifier **ānum** and a headword **swenge**, both in the dative case. It may be observed that OE has two words equivalent to PDE **with**: **mid** (cognate with PD German **mit**) 'in company with, by means of', and **wiþ** 'against'; compare such PDE examples as **Tom walked with** (i.e. 'in company with') **Anne along the road** and **Bill fought with** (i.e. 'against') **Tom**. The verb **slōgon** is governed by the noun phrase **þā hǣþnan** in the previous clause, and is thus preterite plural, indicated by the ending **-on** (see **tugon** in the previous clause). The remaining part of the clause may be translated literally as 'from him concerning the head', an idiomatic construction characteristic of OE.

The passage concludes with a further coordinated clause:

> **and his sāwol sīþode gesǣlig tō Crīste**
> 'and his soul travelled blessed to Christ'

The subject of the clause is the noun phrase **his sāwol** 'his soul'; the possessive pronoun **his** is in the *genitive* case, used in OE to flag possession and still present in PDE, both in pronouns (cf. **his, her, its**) and in nouns (cf. **the woman's book, John's car**, etc.). The verb **sīþode** 'travelled' is in the preterite singular, governed by the singular noun phrase **his sāwol**, and the adjective **gesǣlig** is an apposed adjective phrase also in agreement with **his sāwol**. The clause concludes with the prepositional phrase **tō Crīste**, with the noun **Crīst** marked as dative by the inflexion **-e**.

The passage also illustrates, through its spellings, many features character-istic of the OE sound-system. The pronunciation of <g> as /j/ is exemplified by forms such as **gīet** 'still' (cf. PDE **yet**), and in the frequent prefix **ge-**, e.g. **gelēafan** 'faith', **gesǣlig** 'blessed', **geseah** 'saw'. The mapping of <h> onto [x] is exemplified by final **-h** in **geseah**. The appearance of **ā** where PDE has <o> etc. is exemplified by **ānum** (a dative form, cf. nominative **ān**) 'one', **swā** 'so', and **sāwol** 'soul'. The 'short/long' diphthongal distinction is illustrated by the forms **geseah** 'saw' and **hēafod** 'head'.

Analysis of this short passage of OE illustrates many of the ways in which OE differs in structure from PDE, ways which have been mentioned in earlier chapters. OE is much more of a synthetic language than PDE, with greater use of inflexional endings, and its element-order is more flexible (though still governed by certain stylistic conventions). Much of the vocabulary of OE remains (modified in appearance through the action of sound-changes), but many of these words have changed in meaning, sometimes rather subtly. These issues will be pursued in detail in later chapters.

## 3.3 *The Dream of the Rood*

This chapter will conclude with an examination of part of an OE poem which, since Victorian times, has been known as *The Dream of the Rood*.

*The Dream of the Rood* survives in its fullest version in *The Vercelli Book*, which dates from the end of the tenth century. The poem is a religious dream-vision, in which a dreamer experiences a vision of the Cross on which Christ was crucified. The Cross speaks to the dreamer, as objects often do in the Anglo-Saxon 'riddle' tradition, describing its experiences and subsequent transformation from an instrument of torture to a symbol of triumph.

The Vercelli text draws upon a good deal of traditional material, and is related to a text which survives from several centuries before: the Ruthwell Cross inscription. The passages below are parallel versions of parts of the Vercelli and Ruthwell poems; the Ruthwell text is presented in a transliterated form, using generally accepted scholarly conventions for transliterating runic inscriptions. The dots indicate a runic character which is either damaged or missing. The lines describe how Christ, in an apparent reversal of heroic convention, undresses in preparation for the 'battle'. The Cross trembles when Christ 'embraces' it; the implication is that the Cross, as in origin a tree and part of natural creation, is here being forced to act against its nature. In accordance with present-day methods of reflecting OE metrical practice, the poem is written in alliterating 'half-lines', indicated here by spaces (in OE manuscripts, poems were written out continuously, so there was no visual distinction between poetry and prose). Three translations of the Vercelli text are given to help the reader: a literal word-for-word translation, a prose translation, and a translation in verse by Michael Alexander, a well-known modern poet and critic. Only a literal translation is offered of the Ruthwell text.

*Vercelli text, lines 39–45*

Ongyrede hine þā geong Haeleþ,   þæt wæs God ælmihtig,

strang and stīþmōd.   Gestāh hē on gealgan heanne

mōdig on manigra gesyhþe,   þā hē wolde mancyn lȳsan.

Bifode ic þā mē se Beorn ymbclypte;   ne dorste ic hwæþre būgan tō
                                        eorþan,

feallan tō foldan sceatum,   ac ic sceolde fæste standan.

Rōd wæs ic ārǣred;   āhōf ic rīcne Cyning,

heofona Hlāford;   hyldan mē ne dorste.

[Literal translation: Undressed himself then young Hero, who was God almighty, strong and resolute. Ascended he on gallows high, bold in many's sight, when he wanted mankind to redeem. Trembled I when me the Warrior embraced; nor dared I yet bow to earth, fall to earth's surfaces, but I had firm to stand. Cross was I raised up; lifted up I powerful King, heavens' lord; bow me not dared.]

[Full translation: Then the young Hero, who was God almighty, undressed himself, strong and resolute. He ascended onto the high gallows, bold in many's sight, when he wanted to redeem mankind. I trembled when the Warrior embraced me; nor dared I yet bow to the earth, fall to earth's surfaces, but I had to stand firm. I was raised up a Cross; I lifted up a powerful King, heavens' lord; I did not dare to bow.]

[Poetic translation by Michael Alexander (1966: 107):
Almighty God ungirded Him,
eager to mount the gallows,
unafraid in the sight of many:
He would set free mankind.
I shook when His arms embraced me
But I durst not bow to ground,
Stoop to Earth's surface.
Stand fast I must.]

*Ruthwell text*
..geredæ hinæ god almegttig
þa he walde on galgu gistiga
.odig f.... .... men
.ug.
.... ic riicnæ kyniŋc
heafunæs hlafard hælda ic ni dorstæ

[Literal translation: (un)dressed him(self) god almighty/ when he wished on gallows ascend/proud ... ... men/ ..../ I powerful king/ heaven's lord to bow I not dared/]

The two texts are written in different dialects of OE: the Vercelli text is written in Late West Saxon, for historical reasons the dominant written vernacular of late Anglo-Saxon England, while the Ruthwell text is written in Old Northumbrian of the seventh/eighth century. However, there are definite similarities. Most obviously, in both texts word-order is not the same as in PDE, with verbs frequently in 'initial position' in clauses or delayed until the end of clauses, for example **āhōf ic rīcne Cyning** and **þā hē wolde mancyn lȳsan** in the Vercelli text, **.. geredæ hinæ god almegttig** and **þa he walde on galgu gistiga** in the Ruthwell text. Such flexibility is, of course, made possible in OE because of the range of distinct inflexional endings available to express relationships between words, **-edæ, -æ, -u, -a, -næ, -æs** in the Ruthwell text, **-ede, -ode, -an, -ne, -ra, -um, -e, -a** in the Vercelli text. Of course, some inflexional endings are still found in PDE (e.g. **-'s** to express possession when attached to nouns, **-ed** to express past tense in verbs). Moreover, it is noticeable that both texts share with PDE the method of marking pronouns for function; thus, where PDE distinguishes **he** and **him**, OE has **hē, hine** (Vercelli), **he, hinæ** (Ruthwell).

The poem also illustrates OE verse practices. This passage of verse is of course very challenging; it was chosen not only because it demonstrates linguistic forms but also because it shows the power of literature in OE. Literary qualities are not the focus of this book but the passage does allow us to note some characteristic features. Modern readers will note the use of alliteration, which was structural in OE verse in the same way as rhyme is structural in later poetry. The basic metrical unit of the OE poem was the *half-line*; half-lines were linked together in pairs by alliterating syllables. A line such as:

**heofona Hlāford; hyldan mē ne dorste.**

illustrates the basic pattern; of the four open-class words here (viz. **heofona, Hlāford, hyldan** and **dorste**), the first three alliterate.

## 3.4 **The remainder of this book**

The student who has read carefully through chapters 1, 2 and 3 will have developed a good understanding of the basic structures of OE. The remainder of the book builds on this basis. In what follows, each level of language – spellings and sounds (chapter 4), the lexicon (chapter 5) and grammar (chapters 6 and 7) – is treated in more detail.

In chapter 4 the development of the OE writing-systems is discussed and then an outline, more advanced than presented in chapter 3, is given of the OE phonemic inventory of vowels and consonants, followed by a discussion of OE stress-patterns. This outline is then followed by more complex issues, to do with dialectal variation and sound-change, and the chapter concludes with a controversial problem in the study of OE sounds and spellings, the question of the 'short diphthongs'.

Chapter 5 is concerned with the OE lexicon. The sources of the OE lexicon are discussed, and an account, more developed than in chapter 3, is given of lexical morphology. The chapter then moves to a discussion of the semantic structure of the OE lexicon, showing how the *Thesaurus of Old English* can offer special insights into its organisation.

In chapters 6 and 7, the focus shifts to grammar. In chapter 6, the OE noun phrase, verb phrase and sentence structure are discussed in turn in greater detail than in chapter 2, and in chapter 7 an outline of OE inflexional morphology is offered. This outline is followed by a comparison of these usages with those current in other Germanic languages and with later developments in the history of English.

It is recommended that each of the chapters should be read alongside the study of the texts presented in *Appendix 1*. These texts include portions of some of the most famous works of OE literature – *Beowulf*, the *Anglo-Saxon Chronicle* – but there are also some less well-known works, including dialectal texts such as the various versions of *Cædmon's Hymn* and portions of Mercian and Northumbrian texts, and samples of the very earliest OE writings, some of which are recorded in *runes*.

## Note

1. It should be noted that the final text is hardly prototypical PDE, since it includes some archaic features, e.g. **hallowed, your kingdom come**; in PDE **hallowed** 'sanctified' is a rare word only found in religious registers, and it would be more usual to use an auxiliary verb to express wish or hypothesis, i.e. 'may your kingdom come' rather than 'your kingdom come'.

## Key terms introduced in this chapter

Gothic
Norse
Old High German
alliteration
half-line

# CHAPTER 4

# Spellings and Sounds

## In this chapter …

This chapter discusses the spellings and sounds of Old English in more depth than was possible in previous chapters. We look at the writing-systems of OE and how they mapped onto OE sounds. This chapter also describes how the sounds of OE changed over time, and gives an outline description of the different accents of OE.

### Contents

## 4.1 **Fuþorc and alphabet**

OE differed from PDE in being recorded by means of two distinct writing-systems: a Latin-based alphabet from which the PDE system is derived, and a distinct Germanic writing-system known as *runes*. The set of runes used in OE is generally referred to as the *fuþorc*, after the first six letters in its canonical listing ('f', 'u', 'þ', 'o', 'r', 'c'). Most recorded OE survives in the Latin-based *alphabet*, named after the first two letters in the Greek alphabet from which it was derived (*alpha*, *beta*). However, important material – especially from the earliest period of OE – is attested by the fuþorc, and one or two fuþorc-derived letters were transferred to the Latin-based script used in Anglo-Saxon England.

The OE word **rūn** means 'secret' (**rūnwita** 'counsellor' = 'secret' + 'wise man'), and the term has developed an esoteric meaning which is still widely current in PDE usage, as represented by the availability of runic jewellery in gift shops on the one hand and by the use of runes in fantasy literature on the other. And there is some evidence that Germanic peoples saw the origins of the runes as in some sense mysterious; in Germanic myth, as passed down in later Norse legends, the god Oðinn learned the runes through being nailed to the 'world-ash tree' Yggdrasill for nine days and nine nights. This interpretation of the function of the runes would seem to be supported by their decorative role, and by their use in votary inscriptions and the casting of lots. They were also used for purposes which may be described as broadly literary; perhaps the most famous runic inscription in OE is that which appears on the Ruthwell Cross in south-west Scotland, which records the Cross-poem related to *The Dream of the Rood* discussed in a transliterated version in the previous chapter.

However, these exotic functions of the runes have been exaggerated by later scholars, over-excited by Germanic mysticism. Runes did indeed have a function in Germanic magic, but they were also used throughout the north and west Germanic world with more humdrum functions, as well as for recording literature: for communicating simple messages on perishable materials such as slips of wood, for commemorating the dead on funerary monuments, and for marking ownership of objects. In other words, runes were a writing-system used for a range of functions, in ways similar to those of PD writing-systems.

The evidence suggests that, far from having a divine origin, runes originated, in the first two centuries BC, for the most part as a modification of various alphabets used for inscriptions in the mountainous borderline areas between what is modern Austria and the Roman Empire. These forms were supplemented by other 'pre-runic' symbols, whose function had been hitherto essentially decorative, repurposed with a communicative function. From this area, runes spread north gradually, into modern Scandinavia by the third century AD, and, eventually, into the British Isles.

The earliest or 'Common Germanic' runic system consisted of twenty-four letters, and is usually referred to as the *fuþark*. The fuþark is recorded in several early inscriptions, of which the most complete is that on the Kylver stone, from Gotland, Sweden, dating from the early fifth century AD (see the texts in *Appendix 1*).

The runic system was, in origin at least, a phonographic system in which letters corresponded to sound-segments. As a result, runic systems were sensitive to developments in the sound-systems to which they corresponded, and the first few centuries AD form a period of significant development and divergence among the Germanic dialects. As a result, the various sets of runes evolved to reflect the divergence of sound-systems in Germanic varieties.

There is good evidence of such a modified fuþark in the Ingvaeonic varieties (Frisian, OE) by the sixth century AD, for example the Arum wooden sword inscription from west Friesland, which has the inscription **edæboda**, probably to be interpreted as 'return messenger'. This inscription includes a new rune for 'o', viz. ᛟ, and a changed sound-value for ᚠ, 'æ' (compare Kylver 'reversed' ᚨ 'a', which represents the common Germanic usage). It will be observed that the 'o' rune of the Arum inscription is an obvious modification of the Common Germanic 'a' rune with small upward-angled lines attached to the right 'branches' of the form. The earliest full sequence of these Ingvaeonic runes is recorded on a *scramasax* (i.e. a short one-sided sword) dating from the eighth/ninthcentury AD and found in the River Thames in the middle of the nineteenth century. The Thames scrama-sax inscription, with parallel modern transliterations, appears in *Appendix 1*. Since the new rune 'o' now occupies the fourth position in the sequence, in place of the rune ᚠ now displaced towards the end with a new sound-equivalence, the OE runic system is referred to as the *fuþorc*.

The development of the runes to reflect sound-change is of considerable importance for the history of sounds during the pre-OE and OE periods, and is discussed further, below.

Runes continued to be used for some time in Anglo-Saxon England, but they suffered from certain disadvantages. Their residual pagan associations, it has been argued, may have militated against their use; however, it should be noticed they were used, as on the Ruthwell Cross, for recording a religious text, and the Northumbrian kings of the period when the Cross was erected were notoriously pious, and likely to have forbidden any practice seen as overtly pagan. More significantly, runes, whose prototypically straight lines and avoidance of horizontals made them useful for carving across the grain of wood as well as for use on stone or bone, were not well suited physically for recording long texts on parchment. And of course runes were a Germanic script, not used in the wider European Christian culture which became dominant in England as the Anglo-Saxon period progressed. Runes are recorded in manuscripts from late Anglo-Saxon England, but as an object of antiquarian interest.

Two examples of longer OE runic inscriptions appear in *Appendix 1*: parts of the inscription which appear on the Ruthwell Cross (see also chapter 3, section 3) and on the Franks Casket. These inscriptions are accompanied by transliterations into the Latin alphabet, using the widely-accepted conventions established by Bruce Dickins (see Dickins 1932).

Runes were superseded by the Latin alphabet recorded in the *insular script*, a manner of writing which was developed largely in Ireland and first employed in Britain in Christian Northumbria; insular script commonly appears in late Anglo-Saxon manuscripts. Insular script had characteristic forms for the letters <f, g, r, s>, and some other peculiarities. In the earliest OE texts, <th> was used for /θ/ and <w> for /w/, but these letters were replaced by two adoptions from the runic script: <þ> for /θ/, and <ρ> for /w/, known by their runic mnemonics **þorn** 'thorn' (earlier **þyrs** 'giant, demon, wizard' – the mnemonic seems to have been changed because of potential magical associations) and **wynn** 'joy' respectively. Other letters peculiar to the OE version of insular script were <ð>, an alternative grapheme for thorn now known as **eth** or **edh**, the Old Icelandic name for the letter when it was adopted from OE, and <æ>, known as **æsc** 'ash', derived from the mnemonic name for the equivalent runic letter, ᚨ /æ/. Eth/edh was created by drawing a fine line through the upper part of the vertical bar (the *ascender*) in the insular Latin form of <d>, while ash was a modification of the Latin <æ>.

Insular script was used in Anglo-Saxon England for recording two languages: OE, and Latin. Interestingly, some graphs of the insular script were only used when recording OE; when writing Latin, some distinct graphs were adopted. Thus <g>, for instance, appears in the insular script as both <<g>> and <<ȝ>>; <<ȝ>> was used for copying OE, while <<g>> was used for copying Latin. These distinctions, in line with the general practice of modern scholars, are not made in this book. Concern with such matters is the province of a distinct scholarly discipline, *paleography* (see Roberts 2005).

When Anglo-Saxon studies began in England in the sixteenth century, it was customary, for reasons to do with antiquarian aesthetics, to represent insular script in printing using a special font, a practice which continued into the middle of the nineteenth century. However, from the middle of the nineteenth century onwards it has been usual for editors of OE texts to transliterate the insular script into roman equivalents. Modern editors of OE texts generally retain thorn, eth and ash but replace wynn with <w>, since it can easily be confused with thorn. A few retain the special insular form of <g>, <<ȝ>>, but this practice is rather rare. Modern editors generally add a diacritic mark to indicate long vowels, the macron, but this was not an OE practice; the accent which appears sporadically in Anglo-Saxon manuscripts seems to have been used either to indicate stress or to disambiguate ambiguities when two words were written with the same sequence of letters, e.g. **gōd** 'good', **god** 'God'. Macrons are, however, used in this book, since they perform a valuable philological function.

## 4.2 The OE sound-system: introduction

Our knowledge of the OE sound-system is derived from a variety of sources, notably reconstruction from later states of the language, comparison with related languages, and, in particular, the interpretation of spelling as man-ifested in the insular script.

The OE sound-system differed in a number of ways from those character-istic of many varieties of PDE. The two most important differences are:

- OE had a different inventory of phonemes;
- OE distributed phonemes differently within the lexicon.

Other significant differences include:

- OE distinguished phonemically between long and short consonants and vowels;
- OE seems to have distinguished phonemically between short and long diphthongs, though this is controversial among scholars;
- there was, at least in the earlier period of OE, a wider variety of unstressed vowels than in PDE.

These differences will now each be explored in turn, with special reference to the WS variety.

## 4.3 **The OE consonants and vowels**

The *phonemic inventory* of the WS variety of OE differs from the 'reference accents' of PDE (i.e. 'Received Pronunciation' = RP, the prestigious variety used in England, and 'General American' = GenAm) in a number of ways, both in consonants and in vowels. Here is the consonant inventory for the EWS variety, as reconstructed by most modern scholars:

/b, p, θ, t, d, f, s, ʃ, x, l, r, g, k, j, w, ʍ, tʃ, ʤ, m, n/

For comparison, here is the consonant inventory for RP:

/b, p, θ, ð, t, d, s, z, ʃ, ʒ, h, l, r, g, k, j, tʃ, ʤ, m, n, ŋ/

The comparison shows some substantial differences between the WS and RP consonantal systems. First, WS did not, it seems, distinguish phonemi-cally between voiced and voiceless fricatives; these sounds were in *comple-mentary distribution*, i.e. did not occur in the same phonetic environments, and were thus allophones. Voiceless sounds, therefore, appeared in word-final and word-initial positions, e.g. [f] <f> in **hlāf** 'loaf', **fela** 'many', while voiced sounds appeared intervocalically, e.g. [v] <f> in **yfel** 'evil', **hlāford** 'lord'. Other examples are: **þurfan** 'need' (with word-initial [θ]) beside **ȳþe** 'wave' (with word-medial [ð]), **hūs** 'house' (noun, with word-final [s]) beside **hūsian** 'house' (verb, with word-medial [z]).

Second, WS, like some varieties of PD Northern English, did not seem to have a distinct /ŋ/ phoneme. It seems probable that WS had an allophone [ŋ], but this sound was found only in certain environments, e.g. in the environment of a following /g/. Thus OE **singan** 'to sing', phonemically /singɑn/, was probably pronounced [siŋgɑn] in WS.

Third, most RP speakers no longer distinguish between /w, ʍ/ as does OE (**wæl** 'slaughter', **hwæl** 'whale'; some other accents of PDE, e.g. Scottish English, also make the distinction), and no longer include /x/ in their inventory (though again compare Scottish usage, e.g. /x/ in **loch**). The interpretation of these clusters is problematic; **hw, hl, hn** and **hr** may represent voiceless or 'devoiced' sounds, but it is probably easier to think of them as [hw, hl, hn, hr]. After vowels and consonants, **h** was pronounced much as the sound of **ch** in Scots **loch** or German **nicht** i.e. as /x/, in, for example, **hēah** 'high', **þōhte** 'thought', **riht** 'right'.

Fourth, OE and PDE differ in their use of written symbols to represent the same sounds. OE not only uses the (apparently) alien letters <þ, ð > for /θ/, where PDE uses <th>, but also uses <sc>, <c>, <cg>, <g> where PDE uses <sh>, <(t)ch>, <dg>, <y>.

Not indicated in the phonemic inventory above is the OE distinction between long and short consonants, represented by pairs such as **mann** 'male human', **man** 'one' (pronoun), with /nn/, /n/ respectively. A phonemic distinction between long and short consonants is not a feature of RP, but may be detected phonetically through a comparison of the PDE pronunciation of /d/ in **bad** with /d/.../d/ in **bad debt**.

The monophthongal vowel inventory of OE was as follows:

/i, i:, e, e:, æ, æ:, ɑ, ɑ:, o, o:, u, u:, y, y:/

Examples of words containing these vowels are: **scip** 'ship', **wrītan** 'write', **æsc** 'ash-tree', **wǣron** 'were', **mann** '(male) human', **stān** 'stone', **dol** 'foolish', **gōd** 'good', **full** 'full, complete', **fūl** 'foul', **yfel** 'evil', **fȳr** 'fire'.

The first major difference between the OE system and those common in PDE is the phonemic distinction between short vowels (V) and long vowels (VV), demonstrated by pairs such as **god** 'god' and **gōd** 'good'. Length is no longer a distinctive feature of PDE accents, though all varieties exhibit allophonic vowel-length variation in particular environments: compare the realisation of /i/ in many pronunciations of **beat, bead**.[1]

The second major difference between OE and PDE accents is to do with the range of available vowel-heights. OE is often described as a 'three-height' system, with three sets of front vowels: /i, i:/ (with parallel rounded vowels /y, y:/), /e, e:/, /æ, æ:/, and three sets of back vowels: /ɑ, ɑ:/, /o, o:/, and /u, u:/ (see chapter 2, section 2). Many PDE systems have four heights. Again, Scots and Scottish English are good examples for comparison, since some historic long vowels in these accents have not diphthongised (compare Scottish and Southern English pronunciations of the vowel in **late**, [e] and [eɪ] respectively).

Finally, OE had a pair of close rounded front vowels, /y, y:/. Rounded front vowels are comparatively rare in PDE accents, though again found in Scottish accents (compare Scottish and RP pronunciations of **foot**). There is evidence for a pair of mid rounded front vowels, /ø, ø:/, but these vowels had unrounded to (and thus merged with) /e, e:/ in recorded WS.

Of course, this outline of the inventory of OE monophthongs is likely to be a crude over-simplification, based on reconstructed WS usage. Just as in PDE, it seems likely that OE had a variety of accents, and it is known that there were major differences between, for example, Saxon and Anglian usages. For instance, it may be noted that in the OE vowel inventory given above there seems to be no qualitative distinction between 'short' and 'long' vowels; compare the qualitative distinction /ɪ,i/ in PDE British English pronunciations of the vowels in **bid, beat**. There were probably such distinctions in some accents, as in PDE; the matter, however, is controversial and will not be pursued here.[2]

It is conventional to distinguish three sets of diphthongs in OE, spelt <ea, eo, ie>; <io> also appears sporadically in EWS manuscripts, but is replaced by <eo>. The traditional view, still accepted by many scholars, is that OE distinguished between *monomoric* (i.e. consisting of a single beat or *mora*, V) short diphthongs in words such as **bearn** 'child', **geaf** 'gave', **eorþe** 'earth' and **heofon** 'heaven', and *bimoric* (VV) long diphthongs in words such as **nēah** 'near', **gēar** 'year', **lēoht** 'light', where the diacritic macron may be taken to refer to the two vowels taken together. The digraph <ie> is also found in EWS, in words such as **ieldra** 'older', **giefan** 'give', **hierde** 'shepherd', **hīeran** 'hear', **līehtan** 'give light'; in LWS, <ie> is often replaced by <y>, yielding **hyrde** 'shepherd', **hȳran** 'hear'. There is considerable debate about the sound-significance of the OE spellings <ea, eo, ie>, and the status of the short diphthongs, and for that reason they are discussed further as a special problem at the end of this chapter.

Finally, there are significant differences in the distribution of sounds within the lexicon. These *lexical-distributional* differences are most marked with regard to those words which contained a long vowel in OE, where for example OE **ū** /u:/ appears in **cū, hū, nū, hūs** etc. where PDE has a diphthong /aʊ/ (cf. PDE **cow, how now, house**).

## 4.4 Stressed and unstressed syllables

So far, discussion has focused on individual segments, e.g. the representation of the phoneme /b/ in OE. However, there are of course suprasegmentals, sound-structures other than segments, of which the most important for our purposes are *syllables* and *stress*.

As was noted in chapter 2, section 2, *syllables* are clusters of segments which, in PDE, are generally focused on a vowel, and which consist of an optional *onset*, a compulsory *peak* (or *nucleus*), and an optional *coda*; thus, in a PDE word such as **meat**, **m** is the onset, **ea** is the peak, and **t** is the coda. The combination of peak and coda is known as the *rhyme*. Syllables may be *light* (with rhymes consisting of V, VV or VC), *heavy* (with rhymes consisting of VVC, VCC), or *superheavy* (with rhymes consisting of VVCC). Many handbooks refer to light syllables as *short* syllables and heavy syllables as *long* syllables. In terms of beats, a light syllable consists of one or two morae, a heavy syllable consists of three morae and a superheavy syllable consists of four morae.

*Stress* was assigned in OE verse, it seems, on the basis of the heavy/light distinction between syllables; metrical stress in poetry was prototypically assigned to heavy syllables. Stress in OE verse could also be assigned to words with two short syllables, e.g. **nama** 'name'; the sequence VCV (as in -ama) was evidently deemed equivalent to VVC and VCC in moraic terms. This assignment of stress to the sequence VCV is known as *resolution*.

Stress, as was noted in chapter 2, section 2, is also to do with the assignment of prominence to a particular syllable. Stress moreover is rule-governed; in PDE, stress is assigned to syllables in accordance with a set of rules inherited from Proto-Germanic and modified by contact with other languages such as French and Latin. In Proto-Germanic, stress was assigned to the beginning of lexical words, and this pattern remained basic in OE; thus stress was assigned to the syllables underlined in words such as **niman** 'take', **standan** 'stand', **cyning** 'king', **hlāford** 'lord', **bæcere** 'baker', **micel** 'great', **twentig** 'twenty'; syllables such as -an, -ing, -ord, -ere, -el, -ig etc. were unstressed.

However, OE had many words which derived from the affixation of a prefix or suffix to the word's root, for example: **forniman** 'take away, destroy' (**niman** 'take'), **geloren** 'lost' (past participle, cf. **lēosan** 'lose'), **æftergenga** 'follower' and **bīgenga** 'inhabitant' (cf. **genga** 'companion'), **mægþhād** 'maidenhood'; or through compounding, as in **sciprāp** 'cable' (**scip** 'ship', **rāp** 'rope'). In these cases, different principles of assigning stress apply. The general rule is that prefixes and suffixes are assigned a degree of stress if they have an existence as an open-class lexical word: noun, adjective, verb, or adverb. Thus, since **æfter** can be used as a distinct adverb meaning 'afterwards', it receives a degree of stress when acting as a prefix in **æftergenga**; it has what is known as *secondary stress*. The same applies to **hād** in **mægþhād**; **hād** can be used as a noun meaning 'character, rank, condition'. However, **ge-** in **geloren** does not have a separate existence as a distinct word so it does not receive any degree of stress, and the same applies to inflexional endings such as -an, -e, -es, -um etc. An interesting pair of words is **hlāford** 'lord', **hlāfweard** 'steward' (cf. **hlāf** 'loaf of bread', **weard** 'guardian'); the unstressed suffix -ord is a reduced derivation from -weard but has lost its independent semantic significance.

In short, the assignment of stress was made on semantic principles, which is what we would expect given the role of *prominence* in discourse. Prominence in discourse is to do with the predictability of the item in question; if the item in question is a member of the closed word-classes, for example PDE **the, of,** or a bound morpheme, for example PDE **-ing,** then we would expect that item to be largely predictable from syntactic context and thus not needing to be marked as prominent in terms of stress. However, the open classes of words have in principle an infinite number of members, and are not therefore predictable in the same way; they therefore require a degree of prominence in discourse. Such stressed items in OE, as reconstructed from verse, are invariably either heavy syllables or a sequence of light syllables equivalent to a heavy one in moraic terms (i.e. through resolution). It would seem that affixes of the **-hād, æfter-** type, which are either heavy or resolved, are stressed since they were perceived as quasi-independent lexical items.

## 4.5 Sound-change and dialectal variation

So far in this chapter, the focus has been on the description of WS, a particular variety of OE, at a particular point in time: the EWS period, which is roughly contemporary with the best-known Anglo-Saxon king, Alfred the Great (i.e. the late ninth century). However, the OE period lasted for some six centuries, from the arrival of the Anglo-Saxons in Britain in the fifth century up to and beyond the Norman Conquest in the eleventh: roughly the length of time which separates Chaucer from ourselves. And, just as PDE differs considerably from Chaucer's ME, so the earliest OE – insofar as we can reconstruct it – differed from OE on the eve of William the Conqueror's arrival.

Moreover, the label 'OE' refers to a set of varieties. Older histories of the language often used to describe the history of English as a march towards standardisation; it is now customary to emphasise that the history of any language is, in Lass's words, the history of 'a population of variants moving through time' (Lass 1997). In this section, an outline of sound-changes and dialectal variation, insofar as it refers to accents, will be given. The first part of this outline will refer to the emergence of WS, since that is the best-known OE variety, but this is followed by a discussion of the other OE dialects.

*Sound-change* is usually defined as a phenomenon whereby speakers adjust their phonologies, or sound-systems. Outcomes of sound-change include *mergers* of previously distinct phonemes, the phonemicisation of allophones (*splits*) and the addition of new phonemes to a language's inventory, and the redistribution of phonemes within the lexicon (*shifts*).

Sound-changes seem to be the results of interaction between individuals which diffuse into the wider community; they are thus triggered through contact and then implemented through a process of social monitoring. The process seems to take place as follows: one speaker attempts, consciously or (more probably) unconsciously, to imitate the usage of the other, for reasons of peer-identification. If the individuals become strongly tied socially (for example, within a family group, or in a close-knit work-group) the usage is imitated precisely. However, if the individuals are weakly tied socially, one speaker may 'miss the target' because weak ties do not allow for persistent monitoring of linguistic behaviour. The 'mistaken' outcome can then be passed to another individual. Of course, it is possible that several individuals behave in the same or in similar ways for the same reason, namely group-identification; if such group behaviour occurs, then we might expect the change to be diffused more vigorously or sustained. The triggering, implementation and diffusion of sound-changes is a notoriously controversial matter (see Smith 2007 and references there cited).

Before the arrival of sound-recording, four sources of information are traditionally distinguished for past states of the sound-system of a language: contemporary writers on language, writing-systems, verse practices and information arrived at through the process known as reconstruction. The first of these witnesses is lacking for OE, though some useful information may be derived from contemporary writings on Latin (such as Ælfric's *Grammar*, which dates from the late tenth/early eleventh centuries), and from the anonymous, sophisticated twelfth-century phonologist who wrote a study of the sound-structure of a cognate language, Old Icelandic: *The First Grammatical Treatise* (Haugen 1972). The other sources of evidence, however, are all available, and the following outline derives from a mixture of these sources. For the earliest period, when first Proto-West Germanic and subsequently OE began to emerge as a distinguishable language from the other varieties of Germanic, we depend almost wholly on reconstruction, and this situation persists during the prehistoric period of Anglo-Saxon settlements, when the dialectal map of OE was established.

The outline of sound-changes given here is very brief, and really designed as a precursor to more advanced study. In this outline, 'philological' notation is adopted (after Campbell 1959 and Hamer 1967); the advantage of this notation is convenience for the reader, since it (a) corresponds to a convenient reference model of OE orthographic practice, and (b) avoids commitment to a specific phonological or allophonic interpretation (which can be the point at issue). However, the standard phonetic and phonological conventions are also used: [..] = allophonic/phonetic transcription,

/../ = phonemic transcription; C is used, as hitherto, for any consonant, and V for any vowel. For rules, i.e. descriptive formalisations of developments in sounds, the following conventions are also used:

>    goes to, becomes, is realised as
<    comes from
$    syllable boundary
Ø    zero
/    in the environment: X > Y/A_B = 'X becomes Y in the environment of a preceding A and a following B, i.e. AXB becomes AYB.'

The names of the sound-changes (e.g. *first fronting, breaking, restoration of a*) are those in traditional use in the standard handbooks.

## 4.5.1 Sound-changes affecting vowels in stressed syllables

In what follows, the letters A–M as labels for each sound-change are those used in the handy scheme adopted in Hamer 1967.

*Changes in the Germanic period* (i.e., before the divergence of the Germanic varieties; not all of these features are manifested in all Germanic varieties):

Changes A–C are examples of shifts, often conditioned by particular environments, which cause the redistribution of sounds in the lexicon:

A. Shift **u > o**; the rule is:

   **u > o**, unless /_ C [+ nasal], or /_ $ **u, i/j**

Examples are: **bunden** 'bound' past participle (beside **holpen** 'helped' past participle); **gyden** 'goddess' (beside **god** 'god').

B. Shift **e > i**; the rule is:

   **e > i** /_ C [+ nasal], or /_ $ **u, i/j**

Examples are: **bindan** 'bind' (infinitive), **helpan** 'help' (infinitive).

C. Shift **eu > iu**; the rule is:

   **eu > iu** /_ $ **i/j**

This **iu**, the product of a vowel-harmony, survives in the very earliest OE texts, for example, in **þīustra** 'darkness' in the *Corpus Glossary* (eighth/ninth century); subsequently **īu** became **īo**.

*Changes in the West Germanic and 'Ingvaeonic' periods:*

D. Diphthongal changes; the rule is:

   **ai > ā, au > ǣa** (**ǣa** = later **ēa**), **eu > ēo, iu > īo**

The last two diphthongal changes take place during the OE period, but are included here for convenience. Examples of the first two are **bān** 'bone', **ēage** 'eye'. The older forms are preserved in other Germanic varieties; compare PD German **Bein** 'leg', **Auge** 'eye'. Other examples include one of the words inscribed on the Bucharest (Pietroasa) ring, dating from *c.* 400 AD, **hailag** 'holy', and personal names in the writings of Latin and Greek historians, for example **Radagaisus, Austrogothi**.

E. *First fronting* is sometimes known as *Anglo-Frisian Brightening*, since it is a development which is manifested in both OE and Old Frisian. This change affected the Proto-Germanic open back vowel **a**, which was fronted (thus 'brightened') to **æ** in most environments. The rule is:

> **a > æ**, except /_ C [+ nasal], [w] (despite Campbell 1959: 55; see Hogg 1992).

Thus forms such as **dæg** 'day', **glæd** 'glad', with an open front vowel, appear beside **land** 'land', with an open back vowel. This development did not take place in North or East Germanic varieties, thus Gothic **dags** 'day', Old Norse **dagr**.

*Changes in the period between the divergence of prehistoric Old English and prehistoric Old Frisian, and recorded West Saxon (i.e. the 'pre-West Saxon' period):*

F. *Breaking of front vowels before consonant groups* is a conditioned sound-change, whereby a diphthong appears in place of a monophthong in particular environments; the monophthong is thus 'broken' into a diphthong. The rules are as follows:

(a)   **i > io**/_ **h, hC, rC; e > eo**/_ **h, hC, rC, lh** and sometimes **lc**
(b)   **æ > ea**/_ **h, hC, rC, lC; ī > īo**/_ **h, hC** (but see L, below)
(c)   **ǣ > ēa**/_ **h, hC; ē > ēo**/_ **h** (but this last development is only found in Anglian dialects).

Examples include **feohtan** 'fight', beside **helpan**; **eahta** 'eight', **earm** 'poor', **eald** 'old', **healp** 'helped' (preterite singular), **nēah** 'near'.

G. *Restoration of a*: The **æ** which was the result of first fronting (see E, above) was retracted to **a** when a back vowel appeared as the peak/nucleus of the following syllable. Thus:

> **æ > a**/_ CV[+back], and often also /_ CCV[+ back], where CC = geminate (i.e. two consonants of the same type, e.g. **bb**), or **st, sk**.

Examples include **dagas** 'days' (beside **dæg**), **gladost** 'most glad' (beside **glæd**), **crabba** 'crab'.

H. *Influence of palatal consonants*: The influence of palatal consonants on following vowels operated only in WS and in Old Northumbrian. In WS, if the palatal consonants **g, c, sc** preceded the mid and open front vowels e, æ and ǣ a vocalically close glide developed between the consonant and the vowel, producing the diphthongs ie, ea, ēa (though see section 4.6 below). Thus:

e > ie, æ > ea, ǣ > ēa/ **g, c, sc** _ (where **g, c** and **sc** are palatal consonants).

Examples are **giefan** 'give', **gīet** 'still' (cf. PDE **yet**), **sceal** 'must' (cf. PDE **shall**), **scēap** 'sheep'. This phenomenon in WS is often referred to as *palatal diphthongisation*, although – as is discussed in section 4.6 below – there is considerable scholarly debate about how these digraphs are mapped onto the sound-system. It is indisputable, for instance, that <e> in **geong** is a spelling convention; if <eo> in this word were really mapped onto /e:o/ then the PDE form would be *yeng.

I. *I-mutation (i-Umlaut)*: The processes involves in this sound-change can be paralleled in many of the Germanic languages. I-mutation is a kind of *vowel-harmony*, whereby a back or open vowel took on some of the front/close quality of the vowel in the following unstressed syllable. The rules are as follows:

V[+back] > V[+ front]/_ \$ i, j; V [+front, + open] > V [+front, + close] /_ \$ i, j.

When /i/ or /j/ stood in the following syllable, all stressed back vowels were fronted, thus: a > æ (although a had in most cases become æ before the period of i-mutation), ā > ǣ, o > oe (a rare development), ō > ōē, u > y, ū > ȳ. In the same situation, open front vowels were raised, thus æ > e; it is also possible that e > i. All diphthongs became ie, īe; subsequently, oe, ōē unrounded to become e, ē. The vowels i, ī, ē, ǣ were not affected; e had already become i (see B, above). In many cases the i, j which caused i-mutation had disappeared during the prehistoric period.

Examples are **reccan** 'stretch, tell, wield' (cf. Proto-Germanic *rakjan), **menn** 'men' (Proto-Germanic *manniz), **ele** 'oil' (Latin **olium**), **hǣlan** 'heal' (cf. **hāl** 'whole'), **dēman** 'deem, judge' (cf. **dōm** 'judgement'), **brȳcþ** 'enjoys' 3rd person present singular (cf. infinitive **brūcan**), **gylden** 'golden' (Proto-Germanic *guldin), and **ieldra** 'older', **fieht** 'fights', **smīecþ** 'emits smoke', **nīehst** 'nearest' (cf. OE **eald** 'old', **feohtan** 'fight' = infinitive, **smēocan** 'emit smoke' = infinitive, **nēah** 'near'). I-mutation is of great importance for understanding the morphology of the OE verb in particular, and it will be discussed further in chapter 7.

J. *Back-mutation (back Umlaut)*: Back-mutation is another kind of vowel-harmony, although in this case a short, front vowel develops a back-vowel glide and thus becomes a diphthong when a back vowel appears as the peak of the following syllable. Thus the rule is:

V [+ short, + front] > diphthong/_ C V [+ back].

This sound-change has a restricted manifestation in WS, since æ could not appear in this position, as a result of restoration of **a** (G, above), and it only took place in WS if C = labial (**p, f, w, m**) or liquid (**l, r**). The rule relevant for WS therefore reads:

i > io, e > eo /_ C [+ labial or + liquid] V [+ back].

Examples include: **leofaþ** 'lives' (cf. **libban** 'live' = infinitive), **heofon** 'heaven'.

K. *Loss of h and compensatory lengthening*: When **h** was intervocalic it was lost and the preceding vowel, if short, was lengthened to compensate, e.g. *\*feohes genitive singular > fēos (cf. **feoh** 'cattle, property'). Similar processes occurred with regard to medial **rh, lh**, thus *\*feorhes > fēores (cf. **feorh** 'life'). The rule is:

V > VV/_h, V > VV/_rh, lh

L. A shift, **io, īo > eo, ēo** in WS. This change was still happening in historic times, and the earliest forms of WS often retain <io>-spellings.

M. A series of changes took place during the historic period of OE, i.e. *c.* 700–1100 AD. Of these by far the most important was a pair of *quantitative changes*:

(a)  Late OE: *Lengthening before homorganic consonant groups*, e.g. OE cild, late OE **cīld** (compare unlengthened OE and late OE **cildru**)
(b)  Late OE: *Shortening before non-homorganic consonant groups*, e.g. late OE **cepte** < **cēpte** (compare unshortened OE **cēpan**); **wifman** < **wīfmann** (compare unshortened OE **wīf**)

Homorganic consonants are those made using the same organs of the mouth; thus /l/ and /d/ are homorganic since both are alveolar consonants, whereas /p/ and /t/ are bilabial and alveolar respectively. It seems that, in late OE, homorganic groups such as /ld/ came to be treated as monomoric, C, rather than as bimoric, CC; as a result, the rhyming element in words like **cild** came to be seen as forming a light syllable rather than a heavy syllable of the kind which received stress. The vowel therefore lengthened to compensate. This lengthening did not take place, however, when another consonant followed (as with **cildru**) since that sequence remained heavy in moraic terms. The shortening process derived from a similar rebalancing of syllabic patterns. This development is important for ME rather than OE studies; for a discussion, see Smith 2007: chapter 5.

The reasoning which lies behind the generally accepted chronological ordering may be briefly summarised: *First fronting* must precede the other changes because, where relevant, the forms produced by it are subjected to later developments. The relationship of *breaking* and *restoration of a* is determined by forms such as **slēan** (< *sleahan** with loss of **h** and 'compensatory lengthening' < *slæhan** with breaking < *slahan** with first fronting). If restoration had preceded breaking, the resulting form *slahan** would not have been subject to breaking.[3]

The chronological relationship between *breaking, palatal diphthongisation* and *i-mutation* is, as Campbell (1959: 107) calls it, 'a difficult question'. That palatal diphthongisation follows breaking is traditionally illustrated by forms such as **ceorl** 'peasant', **georn** 'eager' < *kerl-, *gern-; the form **eo** has to be the product of breaking because otherwise *ie** would have developed from an unbroken **e** to produce *cierl, *giern, and **ie** was not subjected to breaking (Campbell 1959: 108). It is now often accepted that palatal diphthongisation precedes i-mutation because palatal diphthongisation does not appear to take place before front vowels produced by i-mutation; the only evidence for this chronological sequence, though, is the reconstructed form *cīese** 'cheese' > Late WS **cȳse**. As reaffirmed by Hogg (1992: 120), Late WS **cȳse** 'cheese' must arise from the sequence **cȳse** < Early WS *cīese** < (subjected to i-mutation) *cēasi-** < (subjected to palatal diphthongisation) < *cæsi-** (subjected to palatalisation of *k-** in the environment of a preceding front vowel) < *kǣsi-**; the form is a loanword into Proto-Germanic from Latin **cāseus**, and Latin **ā** was regularly reflected in Proto-Germanic as **ǣ**. Any other sequential ordering of forms would not yield the historically attested word.

The relationship between *breaking* and *i-mutation* is indicated by the form **ieldra** 'older'; **ie** is the i-mutation of **ea** produced by breaking, and this fact would seem to confirm that breaking precedes i-mutation.

*Back-mutation* must be later than *i-mutation*, because i-mutated forms are subjected to back-mutation: for example, **eowu** 'ewe', derived from the sequence West Germanic *awi** > (through first fronting) *æwi** > (through i-mutation) *ewi**, with a later suffix transference of **-u** to yield **eo** through back-mutation of earlier *e**; see Campbell 1959: 90. The lateness of back-mutation is attested by the fact that in the earliest surviving Anglian texts non-back-mutated forms occasionally appear, e.g. **sitaþ** (transliterated form) on the runic Franks Casket, which dates from *c.* 700.

## *Dialectal distinctions in the OE vowels in stressed syllables*

The following are the main dialectal distinctions in stressed vocalism in OE, with reference to WS and Old Anglian (Old Northumbrian, Old Mercian, varieties of Old Anglian).

(a) Proto-Germanic ǣ (so-called ǣ) is reflected in WS as **dǣd** 'deed' **strǣt** 'road, street', Old Anglian **dēd, strēt**.

(b) *First Fronting* had distinct outputs in WS and Old Anglian. Thus pre-WS \***æld** 'old' which became **eald** (through breaking) is paralleled by Old Anglian **ald**; some scholars consider that the Old Anglian development was subsequent to first fronting (and thus a *retraction* whereby a front vowel became a back vowel again), while others believe that first fronting simply failed to take place in the ancestor of Old Anglian in the environment of a following /l/. A similar distinction may be observed with reference to following /r/-groups, e.g. WS **bearnum**, Old Northumbrian **barnum**.

(c) *Breaking* and 'retraction': see (b) above.

(d) *Influence of palatal consonants* affected WS and Old Northumbrian, but with different outputs, cf. WS **scēap** 'sheep', Old Northumbrian **scīp** (from non-West Saxon \***scēp**).

(d) *Smoothing* is a monophthongisation which affected Old Anglian, producing a contrast between WS **weorc** 'work' and Old Anglian **werc**.

(e) *Back-mutation*, as discussed in 4.5.1 above (change J), had distinct outputs in WS and non-WS varieties; thus WS **witodlīce** 'certainly' contrasts with non-WS **weotudlīce**.

(f) *Second fronting* is a process of raising and fronting which affected the Mercian variety, rather as first fronting had affected all varieties of OE; it took place comparatively late in the history of OE phonology (thus 'second' as opposed to 'first' fronting). Second fronting involved the raising of æ to e, and the fronting of **a** to **æ**. This development accounts for the Old Mercian distinction between **deg** 'day', **dægas** 'days', cf. WS **dæg, dagas**.

## 4.5.2 Sound-changes in the vowels of unstressed syllables

Sound-changes also affected the vowels of unstressed syllables. Changes (a)–(d) below are the most important for the early history of OE sounds, while change (h) is of considerable significance for the later history of the language.

(a) **ai, au > ǣ, ō** in unstressed syllables (compare **ā, ēa** in stressed syllables). In recorded OE, these vowels appear as **e, a** respectively. Examples: **giefe** 'gift' (dative singular), **eahta** 'eight' (compare Gothic **gibai, ahtau**, which retain the older forms).

(b) *First fronting*: except in some words with low sentence-stress (e.g. **þone** 'that' etc.), unstressed **a > æ** (later **e**), e.g. **tunge, ēage**, except in the environment of following nasals.

(c)  *Breaking*: breaking does not take place in unstressed syllables. Rather (according to Campbell 1959: 142) æ is retracted to a (/aː/) /_ lC, rC, with a tendency to develop into o, e.g. **hlāfard, hlāford** 'lord'.

(d)  *I-mutation*: i-mutation was fully operative in unstressed syllables, but oe (long and short) and y became e (long and short) and i in the prehistoric period, and æ > e soon after the earliest writings began to appear. Thus e (long and short) and i were the only remaining products of i-mutation, and these fell together on e at an early stage. Examples: **stānehte** 'stony' (cf. Old High German **-ohti**); medial -i- in weak Class II verbs (from **-ej-** < **-ēj-** < **-ōēj-** < **-ōj-**). See the discussion of weak Class II verbs in section 7.4.

(e)  Early OE loss of unstressed vowels was very frequent, in a variety of positions, for example: **gōdne** 'good' masculine accusative singular (< **\*-anōn**), **hātte** 'called' preterite singular (cf. Gothic **haitada**), **dæglic** 'daily' (cf. Old High German **tagalīh**).

(f)  Early OE shortening of unstressed long vowels: all unstressed long vowels were shortened in prehistoric OE.

(g)  Parasitic vowels appear sporadically, e.g. *Lindisfarne Gospels Gloss* **worohton** 'made' preterite plural (cf. WS **wrohton**); they also arose sporadically for syllabic l, m, n, r, with i (later e) after a front vowel, u (later o) after a back vowel, for example, in the *Epinal-Erfurt Glosses*, **segil-** 'sail', **thōthor** 'ball'. PDE **through, thorough** derive from the OE variants **þurh, þuruh**.

(h)  Reduction in variety of unstressed vowels, exemplified by the interchangeability of -en, -an, -on in late OE texts. Thus, for instance, whereas **hīe bundon** and **hīe bunden** meant different things in early WS, 'they have bound' and 'they might have bound' respectively, the difference in meaning can only be determined from context in late WS.

## 4.5.3 The OE consonants

In common with other varieties of Germanic, OE shows in its distribution of consonants the effects of the First Consonant Shift, generally known as Grimm's Law. It also shows the effects of a development of Grimm's Law known commonly as Verner's Law.[4]

*Grimm's Law* is so-called after the German philologist and folklorist Jacob Grimm (1785–1863) who first gave currency to a coherent account of this sound-change. Grimm showed that there was a predictable set of consonantal differences between the Germanic languages and the other languages of the Indo-European family, dating from the period of divergence of Proto-Germanic from other Indo-European dialects. The effects of Grimm's Law in OE can be seen through comparing groups of *cognates*, i.e. words in different languages with a presumed common ancestor (Latin **co + gnātus** 'born together'), e.g. Old English **fæder** 'father', **fisc** 'fish' corresponding to Latin **pater, piscis** (cf. Italian **padre, pesce**). Here is a general set of correspondences, illustrated from recorded languages. Sanskrit, Lithuanian etc. are archaic; Gothic, OE etc. exemplify the operation of Grimm's Law:

| Proto-IE | Sanskrit (unless otherwise) | Gothic (unless otherwise) |
|---|---|---|
| *p | **pita** | **fadar** 'father' |
| *t | **trayas** | **þrija** 'three' |
| *k | **krnatti** 'spins' | **haurds** 'woven door, hurdle' |
| *bh | **bhrata** | **broþar** 'brother' |
| *dh | **dhama** 'glory' | **doms** 'fame' |
| *gh | **ghnanti** 'they strike' | OE **gūþ** 'battle' |
| *b | Lith. **bala** 'swamp' | PDE **pool** |
| *d | **dasa** | **taihun** 'ten' |
| *g | Lat. **genus** | **kuni** 'kin' |

*Verner's Law* is so-called after the Danish philologist Karl Verner (1846–1896), who accounted for some apparently anomalous deviations from Grimm's Law. Verner was one of the *Neogrammarians*, a group of linguists active particularly in Germany at the end of the nineteenth century, who attempted to place the study of language on what seemed to them to be a 'scientific' basis, comparable in terms of descriptive formalisation with what had been achieved for physics, for example. Their achievements still underpin present-day research in historical linguistics; 'Verner's article probably had a greater effect on historical linguistics than has any other single publication' (Lehmann 1992: 154).

Verner noticed that Proto-Indo-European voiceless plosives became Proto-Germanic voiceless fricatives according to Grimm's Law, but 'in voiced surroundings [e.g. between vowels] these voiceless fricatives, plus the already existing voiceless fricative *s*, became voiced when not immediately preceded by the accent [i.e. when the stress was on the following rather than on the preceding syllable]' (Lehmann 1992: 154). A subsequent stress-shift meant that this environment was later obscured.

An OE example illustrating the process is **fæder**, with medial **d** (from earlier *ð), as opposed to medial θ; cf. Proto-Indo-European *petēr). Verner's Law has morphological implications in OE; medial -r- in **curon** 'chose' (plural) is derived from earlier *z (*rhotacism*); cf. infinitive **cēosan** 'choose'. Here is a set of further examples, where Greek represents IE usages not affected by Verner's Law and OE is representative of Germanic languages:

| Greek | OE |
|---|---|
| **hepta** | **seofon** 'seven' |
| **pater** | **fæder** (cf. Old Norse **faðir**) 'father' |

hekura             **sweger** 'mother-in-law'
**nuos** < *****snuos**     **snoru** 'daughter-in-law'

As well as Grimm's and Verner's Laws, OE shows the marks of other sound-changes affecting consonants. The most important are:

(a) *Fronting and assibilation* is an Ingvæonic change: in both OE and Old Frisian a distinction arose between front or palatal and velar plosives [g, k], whereby front allophones (eventually affricates and approximants) appeared before front vowels and back allophones before back. The process seems to take place after the restoration of **a** before back vowels, proven by forms such as **caru** 'sorrow', **galan** 'sing'. Examples include **cirice** 'church', **georn** 'eager'. Velar consonants, however, remained not only before back vowels, but also before their Umlauts, e.g. **cū** 'cow', **cyning** 'king', since the process was completed before the i-mutation which produced the **y** in OE **cyning**.

(b) *Voicing and unvoicing of consonants (mainly fricatives)*: issues raised here are important for ME studies. As we have seen, OE did not make a phonological distinction between voiced and voiceless fricatives; the sounds were allophones, with voiceless sounds in initial and final position and voiced sounds intervocalically. The phonemic distinction arose in ME with the introduction of loanwords from French and the loss of inflexional endings whereby forms such as **hūsian** 'house' (verb) became **house(n)** and finally lost its ending altogether; compare the PDE distinction between **house** (noun) and **house** (verb).

(c) *Gemination*, or doubling of consonants, took place in various environments and at various times. The rule is as follows:

VC > VCC when syncopation of vowels brought VC /_ **r, l**

Examples include **bettra**, Late WS **blǣddre** 'bladder'.

(d) *Metatheses*, whereby sounds are transposed in sequence, are quite common in many varieties of English at various times in its history, cf. OE **þrīe**, **þridda** beside PDE 'three', 'third'. Thus in OE **āscian** 'ask' often appears beside **āxian, ācsian**, cf. PDE dialectal **axed** 'asked'.

## 4.6 The problem of the 'short diphthongs'

This chapter concludes with a special study of one of the most controversial problems in OE philology: the problem of the interpretation of the spellings <ea, eo, ie>. These spellings have given rise to a whole series of questions, for example: do these spellings really represent diphthongs? What is their weight in moraic terms, i.e. are they to be seen as equivalent to long (heavy) monophthongs, VV? How far are (as conventional wisdom holds) the 'short diphthongs' <ea, eo, ie> to be seen as equivalent to short vowels, i.e. V (vowels with which, historically, they tend to merge)? How are the individual elements within these diphthongs (if that is what they are) to be pronounced? These questions form one of the major conundrums in the study of OE phonology, and continue to give rise to discussion among scholars.

Almost all scholars accept the existence in WS of the long diphthongs spelt <ea, eo>, which represent the reflexes of Germanic diphthongs as well as the products of certain sound-changes (for which see section 4.5 above). These diphthongs were bimoric, i.e. VV in terms of weight, and thus equivalent to long monophthongs.

The problem arises with the so-called 'short diphthongs', which were not the reflexes of Germanic diphthongs but arose as the result of sound-changes such as breaking or 'palatal diphthongisation', and have been believed by many scholars to be monomoric, i.e. V, and thus equivalent in metrical weight to a short monophthong. The key problem is, as David White has pointed out (2004: *passim*), that such short diphthongs are vanishingly rare in world languages, and indeed not found in living languages at all; their presence in standard descriptions is the outcome in all cases of scholarly reconstruction.

One argument offered originally by Marjorie Daunt (Daunt 1939), and recently reiterated by White (2004), is that spellings such as <ea, eo>, when representing the 'short diphthongs', instead are used to indicate the quality of the following consonant. Certainly it is generally accepted that such usages occur in OE, for example spellings such as **secean** 'seek' (beside more common **secan**), or **geong** 'young' (which would have yielded PDE *yeng if <eo> had represented one of the 'short diphthongs'). Richard Hogg sums up this view as follows: '... the traditional position holds that <ea, eo, io> always represented diphthongs both long and short except where the orthographic evidence suggests otherwise or the linguistic development is implausible ...' (1992: 17). It could therefore be argued that <ea, eo> in words such as **eald** 'old', **earn** 'eagle', **weorpan** 'throw', **eolh** 'elk' represent /æ/ or /e/ followed by a 'back consonant'; <eo> in **heofon** 'heaven' would be an attempt to represent /e/ 'coloured' by the back vowel in the unstressed syllable (a 'vowel-harmony'). Old Irish had a phonemic distinction between /l/ and /ł/, with the latter flagged by the use of the preceding digraph <ea> as opposed to <e>. And the Latin alphabet was brought to Anglo-Saxon England by Irish-trained scribes who would be capable of transferring a spelling-distinction from Old Irish to OE, when that spelling-distinction mapped onto a sound-distinction in the target language.

However, there are problems with this analysis. Pairs arose in WS, subsequent to the operation of the sound-change which produced <ea> in **eald, earn** etc, which seem to indicate that <ea> was perceived in WS as phonologically distinct in quality from <æ>, e.g. **ærn** 'house' beside **earn** 'eagle'; despite suggestions to the contrary (e.g. White 2004: 80), it seems likely that, in the conditions of vernacular literacy obtaining in WS, this difference indicates a real distinction in pronunciation (compare the PDE pronunciation of **meet, meat** with the distinction in pronunciation between these words which existed in EModE, that is, [meːt, miːt] respectively). If there were no difference in pronunciation, we would expect variation in spelling between *ǽld and **eald** in WS, and such variation does not occur.

Although some languages (e.g. Scottish Gælic) have a three-way length distinction, viz. V, VV, VVV (see Laver 1994: 442), it seems unlikely that OE had the same system, with the short diphthongs to be interpreted as bimoric (VV) and the long diphthongs as trimoric (VVV). The 'long diphthongs' of OE derive in historical terms from bimoric (VV) Proto-West Germanic diphthongs, and there does not seem to be any good reason to posit a lengthening – especially as, in later stages of the language, they tend to merge with long monophthongs, VV. The 'short diphthongs', in contrast, tend to merge with short monophthongs, V.

Perhaps the most economical explanation would be to see the 'short diphthongs' as consisting of a short vowel followed by a so-called glide-vowel, i.e. Vv. Daunt herself argued that 'there was probably a glide between the front vowel and the following consonant' (Hogg 1992: 18), a point later repeated by Stockwell and Barritt (1951; see Hogg 1992: 19). The distinction between monophthongs-plus-glides and diphthongs is a tricky one, but recent experimental work on, for example, Spanish suggests that a robust distinction is possible (see Hualde and Prieto 2002).

The spelling <ie> is used in EWS to represent the outcome of further sound-changes which affected <ea, eo>, and it therefore seems logical to assume that it, too, represents a diphthong, probably of the same kind (i.e. full vowel plus hiatus vowel).

The most recent full conspectus of relevant scholarship appears in Hogg 1992: 16–24, which gives a full outline of the controversy, with references to date, and also White 2004; readers are also recommended to study the relevant chapters of Lass 1994 and of *The Cambridge History of the English Language (CHEL)*.

## Notes

1. A well-known PD example, which raises controversy about its phonemic status, is the Scottish Vowel-Length Rule, whereby vowels are realised long in the environment of a following morpheme boundary and /r, v, z, d/. Pairs such as **brewed** and **brood** thus exhibit distinct stressed vowels (VV, V respectively). This pattern, which seems to have emerged in Scots in the sixteenth century and to have been sustained in Scots and Scottish English ever since, is known as the Scottish Vowel-Length Rule, otherwise as 'Aitken's Law' after the scholar who first formulated it precisely (see Aitken 1981, Collinge 1992: 3–6).

2. Campbell 1959: 14 makes an interesting point in a classic footnote: 'It is funda-mental to the history of English vowels that the long and short vowels were practically identical in quality till about 1200, and that afterwards they became distinguished by the short sounds becoming more open or more lax than the long sounds to which they previously corresponded.' The evidence for this differ-ence derives from distinct developments in the transitional period between OE and ME; see Smith 2007: chapter 5 for a discussion.

3. There is some slight evidence that breaking might have preceded restoration in Old Northumbrian, yielding historical **slā**; see Hogg 1992: 99–100.

4. The Second, or High German, Consonant Shift was a development which took place in what is now southern Germany, and need not concern us here. For details, see Chambers and Wilkie 1970; for a more advanced account, see Keller 1978.

## Exercises

Exercise 4a  'The relationship between phonological and graphological change is a close one.' Discuss, with special reference to the pre-OE and OE periods.

Exercise 4b  Consider the evidence for sound-change offered by the Old English *fuþorc*.

Exercise 4c  Write notes on the history of the following graphemes: <þ>, <ȝ>, <v>, <y>

Exercise 4d  Write notes on the following forms: **ieldra, dagas, fæder, strǣt**

Exercise 4e  What is phonemicisation? Illustrate your answer with reference to the history of the English fricatives during the Old and Middle English periods.

## Key terms introduced in this chapter

fuþorc, fuþark

runes

alphabet

insular script

palaeography

phonemic inventory

sound-change (mergers, splits, shifts)

Grimm's Law

Verner's Law

mora

# CHAPTER 5

# The Old English Lexicon

## In this chapter …

This chapter takes a closer look at Old English vocabulary. It begins with a discussion of OE word-formation (lexical morphology), and then looks at how OE borrowed words from other languages, such as Latin. Chapter 5 also looks at the semantics of the OE lexicon.

### Contents

## 5.1 **Lexical morphology I: roots, themes and stems**

This chapter deals with *words*, defined in chapter 1 as stable, uninterruptible units of meaning made up from a free morpheme and optional bound morphemes. These words may be grouped into *lexemes*, the overall term for words which are related in *paradigmatic* terms (e.g. **love, loves, loved** are members of one lexeme, **pony, ponies** are members of another). The set of OE lexemes makes up the OE vocabulary or *lexicon*. Study of the lexicon is known as *lexicology* (not to be confused with *lexicography*, i.e. dictionary-making).

The OE lexicon was largely inherited from its Proto-West Germanic ances-tor, and thus shared its practices of *lexical morphology* (often called *word-formation*) with other West Germanic languages. Readers who understand PD German will find many OE practices of word-formation to be very familiar. There are also features of OE which derive from its Proto-Indo-European ancestor, and thus the starting-point for discussion of OE lexicology has to be a discussion of certain structures common to all the Indo-European languages.

The basic lexical element in open-class Indo-European words is the *root*, which carries the primary semantic content of the word. The root is generally followed by a *theme*. Together, the root and theme make up the *stem* of a word, to which an *ending* may, or may not, be added. Thus, in the reconstructed Proto-Germanic form **\*stainaz** 'stone', **\*stain-** is the root, **\*-a-** is the theme, and **\*-z** is the ending. Roots and themes were carefully distinguished in Proto-Germanic, it seems, but in later dialects (such as OE), many themes have disappeared or have become obscured. Distinct themes are better preserved in older varieties of Indo-European, such as Latin and Greek; thus in Latin **manus** 'hand', **man-** is the root, **-u-** is the theme and **-s** is the ending. There were also consonantal themes in Proto-Indo-European, e.g. **-in-** in Latin **hominis**, an inflected form of **homo** 'man' (=**hom-** + **-in-** + **-is**).

It is traditional in advanced OE grammars to classify most paradigms of nouns by their reconstructed themes ('a-nouns', 'ō-nouns' etc.); thus OE **stān** 'stone' is classified as an 'a-noun' since the theme in Proto-Germanic was **\*a**. Nouns with vocalic themes (i.e. vowels) are traditionally known as *strong* nouns. The main groups of strong noun in OE other than a-nouns are ō-, i- and u-nouns, exemplified respectively by **lufu** 'love' (Proto-Germanic **\*lufō**), **dǣd** 'deed' (Proto-Germanic **\*dǣdiz**), **sunu** 'son' (Proto-Germanic **\*sunuz**). Sub-groups of a-nouns are ja- and wa-nouns, as in **ende** 'end' (Proto-Germanic **\*andja**), **melu** 'meal, ground grain' (Proto-Germanic **\*melwam**); sub-groups of ō-nouns are jō- and uō-nouns, as in **synn** 'sin' (Proto-Germanic **\*sunjō**), **sinu** 'sinew' with inflected forms **sinwe, sinwa, sinwum** (Proto-Germanic **\*senawō**).

In Proto-Germanic the most important consonantal theme was -n-; n-nouns are known as *weak* nouns, e.g. **nama** 'name' (Proto-Germanic **\*namōn**), **tunge** 'tongue' (Proto-Germanic **\*tuŋgōn**). Other consonantal themes had generally disappeared by the time of Proto-Germanic, though a few relics survive, e.g. t-nouns, represented in Latin by **nepotem** (an inflected form of **nepos** 'nephew'), cf. **mōnaþ** 'month' (Proto-Germanic **\*mǣnōþ(āz)**).

As has been noted already, themes have in many cases become obscured or lost in OE; however, the classification is useful for making comparisons with other Germanic languages where themes are better preserved. For instance, Gothic, a form of Germanic which is often cited in this and subsequent chapters as providing evidence of archaic usages, retains many themes in parts of its noun-paradigms, e.g. **harjis** 'army' (nominative/genitive singular), a ja-noun.

Themes are important for the lexical morphology of other parts of speech. Adjectives are traditionally classified in the same way as nouns, although there had been a merger of **a-** and **ō-**stem adjectives, and their associated sub-groups, in pre-Germanic. Examples of the various classes of adjective are **blind** 'blind' (Proto-Germanic *blindaz), **wilde** 'wild' (Proto-Germanic *wilþi-jaz), **nearu** 'narrow' (Proto-Germanic *narwaz), **blīþe** 'joyful' (Proto-Germanic *blīþiz), **heard** 'hard' (Proto-Germanic *xarðuz). Germanic adjectives developed *strong* and *weak* forms, the latter with paradigms similar to the weak nouns; the distribution of strong and weak adjectives was governed by syntactic constraints, discussed further in chapter 7, section 3.

Themes were also a feature of the Proto-Indo-European verb system, where e alternated with o. Remnants of such themes appear in Classical Greek, e.g. **leip-e-te** 'you are leaving', **leip-o-men** 'we are leaving'. The so-called *weak* verb in OE derived from those Proto-Germanic verbs where in the present tense thematic e, o was preceded by j-; the themes of the ancestors of OE *strong* verbs were not so preceded. Weak verbs were also distinguished in the Germanic languages by their manner of forming the preterite (past) tense, i.e. through the addition of a dental suffix. An OE example of a weak verb is **lecgan** 'place', **legdon** 'placed' (plural) (cf. Gothic **lagjan, lagidēdum**).

Much core OE vocabulary consists of single stems, many of them mono-syllabic, with optional accompanying endings, e.g. **stān** 'stone', **nama** 'name', **bindan** '(to) bind', **lufian** '(to) love', **gōd** 'good', **cwic** 'alive'. Many of these core items have PDE words descended from them (their *reflexes*), although the spelling and/or pronunciation may have changed. Regular patterns of change over time can be distinguished, and are useful for students who wish to build up their OE vocabulary. Forms such as **scip** 'ship', **biscop** 'bishop', **fisc** 'fish', for instance, reflect the distinct ways in which OE and PDE represent the phoneme /ʃ/ in their writing-systems, while the regular correspondence between OE **ā** /ɑ:/ and PDE /o:/ (in its various realisations) is exemplified not only by **stān** 'stone' but also by forms such as **hām** 'home', **bāt** 'boat', **āc** 'oak', **hlāf** 'loaf', **hāl** 'whole' etc.

Within many roots in PDE there is a regular variation of vowels which seems to relate to meaning and/or grammatical function, e.g. **hot** (adjective) versus **heat** (noun), **bind** (present tense) versus **bound** (preterite tense). This variation also appears in OE. It is a very ancient phenomenon, which may be presumed in Proto-Indo-European. It is known as *vowel-gradation* or *Ablaut*, and words sharing the same root but with vowel-gradation are said to be in a *gradation-relationship*. It is commonly manifested in the conjugation of strong verbs, e.g. **rīdan** 'ride', **rād** 'rode' (3rd person singular), **ridon** 'rode' (plural), **riden** 'ridden'. However, Ablaut is not restricted to the paradigms of such verbs; it is also found, as in PDE, in such pairs as **bēodan** 'command', **gebod** 'an order'.

The origins of Ablaut are obscure. The oldest Ablaut-distinctions seem to have involved a contrast between front and back vowels, while later developments distinguishing a short–long contrast or the reduction/loss of the vowel and its replacement with a 'syllabic consonant' (compare some pronunciations of **-m** in PDE **rhythm** [rɪðm̩]). These alternations, which arose most probably through variant pronunciations in Proto-Indo-European, developed distinct semantic associations, some of which remain in OE and even PDE. Thus front and back vowels commonly, though by no means consistently, have associations with nearness/'present-ness' and distance/'past-ness' respectively, as in the PDE strong-verb distinction between **bear** (present tense), **bore** (preterite tense); cf. OE **beran** (infinitive), **geboren** (past participle).

Ablaut is not the only source of vowel-variation in OE. A second source, which dates from the pre-OE period, is *mutation* or *Umlaut*. A particular kind of Umlaut was briefly mentioned in chapter 4, section 5, namely i-Umlaut. Umlaut relationships are important for the paradigms of all OE verbs and some common nouns, and will therefore be discussed more fully in chapter 7. Umlaut relationships are common in certain parts of the verb-paradigm, e.g. **cēosan** 'choose' (infinitive), **cīest** 'chooses' (3rd person singular); they may also be seen in such pairs as **fox** 'fox', **fyxe** 'vixen, female fox'.

## 5.2 Lexical morphology II: affixation and compounding

OE had in addition other strategies for adding to its wordstock: *affixation*, *compounding* and *borrowing*. *Affixation* at its simplest made it possible to produce derived forms in other word-classes through the addition of affixes (bound morphemes); thus **lȳtel** 'little' is related to **lȳtlian** '(to) diminish' as is **wita** 'wise man' to **witan** 'know'. Here the transfer is carried out by the addition of an inflexional ending to the stem. Other examples are: **gripe** 'grip' (noun) to **grīpan** 'grip' (verb), **dōm** 'judgement, glory' to **dēman** 'judge' (verb), **hryre** 'fall' (noun) to **hrēosan** 'fall' (verb), **cyme** 'arrival' (cf. **cuman** 'come'), **wundor** 'wonder' (noun) (cf. **wundrian** 'wonder (at)' (verb)), **hāl** 'whole' (cf. **hǣlan** 'heal').

Common non-inflexional morphemes used for conversion in OE include the following:

-**dōm**, -**nes** and -**scipe** can be used to form nouns from adjectives, e.g. **wīsdōm** 'wisdom' (**wīs** 'wise'), **beorhtnes** 'brightness' (**beorht** 'bright'), **wǣrscipe** 'caution' (**wǣr** 'cautious, wary').

-end and -ung can be used to form nouns from verbs, e.g. **wrecend** 'avenger', (**wrecan** 'avenge'), **weorþung** 'honour' (**weorþian** 'honour', verb).

-cund, -fæst, -ful, -ig, -isc, -lēas, -lic and -sum can be used to form adjectives from nouns, e.g. **dēofolcund** 'diabolical, devilish' (**dēofol** 'devil'), **wynnfæst** 'pleasant' (**wynn** 'joy'), **synnful** 'sinful' (**synn** 'sin'), **blōdig** 'bloody' (**blōd** 'blood'), **mennisc** 'human' (**menn** 'humans'), **drēamlēas** 'joyless' (**drēam** 'joy'), **munuclic** 'monastic' (**munuc** 'monk'), **wynnsum** 'delightful' (**wynn** 'joy').

-līce can be used to form adverbs from adjectives, e.g. **sōþlīce** 'truly' (**sōþ** 'true').

Many of these affixes can also be used to change the meaning of the word in question without changing its word-class, e.g. for instance, **hlāforddōm** 'lordship' (cf. **hlāford** 'lord'), **geornful** 'eager' (cf. **georn** 'eager'). Other bound morphemes can also be used to modify the meaning of the stems to which they are affixed. Thus the addition of **for-**, mainly to verbs but also to other words, intensifies the meaning of the word, e.g. **forlēosan** 'abandon' (cf. **lēosan** 'lose'), **foroft** 'very often' (cf. **oft** 'often'). Other prefixes can also be used as intensifiers, for example **ārǣran** 'raise up' (cf. less emphatic **rǣran**), **bescūfan** 'hurl' (cf. **scūfan** 'push'), **infrōd** 'very wise' (cf. **frōd** 'wise'), **oreald** 'very old' (cf. **eald** 'old'). The prefix **be-** can also be used to add the sense 'round, over', as in **bebūgan** 'surround' (cf. **būgan** 'turn, bend'), while **in-** can be used with a directional meaning 'in', e.g. **ingān** 'enter' (cf. **gān** 'go'). With verbs, **on-** indicates that an action has been begun, **onlīehtan** 'enlighten' (cf. **līehtan** 'illumine'); alongside **un-**, **on-** can also be used to indicate the opposite of the stem-meaning, e.g. **onbindan** 'unbind' (cf. **bindan** 'bind'), **unrihte** 'unjustly' (cf. **rihte** 'justly').

A common prefix is **ge-**. On verbs, this prefix seems to have been used very often to indicate *perfect aspect*, and it thus appears frequently on *past participles*, compare **gebunden** 'bound' beside **bindan** 'bind' (infinitive). It can also be used to convert verbs from *intransitive* to *transitive* meaning, e.g. **fēran** 'go', **gefēran** 'reach'. On many words, the **ge-** prefix relates to the idea of association, collectiveness etc., for example **gefēra** 'comrade', **gelīc** 'similar', **gehwǣr** 'everywhere'.

Another important method of adding vocabulary was by *compounding*, that is, placing two free morphemes together. Nouns can be formed from the following combinations: noun + noun, like **sciprāp**, or **bōccræft** 'literature' (**bōc** 'book' + **cræft** 'skill'); adjective + noun, e.g. **blīþemōd** 'happy' (**blīþe** 'happy' + **mōd** 'spirit'); adverb + noun, e.g. **inngang** 'entrance' (**inn** 'into' + **gang** 'journey, way'). Adjectives can be formed from the following combinations: noun + adjective, e.g. **dōmgeorn** 'eager for glory' (**dōm** 'glory' + **georn** 'eager'); adjective + adjective, e.g. **scīrmǣled** 'brightly adorned' (**scīr** 'bright' + **mæled** 'adorned'); adverb + adjective, e.g. **welwillende** 'benevolent' (**wel** 'well' + **willende** 'willing'); and even adjective + noun, e.g. **glædmōd** 'cheerful' (**glæd** 'glad' + **mōd** 'spirit').

# 5.3 Borrowing

One difference between OE and PDE strategies of word-formation is that affixation is unnecessary in PDE in transferring a word from one class to another, a process known as *conversion*. Thus the PDE form **buy** remains the same whether functioning as a verb in **to buy a book** or as a noun in **a good buy**; compare OE **bycgan** 'buy' (verb), **bygen** 'purchase' (noun). Another difference is that *borrowing*, whereby a word from one language is transferred to another, is more common in PDE than in OE. This openness to borrowing has been the case in the history of English since the ME period, encouraged by the nature of the contacts between English and other languages, notably varieties of French.

In OE, borrowing was somewhat less common, and largely restricted to particular registers of language where available native words for modification through affixation or compounding were few. The main languages involved were varieties of Celtic and Norse, French, Latin and Greek, although the impact of all of these languages on OE vocabulary, with the exception of Latin, was small.

There are very few loanwords from varieties of Celtic into OE: examples are **torr** 'rock' (cf. Old Welsh **twrr** 'bulge, belly'), **drȳ** 'magician' (cf. Old Irish **drūi**). However, those forms which are usually cited in the handbooks are often disputed by scholars. The form **dunn** 'dun, dingy brown', for instance, is clearly related to Celtic forms, e.g. Welsh **dwn**, Irish **donn**, and could therefore be considered a Celtic loanword. However, the form **dun** is also found in Old Saxon, and it seems likely, therefore, that all these forms derive from a common Proto-Indo-European ancestor *****dusnos**. Similarly problematic are **mattuc** 'mattock, spade', **bannuc** 'bit, small piece' (cf. Welsh **matog**, Gælic **bannach**); **mattuc/matog** may both be derived through independent borrowing of vulgar Latin ***mattēca**, while **bannock/bannach** may come independently from the Latin adjective **pānicium** 'appertaining to bread' (**pānis** 'bread'). OE **gafeluc** 'spear' may be Celtic (cf. Welsh **gaflach**, Irish **gabhla**). Old Norse **gaflak** and Norman French **gavelot** may be loans from OE, but alternative views are possible (see *OED* s.v. GAVELOCK); it is possible that the word was loaned from French to OE before written records began. Some words ultimately derived from Latin may have entered OE via Celtic, e.g. **ancora** 'anchorite, religious recluse' may be from Old Irish **anchara** rather than from Latin **anachoreta** (Campbell 1959: 219–20 and references there cited).

The principal impact on English from Celtic is manifested in names, both place-names and personal names, and this leads us into the area of *onomastics*, or name-study. The behaviour of names is different from other parts of the lexicon, in that names develop what may be termed *onomastic meaning*. Thus a place-name such as PDE **Cambridge**, which originally 'meant' 'bridge over the River Cam', can be transferred to a location near Boston, Massachusetts where there is no River Cam for a bridge to span. In other words, a name may be adopted to refer to a place rather than to any particular topographic characteristic, and the borrower may be completely unaware of the original significance of the name.

The Anglo-Saxons seem to have had no qualms about borrowing such names, many of which survive in PDE. Thus **Malvern** (Worcestershire) derives from Celtic *\*mēlbrynn* 'bald hill' (*\*mēl* 'bald', *\*brynn* 'hill'), **Penge** (Surrey) from Celtic **penngēd** 'chief wood' (*\*penn* 'head, hill', *\*gēd* 'wood') etc. The names of major rivers were commonly borrowed from Celtic, for example **Trent, Thames, Darent, Avon**. The Anglo-Saxons often combined place-names borrowed from Celtic with elements from their own language, e.g. **Berkshire** from Celtic *\*barrōg* 'hilly' combined with OE **scīr** 'district'. Sometimes a Celtic word and an OE word with the same meaning can be combined tautologously, for example **Chetwode** (Buckinghamshire), derived from Celtic *\*cēd* 'wood' and OE **wudu** 'wood'; such tautologies show that the element **chet-** had lost its original topographic meaning and was now being used onomastically.

Recorded Norse loanwords in OE are also few, and restricted to peculiarly Norse concepts or objects, e.g. **ūtlaga** 'outlaw', **wīcing** 'viking, pirate', **griþ** 'truce', **cnearr** 'galley, ship'. We might compare the appearance in ModE of expressions for notions and things with which English-speakers came into contact through trade or conquest, e.g. **chocolate** (from Nahuatl **chocolatl**, via Spanish), or **bungalow** (Gujerati **bangalo** 'belonging to Bengal').

However, it is important to realise that the relationship between Norse and OE was more complex than the limited appearance of Norse loanwords in OE texts might suggest. Most OE from the late Anglo-Saxon period is recorded in Late West Saxon, which had achieved the status of a standardised written language (sometimes referred to by scholars as a *Schriftsprache* 'written language'). First, it seems likely from the rapid appearance of Norse words in ME, after the disappearance of a standardised form of English, that spoken OE contained many more Norse loanwords than the written form of the language. Second, there is some evidence that northern varieties of OE, i.e. Anglian varieties, were so close in form to the language spoken by the Viking invaders that it was possible for Anglian and Norse speakers to have some degree of mutual understanding of each other's language – rather as Italian and Catalan speakers have today. There are some forms in PDE where it is hard to tell whether the word is derived from Norse or from the Anglian dialect of OE.

Despite the arguments of some scholars, it is unlikely that English and Norse combined in northern England to form a *creole*. A creole is formed when a *pidgin*, a 'simplified' language used as a communicative *lingua franca*, becomes the native language of a particular group of people; the interaction between English and Norse in the north and midlands was profound, but the simplified grammar and vocabulary characteristic of pidgins and thus creoles did not result.

However, there is considerable onomastic evidence suggesting that a blend of English and Norse, and even of English, Norse and Celtic, cultures developed in many parts of the country. Thus place-names such as **Grimston**, combining a Norse modifier **Grims-** 'Grim (personal name)' and an OE generic **-ton** 'settlement' (cf. OE **tūn**), appear in areas on the borders of Norse settlement; this form might be compared with fully Norse place-names such as **Grimsby** (with Norse **-by** 'settlement'). And the form **Kirkcudbright**, found in what is now the south-west of Scotland, is a blend of a Norse generic **kirk-** and an OE modifier **cudbright** 'Cuthbert (personal name)', with the ordering of generic and modifier according to Celtic syntax, where the modifier follows the generic (cf. the reverse pattern in Germanic languages).

The only certain example of a loanword in OE from French is **prūd/prūt** 'proud' and its derivative, **prȳt(e)** 'pride'. (For **gafeluc**, see above.) French loanwords are found in early post-Conquest records; their appearance there indicates that such early loans are from the Norman French rather than the Central French dialect, e.g. **werre** 'war' (cf. PD standard French **guerre**), **carpenter** (cf. PD standard French **charpentier**). The great mass of French loanwords – largely from Central French – are found in English texts from the fourteenth century onwards, as writers in ME marked stylistic difference by studding their language with words from high-status languages.

The most important group of loanwords into OE derive from the classical languages, Greek and Latin, though there are distinct phases of borrowing and some uncertainties remain. Some words in OE which have a Greek etymology were probably derived from contact between Greek-speakers and Germanic peoples in the Proto-Germanic or Proto-West Germanic periods. Examples are OE **dēofol** 'devil', Greek **diabolos**; OE **engel** 'angel', Greek **aggelos**; OE **cirice** 'church', Greek **kuriakon**. The first two of these forms also occur in Gothic, as **diabaulus** and **aggilus**, which occurrence supports the hypothesis that such forms were directly transferred from Greek to Germanic. That such borrowings took place after Germanic had diverged from the other Indo-European languages may be demonstrated by the fact that they do not show the impact of such distinctive Germanic developments as Grimm's Law; thus d- is retained in OE **dēofol**, rather than being replaced by *t-.[1]

Most other words which have cognates in both Greek and Latin, however, probably entered OE and the other Germanic languages through contact with either the Roman Empire or the Roman Church. Those very early loanwords which appear in OE may have entered Germanic through contact with the Roman Empire and its characteristic artefacts and institutions. One example is **strǣt** 'road' (Latin **strāta**), which seems to be used for 'paved road'; compare PDE **Watling Street** and **Ermine Street,** in which the word **street** refers to modern British trunk roads rather than, as is usual in PDE, to roads within towns. Other examples of such early loans are **ceaster** 'city' (Latin **castrum, -a**), **cāsere** 'emperor' (Latin **caesar**).

The date of early loans can often be established by their being subjected to prehistoric OE sound-changes. Thus **ǣ** in **strǣt** represents the regular reflex in the WS dialect of Latin **ā**, while later Latin loanwords retain **ā**, e.g. **pāpa** 'pope' (Latin **pāpa**). The diphthong **ea** in **ceaster** is the result of palatal diphthongisation of an earlier **æ** derived through first fronting of the original **a,** while **ā** in **cāsere** is the usual reflex of the Latin diphthong **ae** in early loans. Other forms subjected to prehistoric sound-changes, and thus early loans, include **sealtian** 'dance' (cf. Latin **saltare**), demonstrating breaking, or **cealc** 'plaster' (cf. PDE **chalk**), demonstrating palatalisation of *k-. By contrast, **butere** 'butter' (cf. Latin ***butirum**) must be a later borrowing, since there is no evidence of the effect of i-mutation to be expected in an earlier loan. OE had an alternative Germanic word for this substance, **smeoru** 'grease, fat', cognate with, for example, PD Norwegian **smør** 'butter'.

The stems of Latin loanwords can also receive suffixes through extension of existing OE patterns. Thus, for instance, the suffix **-ere**, cognate with Latin **-āri(u)s**, appears as is expected in **scolere** 'scholar' (cf. Latin **scholāris**), but is also extended to other loanwords, for example **cantere** 'singer' (cf. Latin **cantor**). Unstressed vowels are often lost in loanwords, e.g. **tīgle** 'tile' (cf. Latin **tēgula**).

Many loanwords into OE from Latin appear owing to the influence of the Roman Church; such loanwords often deal with church institutions or religious objects, or are in other ways 'learned'. Examples are **abbod** 'abbot' (Latin **abbas**, inflected **abbātem**), **sealm** 'psalm' (Latin **psalma**), **sanct** 'saint' (Latin **sanctus**), **alter** 'altar' (Latin **altāre**), **māgister** 'master' (Latin **magister**), **gīgant** 'giant' (Latin **gīgas**, inflected **gīgantem** etc.).

A form such as **māgister** raises an important question about the nature of the borrowing process. How far did the Anglo-Saxons consider a word such as **māgister** to be part of their 'own' OE language? It seems clear from the general history of the English language that some words are considered 'more English' than others; thus **spaghetti** may be considered part of current

English discourse whereas **penne** or **farfalle** may be seen as exotics, not quite assimilated to general usage. It seems likely that forms such as **māgister** were even in their own time seen as exotics, a view confirmed by the fact that the PDE cognate **master** was itself borrowed into English from French at a later date, and **magisterial**, the related adjective, arrived in English only towards the end of the ME period.

## 5.4 Lexicon and semantics

It was noted in chapter 2, section 2.5 that many OE words do not mean quite the same thing as their PDE reflexes: for example OE **sǣlig** 'happy, fortunate, blessed' is very different in meaning from its PDE reflex **silly**. This point leads us into the area of *semantics*.

Semantics – the term derives from Greek **semantikos** 'significant' – deals with meaning, and therefore underpins all levels of language, not just vocabulary. Phonemes and graphemes are distinguished one from another through meaning, in that replacement of one phoneme or grapheme by another changes the meaning of the word. Meaning is also expressed grammatically, through the addition of an inflexional ending or the ordering of elements within a sentence. But meaning is perhaps most obviously involved in the lexicon, particularly with reference to those lexemes belonging to the open word-classes.

The traditional view of semantic relations is that lexemes map onto concepts; in Aristotle's definition, 'Words spoken are symbols or signs of affections or impressions of the soul; written words are the signs of words spoken' (*De interpretatione*, cited Waldron 1979: 16). Aristotle's definition was developed in the nineteenth and twentieth centuries by Ferdinand de Saussure and others, who established the notion of *semantic relations*. Semantic relations express the connexions between (1) the *signifier* or acoustic/written expression, (2) the *signified*, or mental concept, and (3) reality itself. Thus, in Kurt Baldinger's words:

> The acoustic image *table* only brings to mind a schematic representation of the thing. If I say, 'Tomorrow I'm going to buy a table', I do not know which table I shall buy. *Table* evokes the category. And if I say, 'Yesterday I bought a table', I know what the table is like in reality, but the person I am speaking to does not; he only has an idea of the category … This may seem very elementary and obvious, but it has far-reaching consequences for language and the science of language. *(Baldinger 1980: 6–7)*

Semantic relations are often expressed in diagrammatic terms, as the *semiotic triangle* (see Figure 5.1, after Ullmann 1962: 55). Lexemes do not, of course, simply map onto single concepts. The 'same' word can have different

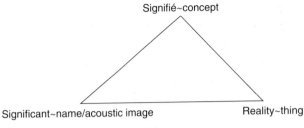

Signifié~concept

Significant~name/acoustic image     Reality~thing

Figure 5.1 The semiotic triangle

conceptual meanings in different contexts and indeed lexemes are defined by their relationship to other lexemes; thus a word like **plane** is likely to mean one thing when accompanied by **hammer, drill, chainsaw** and another thing when accompanied by **airport, runway, pilot**. Lexemes can therefore have more than one meaning, i.e. they can be *polysemous*. Such polysemy is often based on *metaphorical* usage, as with the example of **star**, whose primary denotation may be established from its collocation with words such as **planet, galaxy, moon** but which has developed a secondary denotation, clearly derived metaphorically, when collocated with **film, actor, director**. These conceptual meanings are known as *denotations*.

Of course, lexemes have other meanings as well as denotations. They also have *connotations*, referring to the associated meanings a lexeme may develop, e.g. **beast** denotes the concept 'animate non-human' but has connotations of irrationality, brutality etc. in humans. These connotations can be stylistic; thus, while **commence, begin** and **kick off** denote the same concept, they have different connotations, whereby **commence** is formal, **kick off** is informal, and **begin** neutral.

Such patterns of denotation and connotation can also be found in OE. A word such as **feng**, for instance, can mean 'an embrace' in some contexts but 'captivity' in others. The word **slīdan**, denoting 'slide', can also be used to denote 'fail, lapse, err' or 'be transitory'. The word **weallan** can be used to refer to the movement of water (cf. the PDE verb **well**), but also metaphorically, to do with the human expression of rage, grief or ardour. As we might expect, some metaphorical usages are found generally only in poetry. The most notable of these are the *kennings*, compound words which are a particular feature of OE verse, for example **dægcandel** 'day-candle' (i.e. the sun), **hwælweg** 'whale-way' (i.e. the sea).

Reconstructing the denotations and connotations of OE lexemes, especially stylistic connotations, is a difficult task given the comparatively small corpus and the obvious lack of native informants, but modern scholars have two resources available to help them. First, there are dictionaries of OE. Through the analysis of the co-occurrence and contexts of OE lexemes, scholars are able to reconstruct the denotations and connotations of individual lexemes, i.e. distinguish the components of meaning a lexeme might possess. This process of *componential analysis* is the basis of dictionary-making or *lexicography*. The current standard dictionaries of OE (Bosworth-Toller 1898–1921, supplemented by Campbell 1972, or the student dictionary of Clark-Hall 1960) are somewhat elderly, but the Toronto *Dictionary of Old English* (DOE), based on a comprehensive corpus also available as a concordance, will allow much more precise analysis of OE meaning, especially when combined with other period dictionaries, for example the *Middle English Dictionary* (MED) or in relation to general historical dictionaries such as the *Oxford English Dictionary* (OED). The appearance of certain forms only in particular genres allows for certain conclusions to be drawn about stylistic levels. Thus words such as **hyge** 'thought, mind, heart, disposition, intention' and its compounds are generally restricted to poetry, and are presumably stylistically marked as 'literary'.[2]

Second, scholars now have access to a major new resource for the analysis of the lexicon: the *Thesaurus of Old English* (TOE). TOE (now online as well as in print form) is a notional classification of OE vocabulary, rather as *Roget's Thesaurus* is a notional classification of the vocabulary of PDE. Combined with traditional dictionaries, *TOE* allows for the investigation of a complete area of the lexicon, or *semantic field*.

To demonstrate the usefulness of *TOE*, we might examine once again the lexeme **hyge**. This lexeme appears in three *TOE* classifications, 'The head (as seat of thought)' (*TOE* category 06.01), 'Courage, boldness, valour' (06.02.07.06) and 'Pride' (07.06). These categories are numbered in *TOE* as 06.01, 06.02.07.06, and 07.06; for convenience here we will refer to them as categories (a), (b) and (c) respectively. *TOE* flags vocabulary as 'rare', 'poetic' or 'restricted to glosses'; such forms are marked here. Within (a), **hyge** appears within the subcategory 'mind, intellect' alongside **heorte** 'heart', **hordgeþanc** 'mind' (rare), **(ge)mōd** 'spirit' (cf. PDE 'mood'), **gemynd** 'memory' (cf. PDE 'mind'), **myne** 'memory', **sefa** 'mind', **gewitloca** 'mind' and **(ge)witt** 'understanding' (cf. PDE 'wit'). Within (b), it appears alongside **anmēdla** 'pomp', **bealdnes** 'boldness' (rare), **(ge)bield(o)** 'courage', **ellen** 'zeal', **eorlscipe** 'manliness' (poetic), **hwætscipe** 'bravery', **hygeþrymm** 'courage' (rare, poetic), **mōd** 'courage', **mōdsefa** 'purpose' (poetic), **mōdþracu** 'courage' (poetic), **snellscipe** 'boldness' (rare), **þegnscipe** 'valour', while within (c) it appears alongside **bælc** 'arrogance' (poetic), **blǣd** 'glory', **gāl** 'proud, wicked', **hēahmōdnes** 'pride' (rare, cf. **hēahmōd** 'proud', poetic), **oferhige** 'pride' (rare, poetic), **oferhogodnes** 'pride' (rare), **oferhygdig** 'pride' (also adj. 'haughty'), **ofermēde** 'pride' (also adj. 'proud'), **orgello** 'pride', **orgelnes** 'pride' (restricted to glosses), **unmōdnes** 'pride' (rare), **wlenc(o)** 'haughtiness'.[3]

A few points may be noted about the vocabulary in these categories. First, very few have reflexes in PDE. Consultation of the equivalent categories in

*Roget's Thesaurus* shows that most of these words have been replaced by words derived from French or Latin, while words such as **mood, mind, wit** have changed their meaning since Anglo-Saxon times (for information about these changes, see *OED* s.v. MOOD, MIND, WIT). Second, a fair number are compound words based on a few stems, e.g. words incorporating **mōd**, (anmēdla, mōdþracu etc.), or incorporating **hyge**. Finally, a fair number of these words are restricted to poetic contexts, or are otherwise rare (restriction to glosses, notoriously in Anglo-Saxon times lists of 'hard words' designed to demonstrate the author's learnedness, is an indicator of such). These restrictions on usage, or failures to survive in the core lexicon of English, suggest that such words are stylistically restricted, and this contextual information can be used to draw at least tentative conclusions about lexical connotations.

The kind of exhaustive analysis undertaken by scholars in order to reconstruct precise meanings, both denotations and connotations, may be illustrated from Carole Biggam's use of 'interdisciplinary semantics' in her analysis of colour terms (Biggam 1997, 1998), which looks at language in relation to optics, botany, zoology, historical evidence etc. Optical variables involved in the analysis of colour are:

*hue* (bands on the 'colour spectrum');
*tone* (the amount of black, grey or white mixed with hue, producing 'dark' or 'pale' colours);
*saturation* (specifically the amount of grey mixed with hue; a fully saturated hue contains no grey at all, and is 'bright' or 'vivid', while unsaturated hues contain varying amounts of grey, and are 'dull' or 'greyish');
*surface effects* (e.g. 'shiny' or 'matt') (see Biggam 1997: 15–16).

Through exhaustive analysis of the occurrences and collocations of OE vocabulary referring to 'blueness', Biggam was able to offer precise definitions of each word in turn in terms of optical variables and any special restrictions in usage, thus:

| | |
|---|---|
| **blǣhǣwen** | 'dark blue (dark grey), of dyes and textiles' |
| **blǣwen** | 'dark blue, of dyes and textiles' |
| **glǣsen** | 'shiny pale grey/blue' |
| **hǣwen** | 'blue (grey)' |
| **hǣwengrēne** | 'blue-green (grey-green)' |
| **swearthǣwen** | 'dark blue' |
| **wǣden** | 'blue, possibly restricted to dyes and textiles' |
| **wannhǣwen** | 'dark blue' |
| **hauiblauum** | 'a blue (grey) woad dye' |
| **wād** | 'a blue woad dye' |

Biggam shows that the basic colour term emerging in OE was **hæwen**, with compounds used to define tone, particularly darkness. This pattern of compounding seems to have been necessary since **hæwen** on its own 'was tonally restricted to pale, at least in its early phase as a colour term' (Biggam 1997: 303). However, as **græg** became used for 'grey' and **grēne** for 'green', **hæwen** increasingly developed as the basic colour term for 'blue', particularly amongst learned groups in Anglo-Saxon society who wished to find a gloss for equivalent terms in Latin (which had a more 'advanced' system of colour-distinctions; see further Biggam 1995). Some terms were stylistically restricted to technical contexts, in producing dyes; it is no surprise, therefore, to find technical nouns in this area: **hauiblauum** and **wād**. The form **blæwen** was also restricted to technical contexts to do with dyes and textiles, contrasting with developments in other Germanic languages where cognate forms developed as the basic colour term, yielding, for example, Old Icelandic **blār**, Old High German **blao** (words cognate to **hæwen** in these languages seem to have retained an older specialised meaning of 'mouldy, downy'). However, this pattern changed with the Norman Conquest. Old French supplied English with the form **bleu** (yielding PDE **blue**); **hæwen** generally died out, though retained in certain varieties of Scots until the end of the eighteenth century (see *OED* s.v. HAW). Biggam points out that **bleu** was itself ('ironically') a loanword in French from Germanic (1997: 302–3).

## Notes

1. Present-Day German **Teufel** 'devil' with initial /t/ exemplifies a distinct, later development which differentiated High German from the other West Germanic varieties: the Second Consonant Shift, which took place from the middle of the first millennium AD (see Chambers and Wilkie 1970: *passim*, or Keller 1978: 167–77 for a full account). OE -f- in **dēofol** for Greek -b- is to be expected; Greek -b- was pronounced as a bilabial fricative [β], as was Gothic intervocalic -b- (Wright 1954: 77). The reflex of Proto-Germanic [β] was a fricative in OE: /f/, allophonically [v].

2. One source of 'new' OE vocabulary, now being increasingly exploited by scholars, is place-names. Place-names often contain evidence for lexemes which do not survive in the corpus of literary and documentary texts on which the standard dictionaries are generally founded, e.g. *bagga 'badger', *padduc 'frog', *todd 'fox'. For some fascinating discussion of such vocabulary, see for example Hough 2001, who identifies the form *pohha/*pocca as 'fallow deer' and even suggests the existence of a possible diminutive *pohhel/*poccel as a designation for the creature's fawn.

3. The PDE glosses given for these words are selective, and simply to help the reader. Thus, for instance, **(ge)witt** is glossed fully in Clark-Hall (1960) as 'understanding, intellect, sense, knowledge, conscience'.

# Exercises

| | |
|---|---|
| Exercise 5a | Write on the role of language contact in the evolution of the OE lexicon. |

| | |
|---|---|
| Exercise 5b | Give an account, with full examples, of the structure of OE words. |

| | |
|---|---|
| Exercise 5c | How Germanic is the PDE lexicon? |

| | |
|---|---|
| Exercise 5d | Compare Category 05.13 *Changeableness, change* in *TOE* with Category 143 *Change* in a modern edition of *Roget's Thesaurus of English Words and Phrases*. What seem to you to be the major differences? |

| | |
|---|---|
| Exercise 5e | Using the *OED*, trace the history of the meanings of the words **sad, silly** and **stench** from their OE origins to PDE. |

## Key terms introduced in this chapter
lexical morphology (word-formation)
lexicology
root
theme
stem
word-ending
Ablaut (gradation)
Umlaut (mutation)
affixation
compounding
conversion
borrowing (loanwords)
onomastics
denotation
connotation
polysemy
semantic field
kenning

# CHAPTER 6

# Old English Grammar I: Syntax

## In this chapter ...

This chapter looks in more depth at the syntax of Old English, giving a variety of illustrative examples. Topics covered include the noun phrase, the verb phrase and the order of elements in a sentence.

**Contents**

## 6.1 Introduction

The term *grammar* has been used variously by scholars. Some use the term to refer to all levels of language except lexicography. Others have used it to refer to everything to do with word-form; thus Alistair Campbell's *Old English Grammar* (1959) dealt with OE spellings, sounds and morphology (lexical and inflexional) but did not address OE syntax. In this book, the term 'grammar' will be used somewhat narrowly to refer to *inflexional morphology* and *syntax*, i.e. it will deal with the various forms of lexemes and the functions carried out by these forms. Chapter 6 will deal with syntax; chapter 7 will address OE inflexional morphology. However, the relationship between form and function is relevant to both chapters, and will be discussed here. In both chapters, the focus is on the EWS variety, though some other dialects are discussed at the end of chapter 6.

As was pointed out in chapter 2, many PDE lexemes demonstrate a correlation between word-form and word-function. We might for example compare the simple clauses:

(1) **She loved him.**

(2) **He loved her.**

A characteristic feature of the PDE pronominal system is that the form of a pronoun changes with its function. Thus, in (1) and (2) above, **she** and **he** are used when the feminine and masculine pronouns have subject functions, and **her** and **him** when they are being used as direct objects. The set **she** and **her** form one *paradigm*, that of the so-called 3rd person feminine singular pronouns, while **he** and **him** (along with **his**) form another, that of the 3rd person masculine singular pronouns. These distinctions are not only to do with grammatical categories such as *person*, *gender* and *number*; they are also to do with *case*, a phenomenon whereby functions such as subject or direct object are flagged through inflexional morphology. It is traditional to refer to forms such as **she** and **he** as being in the *nominative case*, and forms such as **her** and **him** (when functioning as direct objects) as being in the *accusative case*. Indirect objects can also be flagged through case; thus in:

(3) **He gave her some flowers.**

the phrase **some flowers** is the direct object while **her** is the indirect object. Indirect objects are considered to be in the *dative case*.

Such paradigms are found in other parts of speech as well. In the noun, for example, the lexeme **book** has four forms marked as different within our writing-system: **book** (singular), **books** (plural), **book's** (singular possessive) and **books'** (plural possessive). The latter two forms are characteristically found as modifiers within noun phrases, for example:

(4) **The book's contents surprised the pupils.**

The subject-phrase of sentence (4) is **The book's contents**, consisting of a headword **contents** preceded by a modifying possessive phrase **The book's**. Forms such as **book's** and **books'** are often referred to in terms of case, here *genitive case*.

Perhaps the most complex PDE paradigms are to be found in verbs. PDE expresses a whole series of distinctions to do with *tense* and *aspect* by means of special endings and/or through the use of auxiliary verbs. Tense distinctions are to do with time; thus PDE verbs distinguish between *present tense*, as in:

(5) **I love books.**

and *preterite tense*, as in:

(6) **She loved bananas.**

Other tenses (e.g. *future*) are expressed by means of auxiliary verbs such as **will** or **shall**, as in:

(7) **They will love that play.**

Aspect distinctions are to do with whether an action is completed (*perfect*) or ongoing (*imperfect* or *progressive*). These distinctions can be expressed either through *simple verb phrases*, consisting of an unmodified headword, or through the use of *complex verb phrases*, consisting of modifying auxiliaries followed by headwords. The following sentences contain perfect verb phrases:

(8) **John loved books.**

(9) **We have eaten our lunch.**

(10) **They had finished their homework.**

The following sentences contain imperfect verb phrases:

(11) **They were enjoying their sandwiches.**

(12) **I am having a good time.**

(13) **The girls will be leaving the train.**

In PDE, verb-lexemes fall into three classes, classified by their way of forming their paradigms. Most PDE verb-paradigms are formed by the addition of inflexional endings, thus: **love, loves, loved, loving**; these verbs are known as *weak* verbs. Some common verbs form their paradigms through changing the vowel in their roots in accordance with Ablaut, thus: **sing, sang, sung**; these verbs are known as *strong* verbs. Finally, some very common verbs form their paradigms *irregularly*. Irregular verb-paradigms are formed either by merging what were, historically, distinct paradigms (*suppletion*), as in **be, am, is, are, was, were, being, been**, or they may have defective paradigms, lacking, for example, infinitives or participles, as with **shall, should**, or **may, might**.

As was stated above, these features of form, or inflexional morphology, and function, or syntax, make up the level of language known as grammar. OE grammar clearly differs from that of PDE. It is traditional to describe OE as a *synthetic* language while PDE is seen as *analytic*. A synthetic language expresses the relationship between lexemes by means of inflexional endings, while element-order and 'function words' are used for this purpose in analytic languages. As was pointed out in chapter 2, section 4, inflexions are significant at every level within the OE grammatical hierarchy: they relate words to each other within *phrases*, they relate phrases to each other within *clauses*, and they relate clauses to each other within *sentences*.

However, the synthetic–analytic relationship is clinal rather than discrete, i.e. 'more-or-less' rather than 'either/or'. OE certainly had more inflexional distinctions than has PDE, and is thus a more *synthetic* form of the language; but PDE forms and functions are largely inherited from OE, and there are clear continuities between the OE and PDE grammatical systems, for example in the weak/strong distinction in verb-paradigms. Other Indo-European languages such as Latin and Sanskrit, or non-Indo-European languages such as Finnish or Zulu, are much more synthetic than OE, while languages such as Chinese are much more analytic than PDE. Even within the Germanic group there are recorded varieties which are more synthetic than OE. Gothic, for instance, makes distinctions in form between nominative and accusative which have disappeared in OE: compare OE **stān** 'stone' (nominative and accusative singular) and **stānas** (nominative and accusative plural) beside Gothic **stains** (nominative singular), **stain** (accusative singular), **stainōs** (nominative plural), **stainans** (accusative plural). OE, it seems, had in comparative terms developed some way down the path from synthesis to analysis; as Bruce Mitchell has put it, beginning students are sometimes left 'with the impression that Old English depended on inflexions to a larger degree than in practice it did' (1985a: 4).

It will have been noted that some features (e.g. morphology, Ablaut) have already been discussed in chapter 5. There is a fuzzy area between grammar and lexicology and this fuzziness is to be expected, since both levels of language are carriers of meaning. It also has implications for historical and dialectal study, since meaning can be carried variously, i.e. through the lexicon rather than grammar and *vice versa*, at different periods and in different varieties of a language.

The remainder of this chapter deals with three areas of syntax: the noun phrase, the verb phrase and sentence structure. Inflexions are dealt with in chapter 7.

## 6.2 The OE noun phrase: functions

*Noun phrases* were defined in chapter 2 as phrases prototypically having nouns as headwords, with adjectives and determiners as optional modifiers. Thus, in a sentence such as:

(14) **The good girl loves her pony.**

the phrase **The good girl** is a noun phrase consisting of a headword **girl** preceded by the modifiers **The** and **good**. Other phrases are also generally classified as noun phrases, i.e. those consisting of pronouns (*pronominal phrases*), those preceded by a preposition (*prepositional phrases*) and those marked by inflexions such as -'s, -s' (*genitive phrases*). There are also *adjective phrases*, which prototypically function in the same way as noun phrases, and *adverb phrases*; these two latter phrase-classes will also be discussed in this section.

In PDE, these phrases all have prototypical functions. Noun phrases and adjective phrases prototypically function as the subjects, objects and complements of clauses. Prepositional phrases and adverb phrases prototypically function as adverbials, i.e. they qualify the meaning of an entire clause. Genitive phrases prototypically function as modifiers within a noun phrase (i.e. they are *subordinated*; see section 6.6 below).

OE had a similar set of phrases with similar functions. In:

(15) **Se gōda wer band þone yflan mid strangum rāpum.**
'The good man bound the evil (one) with strong ropes.'

there are a whole series of noun phrases. Prototypical is the subject **Se gōda wer** 'The good man', consisting of a noun **wer** as headword preceded by modifying determiner **Se** and adjective **gōda**. The object **þone yflan** 'the evil (one)' is an adjective phrase, with the adjective **yflan** 'evil' as the headword in place of a noun, while **mid strangum rāpum** 'with strong ropes' is a prepositional phrase functioning as an adverbial, consisting of a preposition **mid** 'with' followed by a modifying adjective **strangum** 'strong' and a noun **rāpum** 'ropes' as headword.

Other kinds of noun phrase may also be simply illustrated in OE. In:

(16) **Þæs cyninges hlǣfdīge fērde swīþe blīþelīce tō þǣre stōwe.**
'The king's lady travelled very happily to the place.'

the subject consists of the noun phrase **Þæs cyninges hlǣfdīge** 'The king's lady', containing a modifying subordinated genitive phrase **Þæs cyninges** 'The king's'. The adverb phrase **swīþe blīþelīce** 'very happily', functioning as an adverbial, consists of two adverbs, one of which is the headword (**blīþelīce** 'happily') and the other the modifier (**swīþe** 'very'). The prepositional phrase **tō þǣre stōwe** 'to the place', consisting of a preposition followed by a determiner and a noun, is another adverbial.

Noun phrases can also function as complements. In:

(17) **Sēo cwēn wearþ hālig wīf.**
'The queen became (a) holy woman.'

the noun phrase **hālig wīf** '(a) holy woman' functions as a complement. Adjective phrases are commonly used as complements, as in:

(18) **Se wer wæs dysig.**
  'The man was foolish.'

and

(18a) **Se wer wæs swīþe dysig.**
  'The man was very foolish.'

In (18), the adjective phrase consists of a single headword **dysig** 'foolish', while in (18a) it consists of a headword **dysig** preceded by a modifying adverb **swīþe** 'very'.

As in PDE, OE pronouns function as, and are categorised as, noun phrases. For instance, in:

(19) **Hē wæs gōd wer.**
  'He was (a) good man.'

**Hē** 'He' functions as the subject of the sentence, while in:

(20) **Hiere hlāford wæs hālig.**
  'Her lord was holy.'

**Hiere** 'Her' functions as a genitive phrase modifying **hlāford** 'lord'.

So far, the focus has been on similarities between OE and PDE. However, understanding the syntax of the OE noun phrase depends on understanding the operation of four key grammatical categories already flagged in chapter 2: *case*, *number*, *gender* and *agreement*. A fifth category, *person*, is also important. These categories are all relevant to PDE as well as OE, but there are differences in the way in which they operate in the earlier stage of the language.

The notion 'case' is crucial for understanding the syntax of the OE noun phrase. In OE, as in PDE, pronouns vary in form depending on their function; these various forms are called cases; and, as in PDE, nouns are marked for *genitive* (i.e. possessive) case. But case-inflexions are also found elsewhere: as endings on noun-stems, marking cases other than genitive, and on the stems of adjectives. Determiners, like pronouns, are also marked for case, as will be apparent from the examples given above (**se, þone, þæs** etc.).

This extension of case to word-classes other than pronouns and the possessive forms of nouns relates to another category, *agreement*. Agreement (sometimes called *concord*) is demonstrated when a noun, along with any modifier(s) applying to it, is assigned the appropriate case-ending required by the function of the whole phrase in the clause. Thus, in:

(21) **Se gōda hlāford band þone yflan cnapan.**
  'The good lord bound the evil servant.'

there are two noun phrases: **Se gōda hlāford** and þone yflan cnapan. The first noun phrase is the subject of the clause, while the second is the object; all three words in both phrases are marked for case, nominative and accusative respectively.

Cases other than nominative, accusative and genitive are traditionally identified in OE grammars as *dative* and *instrumental*; a *locative* case is also sometimes distinguished. For practical purposes, all these three cases may be subsumed under the dative. The dative case is used to flag indirect objects; it is also prototypically used in prepositional phrases, with many prepositions described as 'taking' the dative. This case appeared in the prepositional phrases **mid strangum rāpum** and **tō þǣre stōwe** in:

> (15)  **Se gōda wer band þone yflan mid strangum rāpum.**
> 'The good man bound the evil (one) with strong ropes.'

and

> (16)  **Þæs cyninges hlǣfdīge fērde swīþe blīþelīce tō þǣre stōwe.**
> 'The king's lady travelled happily to the place.'

In both examples, the determiners, adjectives and nouns in the prepositional phrase were given dative inflexions, underlined here. It should be noted that some prepositions cause the other elements in the phrase in which they appear to inflect in the accusative, and a few 'take' the genitive. In PDE, prepositions always appear at the beginning of prepositional phrases; in OE, they can occasionally appear at the end, especially when the rest of the phrase consists of a single pronoun, e.g. **him tō** 'to him'. Sometimes the dative case is used on its own to signal a meaning which would in PDE require a preposition; such 'prepositionless prepositional phrases' are relics of a period when prepositions were optional elements which were originally part of the same word-class as adverbs (compare PDE **to**, which can be classed as a preposition in **I went to the city** but as an adverb in **I walked to and fro**).

In OE, modifiers agree with the nouns to which they apply not only in case, but also in *number* and *gender*. Number is a comparatively simple concept; it refers to whether the word is singular or plural. As with PDE, there are inflexions on noun-stems to indicate plurality, and pronouns are also marked for number; however, there are also inflexions on adjectives, and marking for number on determiners – restricted to **these, those** in PDE – is much more extensive. Thus, in:

> (21a)  **Þā gōdan hlāfordas bundon þone yflan cnapan.**
> 'The good lords bound the evil servant.'

all lexemes in the subject noun phrase, **Þā gōdan hlāfordas**, are marked for plural number as well as case (compare the singular noun phrase **Se gōda hlāford** 'The good lord' in (21)).

Gender is a little more complex for PDE speakers to understand, since it has no real equivalent in PDE grammar. Nouns and pronouns in OE belong to one of three gender-classes, and this categorisation affects the endings they have, and in turn the endings that any of their modifiers have. Traditionally, these three classes are known as *masculine, feminine* and *neuter* genders. Sometimes this *grammatical gender* corresponds to biological or *natural gender*, but sometimes it does not. For example, OE **stān** 'stone' is classified as a masculine noun, OE **wīf** 'woman' is neuter and OE **giefu** 'gift' is feminine. Any determiners and adjectives modifying or complementing these nouns need to be inflected, through agreement, according to this grammatical gender. In principle, an OE pronoun should also be in the same gender as the noun to which it refers; however, towards the end of the OE period this rule began to be ignored and pronoun choice between, for example, **hē, hēo, hit** began to be determined by natural gender. OE grammatical gender is comparable with that in PD French, where all nouns, however 'sexless' they may be in terms of natural gender, are categorised as either masculine or feminine, e.g. **la table** 'the table' (feminine), or with that in PD German, which is very similar to the OE pattern; for example, **das Weib** 'the woman' (neuter).

As in PDE, OE pronouns are categorised by *person*. First-person pronouns are the equivalent of PDE **I, we** etc.; 2nd person pronouns are the equivalent of PDE **you** (and EModE **thou, ye** etc.); 3rd person pronouns are the equivalent of PDE **he, she, it, they** etc. The indefinite pronoun **one** (cf. OE **man**) is also considered a 3rd person pronoun. The category 'person' is relevant to the conjugation of verbs, and will be discussed further in section 6.3 below.

*Numerals* form a special category of word, and are probably best dealt with as part of the noun phrase. As in PDE, numerals fall into two main groups: *cardinal* (**one, two** etc.) and *ordinal* (**first, second** etc.). In PDE and in OE, both cardinal and ordinal numbers prototypically function as modifiers within noun phrases, e.g. **two books, the fifth floor**. Of the OE cardinals, 1–3 (**ān, twā, þrēo**) inflect like adjectives; thus **ān wer** 'one man', **mid twǣm cnapum** 'with two servants', **tō þrim stōwum** 'to three places'. Cardinal numbers from **fēower** 'four' onwards are generally undeclined, but cause the noun they modify to appear in the genitive case, e.g. **hund scipa** 'a hundred ships' (literally 'a hundred (of) ships'). The numbers 4–12 can be declined when not immediately before the noun they modify, e.g. **stānas nigene** 'nine stones' (literally 'stones nine'), cf. uninflected **nigon** 'nine'. Certain other words behave in the same way, and seem to have been classified with numerals: **fela** 'many', which causes the noun it modifies to appear in the genitive, and **bā** 'both' which is declined in the same way as **twā** 'two'. Ordinal numbers (**forma, ōþer, þridda** etc.), like adjectives, agree with the nouns they modify, and are always declined in accordance with the weak adjective paradigm, e.g. **se þridda wer** 'the third man'. The exception is **ōþer**, which is always declined strong, as in **se ōþer cyning**.

## 6.3 The verb phrase: functions

Verb phrases function prototypically as *predicators* within a clause:

(22) **The girl** <u>reads</u> **the book.**

(22a) **The girl** <u>was reading</u> **the book.**

Verb phrases in PDE fall into two groups: *simple verb phrases*, consisting of a lexical verb (as in (22) above), and *complex verb phrases*, consisting of a lexical verb as headword preceded by one or more auxiliary verbs as modifiers (as in (22a) above). There are also special grammatical categories associated with verb phrases: *agreement, person, number, finiteness, tense, mood, aspect, voice, transitivity, negation*. These categories are applicable to both PDE and OE verb phrases.

The categories of *agreement*, *person* and *number* may be taken together. In PDE, there is agreement between the subject of a clause and the verb phrase which the subject governs, e.g. **I** <u>love</u>, **they** <u>love</u>, beside **she** <u>loves</u>. Agreement is marked by inflexion; the choice of inflexion depends on the number and person of the subject. Thus a 1st person singular subject **I**, or a 3rd person plural subject **they**, means that the form of the verb appears as **love**, whereas the 3rd person singular subject **she** means that the verb appears as **loves**. Such patterns of agreement also appear in OE, though the range of inflexions marking agreement is much more extensive, e.g. **ic lufige** 'I love', **hēo lufaþ** 'she loves', **hīe lufiaþ** 'they love', **þū lufodest** 'you (singular) loved', **wē lufodon** 'we loved'.

All the forms listed in the preceding paragraph are *finite* verbs. Finite verbs in both OE and PDE agree with their subjects. *Non-finite* verbs are the *infinitive* (base-form) and *participles* (present and past). The infinitive form of the verb may be regarded as the base-form from which other parts of the verb-paradigm can be derived. Participles are grammatical units somewhere between the verb and the adjective and deriving characteristics from both. For example, in **The ship was abandoned, abandoned** is clearly derived from the infinitive of the verb **abandon**; but the word **abandoned** occupies the same grammatical 'slot' as **beautiful**, an adjective, in **The ship was beautiful**. The **-ed** form of the verb is in this context a *past participle*.[1] The *present* *participle* in **-ing** is similarly poised between categories; compare the difficulty of analysing PDE **The cat was grinning**. Participles characteristically appear in PDE as the final elements in complex verb phrases, e.g. **was <u>loved</u>, am <u>loving</u>, have been <u>loved</u>**, as can infinitives, e.g. **We shall <u>love</u>**. Participles can also appear as the predicators of certain subordinate clauses, e.g. **<u>Eating</u> a banana, she left the room**. In PDE, non-finite verbs in complex verb phrases are not marked for agreement with a subject.

The categories of *tense* and *mood* affect the pattern of inflexion for finite verbs in both PDE and OE. Tense is a category to do with time, the word coming from Old French **tens** 'time' (cf. Latin **tempus**, PD French **temps**); finite verbs in PDE and OE have special forms depending on whether they are in the *present* or *preterite* tense, e.g. **ic binde** 'I bind', **ic lufige** 'I love' (present), **ic band** 'I bound', **ic lufode** 'I loved' (preterite).

*Future* time (as in PDE **I shall go, she'll go** etc.) was generally expressed in OE simply through the present tense, and futurity was inferred from the context of the phrase:

> (23) **On morgenne, gā ic tō þǣm dūnum.**
> 'In the morning, I shall go to the hills.' (literally, 'In morning, go I to the hills')

The ancestors of PDE **will, shall**, OE **willan** and **sculan**, could be used to express futurity as part of a complex verb phrase, i.e. **willan/sculan + infinitive**, as in:

> (24) **Þā Darius geseah þæt hē oferwunnen bēon wolde…**
> 'When Darius saw that he would be overcome …' (literally, 'When Darius saw that he overcome be would …')

and

> (25) **Ic sceal rǣdan tō merigen.**
> 'I shall read tomorrow.'
> (examples taken from Mitchell 1985a: 426–7).

However, **willan** and **sculan** are more prototypically used with a lexical meaning, to express *volition* and *obligation* respectively. Thus **ic wille gān** means 'I want to go' rather than 'I will go', while **hēo sceal gān** means 'she must go' rather than 'she'll go'.

Mood is a verbal category to do with different degrees of possibility. Three moods are traditionally distinguished: *indicative, subjunctive* and *imperative*. Indicative mood forms are those where the form chosen indicates that the action referred to is a real action, as in **I <u>ate</u> my breakfast**. Subjunctive mood is used to suggest hypothesis, conjecture or volition, as in **I <u>may eat</u> my breakfast**, while imperative mood is used for commands, as in **<u>Eat</u> your** breakfast! In OE, special forms of the finite verb are used to distinguish moods, e.g. **hē lufaþ** 'he loves', **hīe bundon** 'they bound' (indicative), **hē lufige** 'he may love', **hīe bunden** 'they might have bound' (subjunctive), **lufa** 'love!' (imperative singular), **lufaþ** 'love!' (imperative plural). In PDE, a few relics of the old subjunctive survive, e.g. **God <u>save</u> the Queen, If <u>I were</u> you**, but it is usual to express subjunctive mood through complex verb phrases, e.g. **he <u>might eat</u> his apple**.

Although OE expressed subjunctive mood through inflexions, complex verb phrases were used to express further grammatical categories, notably *aspect* and *voice*. Aspect is a category to do with such things as whether the action is completed (*perfect*) or continuous (*progressive*): compare the distinction between PDE **he was eating** (progressive aspect), **he ate** (perfect aspect), **he has been eating** (progressive aspect), **he had eaten** (perfect aspect). The category 'voice' indicates whether the subject governing the form of the finite verb is the agent of the action, i.e. *active*, or the target, i.e. *passive*: compare PDE **she <u>loved</u> her dog** (active voice), **she <u>was loved</u> by her dog** (passive voice).

In PDE, aspectual and voice distinctions are often made using complex verb phrases, and these distinctions, it seems, could also be so made in OE. Available constructions in OE were (1) **wesan** 'be' + present participle, and (2) **habban, wesan, weorþan** + past participle. Examples of (1) used to express progressive aspect are **ic eom singende** 'I am singing', **hīe wǣron wuniende on þǣre stōwe** 'they were dwelling in that place'. However, non-progressive forms (**ic singe, hīe wunedon**) were much more commonly used in OE than in PDE, to such an extent that OE frequently distinguishes aspect not through the form of the verb phrase but through the use of, for example, adverbs, such as **oft** 'often', in **oft ic singe** 'I sing often'.[2]

Construction (2) is much more common, and is used to express perfect aspect and passive voice. When the construction consists of **wesan** or **weorþan**, then the past participle, particularly in early texts, prototypically agrees in case, number and gender with the subject of the sentence; when the auxiliary verb is **habban**, the past participle agrees with the direct object. The past participle is declined as a strong adjective; thus in OE it is difficult, if not impossible, to determine whether the past participle is a 'verbal' adjective or an 'adjectival' verb. Thus **hīe wurdon gebundene** 'they were bound' (literally 'they became bound'), **hīe hæfdon hine gebundenne** 'they had bound him'.

Although there are counter-examples in the OE corpus, suggesting that the PDE usage whereby **have** + past participle as the dominant pattern was emerging, OE seems to have distinguished **habban** + past participle and **wesan, weorþan** + past participle on the grounds of *transitivity*. Transitivity is a grammatical category to do with whether or not verb phrases govern direct objects; *transitive* verb phrases do, *intransitive* verb phrases do not. In OE, while **habban** + past participle is used commonly to express perfect aspect of transitive verb phrases, **wesan** + past participle is used commonly to express perfect aspect of intransitive verb phrases, e.g. **hīe sind gecumene** 'they have come' (literally 'they are come'). Inflexional patterns suggest that past participles were seen as much closer to the adjectival category in earlier OE, i.e. as part of the object rather than the predicator when accompanied by **habban**, and as complements when accompanied by **wesan, weorþan** (see Mitchell 1985a: 415).

**W**esan + past participle constructions can be used to express passive voice, as can **weorþan** + past participle, e.g. **hē wearþ geslægen** 'he was struck' (literally 'he became struck'). However, OE often avoided expressing the equivalent of PDE passive voice with such constructions, instead using the impersonal pronoun **man** 'one', as in **man Horsan ofslōg** 'Horsa was slain' (literally 'one slew Horsa'). Indeed, other alternatives to the **habban, wesan, weorþan** + past participle constructions were common in OE. Not only were simple verb phrases used in their place, but adverbs were frequently employed, as in **ic lufode ǣr** 'I had loved' (literally 'I loved formerly').

*Negation* in OE is expressed adverbially, as in PDE. The most common negator is **ne**, frequently assimilated to the words it precedes, e.g. **nis** 'is not' (= **ne/ni** + **is**); such contractions, it appears, were particularly common in West Saxon dialects (Mitchell 1985a: 479 and references there cited). Double or multiple negation (as in PDE stigmatised **I ain't got nothing**) was entirely acceptable in OE, e.g. **Hit nā ne fēoll** 'it did not fall'. Multiple negation, it seems, was less common in OE poetry than in OE prose (see Mitchell 1985b: 992–3).

# 6.4 Sentence structure I: element-order

In chapter 2, it was noted that the OE inflexional system was much more extensive than that of PDE, and that in principle OE *element-order* was much more flexible than that of PDE. Thus, again in principle, the clauses:

(26) **Se hlāford bindeþ þone cnapan.**

and

(27) **Þone cnapan bindeþ se hlāford.**

'mean' the same, 'The lord binds the servant.'

However, the flexibility of OE element-order should not be exaggerated. Examination of the surviving corpus of OE suggests that there were prototypical usages from which – unsurprisingly! – individual authors could depart for stylistic reasons; and these prototypical usages were clearly necessary when, as was commonplace, there were no inflexional means of distinguishing, for example, subject from object. Thus, for instance, in the clause **þæt wīf bindeþ hit** 'the woman binds it', it is not possible to determine the respective roles of the noun phrases **þæt wīf** and **hit** because the nominative and accusative forms of these words are not differentiated.

Three types of OE element-order are usually distinguished:

(a)  SP, where the predicator (= verb phrase) immediately follows the subject;
(b)  S...P, where other elements of the clause come between the subject and the predicator;
(c)  PS, where the subject follows the predicator.

SP is the usual order in main clauses; S...P is most commonly found in subordinate clauses; and PS occurs often in questions, and also commonly in main clauses introduced by certain adverbials, notably **þā** 'then', **þǣr** 'there', **þider** 'thither'. Examples are:

> (28)  **Se cnapa lufode þone gōdan hlāford.**
> 'The servant loved the good lord.'

with SP in a main clause;

> (29)  **For þǣm þe se cnapa þone gōdan hlāford lufode, hē fērde tō þǣm dūnum.**
> 'Because the servant loved the good lord, he travelled to the hills.'
> (literally 'Because the servant the good lord loved, he travelled to the hills')

with S ... P in a subordinate clause (**For þǣm þe ... lufode**); and:

> (30)  **Þā fērde hē tō þǣm dūnum.**
> 'Then he travelled to the hills.'
> (literally 'Then travelled he to the hills')

with PS in a main clause beginning with **þā** 'then'.

However, OE writers frequently departed from these norms for stylistic effect. PS, for instance, was commonly used to introduce new information (facts, ideas) or to shift emphasis (see Mitchell 1985b: 978).

When the predicator consists of a complex verb phrase, in both main and subordinate clauses, the two parts of the predicator may be separated; the auxiliary verb can follow directly after the subject, and the lexical verb may be left to the end of the clause. In the following examples (31)–(32), the 'split' verb phrases are underlined.

> (31)  **Þā se ealda wer <u>wæs</u> tō þǣre stōwe <u>gecumen</u>, þā band hē his sunu.**
> 'When the old man had come to that place, he bound his son.'

(32) Se ealda wer <u>hæfde</u> his sunu <u>gebundenne</u>.
    'The old man had bound his son.'

However, other patterns are also possible, for example:

(33) Þā se ealda wer tō þǣre stōwe gecumen wæs …
    'When the old man had come to that place…'

## 6.5 Sentence structure II: clauses

In chapter 2, two kinds of clause were distinguished: *main* and *subordinate*. Main clauses can stand as sentences on their own, while subordinate clauses function as units within a main clause, as phrases do, or as subordinate elements within a phrase, like words. Subordinate clauses are generally further classified by grammarians as *noun clauses, adverb clauses, relative clauses* and *comparative clauses*. Some PDE examples containing subordinate clauses follow in (34–40):

(34) **He ate a banana because he was hungry** (with the subordinate clause **because … hungry** functioning as an adverbial = adverb clause)

Adverb clauses are often linked to the main clause by a *subordinating conjunction*, e.g. **because, although, until** etc., but these conjunctions are not a defining characteristic of adverb clauses. In:

(34a) **Feeling hungry, he ate a banana** (with subordinate clause **Feeling hungry** functioning as an adverbial = adverb clause)

the subordinate clause has a non-finite verb as predicator.
    Other kinds of subordinate clause are:

(35) **What I want is a banana** (with subordinate clause **What I want** functioning as a subject = noun clause)

(36) **A banana is what she wanted** (with subordinate clause **what she wanted** functioning as a complement = noun clause)

(37) **He gave her what she wanted** (with subordinate clause **what she wanted** functioning as a direct object = noun clause)

(38) **The banana which she wanted was on the table** (with subordinate clause **which she wanted** functioning as a modifying element within the noun phrase **The banana which she wanted** = relative clause)

(39) **The boy was eating more bananas than she could afford** (with subordinate clause **than she could afford** functioning as a modifier

within the noun phrase **more bananas than she could afford** = comparative clause)

(40) **The boy was eating the banana more greedily than she thought polite** (with subordinate clause **than she thought polite** functioning as a modifier within the adverb phrase **more greedily than she thought polite** = comparative clause)

It will have been observed that relative and comparative clauses overlap in functions. However, comparative clauses can modify adjectives and adverbs as well as nouns, and there is an element of comparison (hence the name) with the element being modified. Relative clauses are often linked to the headwords they modify by *relative pronouns*, e.g. **who, which, that**; comparative clauses are linked to their headwords by *comparative conjunctions*, e.g. **than, as**.

Clauses may be linked to others by a conjunction but not function as a subject, or complement or object or adverbial:

(41) **She went downstairs and ate a banana.**

(42) **He wasn't hungry but still ate the banana.**

Such clauses are known as *coordinated* clauses, linked by coordinating conjunctions such as **and** or **but**.

Similar constructions appear in OE, although there are some interesting differences. Thus clauses can be coordinated, linked by coordinating conjunctions such as **and** 'and', **ac** 'but' etc., as in:

(43) **Se hlāford lufode þone cyning, ac sēo hlǣfdīge hiere cnapan lufode.**
'The lord loved the king, but the lady loved her servant.'

It will have been observed in (43) that the element-order in these coordinated clauses is sometimes that more characteristic of subordinate clauses, with the lexical verb in final position. This fact suggests that the Anglo-Saxons did not draw as clear a distinction between subordinated and coordinated clauses as is the case in PDE.

Subordinating conjunctions in OE include: **forþon, forþǣm, forþǣm þe** 'because'; **oþ, oþ þæt** 'until'; + **gif** 'if'; **þā, þā þā** 'when'; + **þæt** '(so) that'; + **þēah, þēah þe** 'although'; + **ǣr, ǣr þan þe** 'before'; + **æfter, æfter þan/þǣm þe** 'after'; + **þȳ lǣs, þȳ lǣs þe** 'lest'. Comparative conjunctions include **þonne** 'than', + **swā swā** 'like'.

Several of these subordinating conjunctions are composed of a number of words, but they may be considered as single units. Some require the finite verb to be inflected according to subjunctive mood in the subordinate clause involved; conjunctions which can require finite verbs in the subjunctive are marked with a 'plus' sign in the list above. Indicative mood is generally used when the event in the subordinate clause is complete or certain; subjunctive mood is used when the action in question has not yet happened or is hypothetical. Thus **æfter þǣm þe** etc. 'after' – where the action referred to has, by definition, already occurred – would require the verb in the subordinate clause to be in the indicative mood, while **ǣr þǣm þe** etc. 'before' would require the subjunctive. [3]

Examples of adverb and noun clauses in OE are:

(44) **For þǣm þe hē wīs wer wæs, hē weorþode his cyning.**
'Because he was a wise man, he honoured his king.'
(with indicative finite verb in the adverb clause **For þǣm þe ... wæs**)

(45) **Ær þǣm þe hīe þone wer ofslōgen, hīe bundon hine.**
'Before they slew the man, they bound him.'
(with subjunctive finite verb in the adverb clause **Ær ... ofslōgen**)

(46) **Se cyning geseah þæt hīe ānmōde wǣron.**
'The king saw that they were unanimous.'
(with indicative finite verb in the noun clause **þæt ... wǣron**)

(47) **Se hlāford bæd þæt his cnapan þone gōdan cyning binden.**
'The lord commanded that his servants should bind the good king.'
(with subjunctive finite verb in the noun clause **þæt his cnapan ... binden**)

(48) **Singende þus, se cnapa fērde tō þǣm dūnum.**
'Singing thus, the servant travelled to the hills'
(with non-finite verb in the adverb clause **Singende þus**)

**Gif**, meaning 'if or 'whether', can be used to introduce a noun clause (cf. PDE **Whether she does this is up to her**), but it is generally used to introduce a conditional adverb clause with the verb in the subjunctive:

(49) **Gif þū þone wer binde, se hlāford lufige þē.**
'If you bind the man, the lord (will) love you.'

A particular kind of noun clause is the so-called *accusative and infinitive construction*, where the subject of the subordinate clause is in the accusative case and the verb of the subordinate clause is in the infinitive. This construction is frequently used after verbs of saying or thinking (cf. PDE **know, order, tell** etc.):

(50) **Hē hēt þone wer hine bindan.**
'He commanded the man to bind him.'
(literally 'him to bind')

An important group of OE clauses equivalent to PDE adverb clauses are those which occur in *correlative constructions*, whereby two clauses are linked together by *correlative words*, e.g. **forþon ... forþon ..., þonne ... þonne ...** etc. The most common involves the use of **þā ... þā ...** Now it is usual to assign two meanings to **þā** in such constructions, namely, 'then' and 'when', and to distinguish these meanings by the element order of the clauses in question. Thus, if **þā** is followed by the subject of the clause and the clause's verb is in final position, it may be interpreted as a subordinating conjunction 'when'; but, if **þā** is followed by the lexical verb and then the subject of the clause, it may be interpreted as an adverb functioning as an adverbial, meaning 'then'. Thus:

(51) **Þā hēo þone wer geseah, þā lufode hēo hine.**

may be translated as 'When she saw the man, then she loved him', a perfectly acceptable translation. However, it is worth noting that, in the PDE translation, 'then' seems rather redundant; the OE liking for repeating the 'same' word possibly relates to certain devices of cohesion favoured in oral delivery (see section 6.6 below, and also Mitchell 1985a: 777).

An example of a comparative clause is:

(52) **Sēo cwēn dēmde hine rihtlicor þonne dyde se cyning.**
    'The queen judged him more justly than the king did.'

with the comparative clause **þonne ... cyning** modifying the adverb **rihtlicor** 'more justly'; the finite verb in the comparative clause is indicative.

Relative clauses are constructed distinctively in OE. The indeclinable *relative particle* **þe** (cf. PDE **who(m), which, that** etc.) is frequently used on its own to introduce a relative clause:

(53) **Se wer þe his hlāford lufaþ**
    'The man who loves his lord'

(54) **Se cnapa þe þā lēode Ælfred nemnaþ**
    'The servant whom the people call Alfred'

However, there are alternative usages which seem to be constrained by a whole series of factors (see Mitchell 1985b: 160 ff. for a discussion). **Þe** is often accompanied by a defining determiner declined according to its function in the relative clause. Thus sentences (53) and (54) above could be rephrased as follows:

(53a) **Se wer se þe his hlāford lufaþ**

(54a) **Se cnapa þone þe þā lēode Ælfred nemnaþ**

Commonly, and especially when the noun being modified by the relative clause is not preceded by a determiner or adjective, a determiner is used in place of þe, as in:

(55) **Wer se þone Ælmihtigan lufaþ sceal blīþe wesan.**
'A man who loves the Almighty must be happy'

Sometimes no relative particle or determiner is used at all:

(53b) **Se wer his hlāford lufaþ**

(54b) **Se cnapa þā lēode Ælfred nemnaþ**

## 6.6 Sentence structure III: special features

Stylisticians – students of the ways in which speakers and writers, both literary and non-literary, arrange language to achieve their effects – have for many years been interested in the notion of *cohesion*. Cohesion is to do with the range of linguistic devices, or *cohesive ties*, which are used to connect words, phrases, clauses and sentences in a piece of discourse (see further Halliday and Hasan 1976). An obvious example of a cohesive tie in PDE is to do with the handling of pronouns; we use the pronoun **she** to refer back (*anaphoric reference*) or forward (*kataphoric reference*) to a noun phrase which maps semantically onto a female entity. Patterns of cohesion can change over time; thus in OE pronouns were used for the same purpose, but grammatically, in that **hēo** refers forward or back to a noun phrase which was grammatically feminine (but not necessarily female).

One cohesive tie in OE which seems clumsy to PDE readers – though it is actually still common in spoken discourse – is the use of *recapitulation and anticipation*. Expressions such as **the people who lived here, they loved wisdom** and **they learned that thing, that they were foolish** strike PDE readers as clumsy; in formal PDE, the commas and words underlined would be omitted. Such expressions were, however, entirely acceptable in written OE:

(56) **Ure ieldran, þā þe þās stōwa þær hēoldon, hīe lufodon wīsdōm.**
'Our forefathers, those who formerly held these places, they loved wisdom.'
(see Mitchell and Robinson 1992: 66)

It has been argued that this pattern of recapitulation and anticipation, as with correlation, derives from a 'feeling of insecurity in the face of the complicated sentence' (Mitchell and Robinson 1992: 68; see also Mitchell 1985a: 777).

Another characteristic of OE syntax, *the splitting of heavy groups*, may arise from a similar 'insecurity' (Mitchell 1985a: 616). It is characteristic of

OE to 'split' long phrases and modifiers, which were apparently regarded as clumsy. Thus, usages prototypical of PDE, such as **Tom and Dick were walking along the road** or **She was a good and beautiful woman**, contrast with a common OE construction equating to **Tom was walking along the road, and Dick** or **She was a good woman, and beautiful**. An example is:

(57) **Hē fērde mid twǣm cnapum tō þǣm dūnum, and Isaāc samod.**
'He and Isaac travelled with two servants to the hills.'
(Literally 'He travelled with two servants to the hills, and Isaac as well.')

Such usages are of course found in PDE, but they may be regarded as stylistically salient, e.g. **Inspired by British Cheers and Loud/Proceeding from the Frenzied Crowd** (Belloc, *Matilda*, lines 21–2).[4] Stylistic, notably emphatic, uses of the OE construction are found in OE (see Mitchell 1985a: 616 for examples and discussion).

A characteristic feature of OE writing, more common than in PDE formal usage, is the habit of employing *parataxis*. Parataxis means the juxtaposition of two or more simple clauses rather than the subordination of one clause to another, which is called *hypotaxis*. Parataxis can be of two kinds: *syndetic* (with coordinating conjunctions, such as in PDE **and** or **but**) or *asyndetic* (without such conjunctions). Parataxis has been regarded by some scholars as more 'primitive' than hypotaxis, and another example of how Anglo-Saxon writers avoided the use of 'complicated sentences'. However, the use of parataxis in quite sophisticated prose (as in that of Ælfric) suggests otherwise; it is perhaps more plausible to see parataxis as relating to the author–audience relationship, since parataxis places responsibility for the interpretation of a speech or passage on to the listener/reader rather than on the author, whereas hypotaxis characteristically allows the author rather than the listener/reader to make causal connexions.

Mitchell and Robinson (1992) give the following PDE examples to illustrate the difference between hypotaxis and different kinds of parataxis:

(58) Hypotaxis: **When I came, I saw. When I saw, I conquered.**

(59) Asyndetic parataxis: **I came, I saw, I conquered.**

(60) Syndetic parataxis: **I came and I saw and I conquered.**

A good OE example of a paratactic passage is from the *Anglo-Saxon Chronicle*:

(61) **And þā gefeaht Æþered cyning and Ælfred his brōþor wiþ þone here æt Meretūne, and hīe wǣron on twǣm gefierdum, and þǣr wearþ micel wælsliht on gehwæþere hond, and þǣr wearþ Hēahmund biscop ofslægen.**

'And then king Æthered, and his brother Alfred, fought against the army at "Meretown", and they were in two armies, and there was great slaughter on either side, and there Bishop Heahmund was killed.'

## Notes

1. The term 'past participle' has been criticised as conflating distinct categories; see Mitchell 1985a: 12–13 and references there cited. However, the term is widely used in the scholarly literature, and is also handy as a description of a particular form, albeit with several functions, so it will be retained here in preference to Mitchell's suggested replacement, *second participle*.
2. For the origins and meanings of the **wesan** + present participle construction, see especially Mitchell 1985a: 272–80. The category 'aspect' is a problematic one for historians of Germanic languages. For an important, if polemical, discussion of the difficulties involved with OE aspect, see Mitchell 1985a: 363–9 and references there cited.
3. For the origin of OE conjunctions, see Mitchell 1985b: 240–6 and references there cited. The fact that þe is an element, often optional, in the make-up of OE conjunctions is interesting, since the word is also used in relative clauses. Mitchell 1985b: 243 suggests that the role of þe might be better understood if it is translated as 'namely', and refers to it as a *subordinating particle*.
4. For a text of *Matilda* by Hilaire Belloc (1870–1953), see http://www.poetry-archive.com/b/matilda.html.

## Exercises

Exercise 6a    'Old English element-order seems to be completely arbitrary.' Discuss.

Exercise 6b    What seem to you to be the principal differences between OE and PDE verb phrases?

## Key terms introduced in this chapter

inflexional morphology
case (nominative, accusative, genitive/possessive, dative)
gender (masculine, feminine, neuter)
number (singular, plural)
tense (present, preterite)
aspect (perfective, imperfective)
mood (indicative, subjunctive, imperative)
negation
finiteness
transitivity
synthetic vs. analytic languages
cohesion

# CHAPTER 7

# Old English Grammar II: Inflexional Morphology

## In this chapter …

This chapter looks in more depth at the inflexional morphology of Old English, notably of nouns and verbs.

### Contents

## 7.1 Inflexional morphology I: nouns

In PDE, most noun-paradigms, or *declensions*, have a simple pattern of inflexional morphology, taking account of number and possession (= genitive case), thus: **pig, pig's, pigs, pigs'**. OE nouns have to take account not only of a more complex case-system but also of grammatical gender. PDE has a few irregular sequences, for example **child, child's, children, children's**, or **mouse, mouse's, mice, mice's**; these irregularities go back to OE times, and were found in the inflexional morphology of many more nouns.

OE nouns can be classified into five declensions, as follows:

General masculine declension
General feminine declension
General neuter declension

The **-an** declension
Minor declensions

The first three declensions above are often referred to as the *strong declensions*, while the fourth is the *weak declension*. For the 'strong/weak' terminology with reference to nouns, see chapter 5, section 1. The following are typical paradigms for each of these declensions.

## 7.1.1 General masculine declension

The general masculine declension is one of the most common patterns of noun in OE.

> Singular:
> **stān** 'stone' (nominative, accusative)
> **stānes** (genitive)
> **stāne** (dative)
> Plural:
> **stānas** (nominative, accusative)
> **stāna** (genitive)
> **stānum** (dative)

Many masculine nouns decline on the same pattern as **stān**, e.g. **hund** 'dog', **wer** 'man', **hlāf** 'loaf'. Some nouns follow this pattern with some variation in the paradigm caused through sound-change; thus **dæg** 'day' has the same inflexions as **stān** but changes the vowel of its root to **a** in the plural, yielding **dagas, daga, dagum**. Nouns ending in -h lose this ending when an inflexion is added, e.g. **mearh** 'horse', **mēares** (genitive singular) etc.; it will be observed that compensatory lengthening for the loss of the consonant can take place. In disyllabic words, the unstressed vowel of the second syllable is lost when an inflexion is added, as in **engel** 'angel', **engles** (genitive singular), **englas** (nominative/accusative plural).

The general masculine declension is sometimes further sub-divided by scholars according to the theme in Proto-Germanic (see chapter 5, section 1), namely, as **a**-nouns, **ja**-nouns, **wa**-nouns, **i**-nouns. Although these distinctions do not affect the system of endings in OE, there are some differences in the appearance of inflected forms. All the nouns listed above are **a**-nouns, and these are the commonest type. However, **ende** 'end' (genitive singular **endes**, nominative/accusative singular **endas**) is a **ja**-noun (cf. Proto-Germanic nominative singular *****andjaz**). Other examples of masculine **ja**-nouns are **hyll** 'hill' (genitive singular **hylles**, nominative plural **hyllas**), **here** 'army' (genitive singular **herges**, with retained -g- in inflected forms). Masculine **wa**-nouns include **bearu** 'grove' (cf. Proto-Germanic *****barwaz**, genitive singular **bearwes**), **þēaw** 'custom' (genitive singular **þēawes**); the -w- is retained in the inflected forms, but has disappeared in the nominative singular. There are many i-nouns, e.g. **giest** 'guest' (cf. Proto-Germanic *gas-tiz), **dæl** 'part, share', and these decline like **stān**. One group of i-nouns, however, e.g. **wine** 'friend', **cyre** 'choice', **mete** 'food', **mere** 'lake', can decline like **stān** but variant forms appear in the nominative/accusative plural which are the same as the nominative/accusative singular. There are also masculine **u-nouns**, but these form a distinct, irregular group (see section 7.5.1 below).

Some nouns, though of distinct origins, have been transferred to this group through analogy, e.g. **-nd** nouns, derived from the present participle of verbs, such as **hælend** 'saviour', **wealdend** 'ruler'. Such nouns can appear either with or without inflexions in nominative and accusative plural, and appear in the genitive plural with an intrusive -r-, e.g. **wealdendra**.

Comparison between OE and Gothic shows how *syncretism*, the loss of inflexional distinctiveness, has proceeded in Germanic. Here again is the OE set:

Singular:
**stān** 'stone' (nominative, accusative)
**stānes** (genitive)
**stāne** (dative)
Plural:
**stānas** (nominative, accusative)
**stāna** (genitive)
**stānum** (dative)

For comparison, here is the Gothic paradigm:

Singular:
**stains** 'stone' (nominative)
**stain** (accusative)
**stainis** (genitive)
**staina** (dative)
Plural:
**stainōs** (nominative)
**stainans** (accusative)
**stainē** (genitive)
**stainam** (dative)

It will be observed that Gothic, representing an earlier stage of Germanic, sustains a distinction between nominative and accusative which OE no longer has.

## 7.1.2 General feminine declension

The general feminine declension is typified by the following:

> Singular:
> **lār** 'teaching' (nominative)
> **lāre** (accusative, genitive, dative)
> Plural:
> **lāra/lāre** (nominative, accusative)
> **lāra/lārena** (genitive)
> **lārum** (dative)

Many feminine nouns decline like **lār**, e.g. **lāf** 'remainder', **rōd** 'cross', **wund** 'wound', **sorg** 'sorrow'. Another group ending in -**u** in the nominative singular otherwise decline like **lār**, e.g. **giefu** 'gift', **faru** 'journey', **lufu** 'love'. The distinction between these two groups is that **lār** etc. consists in the nominative singular of a single long syllable, with either a long vowel followed by a single consonant or a short vowel followed by two consonants, while the stressed syllable **gie-** in **giefu** etc. is short. As with the general masculine declension, syncopated forms are found, e.g. **sāwol** 'soul' (nominative singular), **sāwle** (accusative singular etc.).

As with the masculine nouns, scholars sometimes further sub-divide feminine nouns on the basis of their Proto-Germanic themes, although these divisions have in general little significance for the OE inflexional pattern. Those listed above are **ō**-nouns; there are also **jo**-, **wō**- and **i**-nouns. **jo**-nouns include **synn** 'sin' (cf. Proto-Germanic *__sunjō__), **brycg** 'bridge', **benn** 'wound', **wylf** 'wolf'; **wō**- nouns include **sinu** 'sinew' (cf. Proto-Germanic *__senawō__, accounting for the -**w**- in OE inflected **sinwe**); **i**-nouns include **dǣd** 'deed' (cf. Proto-Germanic *__dǣdiz__). Also, as with the masculines, there is a small group of **u**-nouns; see section 7.5.1, below.

## 7.1.3 General neuter declension

The following is a prototypical general neuter noun:

> Singular:
> **scip** (nominative, accusative)
> **scipes** (genitive)
> **scipe** (dative)
> Plural:
> **scipu** (nominative, accusative)
> **scipa** (genitive)
> **scipum** (dative)

With the exception of the nominative/accusative plural, the endings of the general neuter declension are identical with those of the general masculine.

Many neuter nouns are declined according to this pattern, e.g. **god** 'god', **gewrit** 'writing'. A large variant group, generally with stems consisting of long syllables or disyllables, decline like **scip** but drop the -u inflexion in the nominative/accusative plural, e.g. **word** 'word', **wīf** 'woman', **sweord** 'sword', **dēor** 'animal', **gēar** 'year', **werod** 'troop'. As with the masculine, sound-changes have produced paradigmatic variation in **fæt** 'vessel' (nominative/accusative singular), **fatu** (nominative/accusative plural). Syncopated forms are also found, e.g. **hēafod** 'head', cf. **hēafdes** (genitive singular), but cf. **werod** 'troop', **werodes** (genitive singular).

Neuter nouns have the same set of themes in Proto-Germanic as the masculines, except there are none with **u-**. The above are all a-nouns. ja-nouns include **bedd** 'bed' (declined like **word**), cf. Proto-Germanic *\*baðjaz*, and **wīte** 'punishment' (declined like **scip**). wa-nouns include **teoru** 'tar' (**teorwes** genitive singular, cf. Proto-Germanic *\*terwaz*), **cudu** 'cud', **smeoru** 'grease'. i-nouns include **dyne** 'din' (cf. Proto-Germanic *\*duniz*).

## 7.1.4 The -an declension

This declension includes masculine, feminine and neuter nouns. The feminine nominative singular ends in -e, as do the neuter nominative and accusative singular; otherwise, they do not differ from the masculine paradigm:

> Singular:
> **nama** 'name' (nominative)
> **naman** (accusative, genitive, dative)
> Plural:
> **naman** (nominative, accusative)
> **namena** (genitive)
> **namum** (dative)

Like **nama** are **guma** 'man', **cnapa** 'servant, boy' and many others.

Feminines include **heorte** 'heart', **tunge** 'tongue', **hlǣfdīge** 'lady' etc. There are only two neuters, **ēage** 'eye', **ēare** 'ear'. Syncopated forms are found, commonly in poetry, e.g. **ēagna** 'eyes' (genitive plural) beside **ēagena**. A few nouns whose roots end in vowels decline thus:

> Singular:
> **frēa** 'lord' (nominative)
> **frēan** (accusative, genitive, dative)
> Plural:
> **frēan** (nominative, accusative)
> **frēana** (genitive)
> **frēam** (dative)

Singular:
**bēo** 'bee' (nominative)
**bēon** (accusative, genitive, dative)
Plural:
**bēon** (nominative, accusative)
**bēona** (genitive)
**bēom** (dative)

Masculines in this group include **frēa, rā** 'roe deer', **gefā** 'enemy, foe', **twēo** 'doubt'; feminines include **bēo, dā** 'doe', **tā** 'toe', **cēo** 'chough'. The form **lēo** 'lion(ess)', a loanword from Latin which is both masculine and feminine, can be declined like **bēo**, but can also appear with an intrusive **-n-**, as in **lēonan, lēonum**.

The **-an** declension, often described as the weak noun, had a consonantal theme in Proto-Germanic, **-n-**. This thematic element derived from Proto-Indo-European themes in \*-en-, with the vowel subject to Ablaut variation (see chapter 5, section 1), yielding \*-on-, lengthened grades \*-ēn- and \*-ōn-, and the reduced or 'zero' grade \*-n-. One example of reduced or zero grade survives in OE, namely **oxna** 'oxen' (genitive plural) as opposed to \*oxena, cf. **oxa** 'ox' (nominative plural).

## 7.1.5 Minor declensions

There are several minor declensions, classified by their way of forming the nominative and accusative plural. The most important are the *-a plurals*, *uninflected plurals*, and *'mutation' plurals*. There are also a few *irregular nouns* which do not fall into any other category.

*The -a plurals*, both masculine and feminine, decline as follows:

Singular:
**sunu** 'son' (nominative, accusative)
**suna** (genitive, dative)
Plural:
**suna** (nominative, accusative, genitive)
**sunum** (dative)

These nouns derive from Proto-Germanic nouns with thematic **u**, e.g. the masculine **sunu** 'son' (cf. Proto-Germanic \*sunuz). Other masculines are **wudu** 'wood', **medu** 'mead'; feminines are **duru** 'door', **nosu** 'nose'. A subgroup whose stem ends in two consonants declines like **sunu** but without **-u** in the nominative/accusative singular, e.g. masculine **feld** 'field' and the feminines **cweorn** 'hand-mill, quern' (cf. Proto-Germanic \*kwernuz) and **hand** 'hand'.

In general, *uninflected plurals* decline like the general masculine, feminine and neuter declensions listed above, except that (as their name suggests) the nominative and accusative plural are the same as the nominative and accusative singular. The most important of these are the relationship nouns **brōþor** 'brother' and **dohtor** 'daughter', which decline as follows:

Singular:
**dohtor** (nominative, accusative, genitive)
**dehter** (dative)
Plural:
**dohtor** (nominative, accusative)
**dohtra** (genitive)
**dohtrum** (dative)

**Brōþor** follows the same pattern, with dative singular **brēþer**. Other relationship nouns vary somewhat from this pattern; thus **mōdor** 'mother' follows the same pattern as **dohtor** in the singular, but has nominative and accusative plural forms **mōdra, mōdru**. **Fæder** 'father' appears uninflected throughout the singular, but follows the general masculine paradigm in the plural; **sweostor** 'sister' similarly does not inflect in the singular, but varies between the **dohtor**- and **mōdor**-paradigms in the plural.

*'Mutation' plurals* are still to be found in PDE, e.g. **foot, feet, man, men** or **mouse, mice**. They were more common in OE. The following paradigms of **fōt** 'foot', a masculine noun, and **bōc** 'book', a feminine noun, are typical:

Singular:
**fōt** 'foot' (nominative, accusative)
**fōtes** (genitive)
**fēt** (dative)
Plural:
**fēt** (nominative, accusative)
**fōta** (genitive)
**fōtum** (dative)

Singular:
**bōc** 'book' (nominative, accusative)
**bēc, bōce** (genitive)
**bēc, bōc** (dative)
Plural:
**bēc** (nominative, accusative)
**bōca** (genitive)
**bōcum** (dative)

Other examples include the masculines **mann** 'man' (nominative plural **menn**), **tōþ** 'tooth' (nominative plural **tēþ**); feminines include **gāt** 'goat' (nominative plural **gǣt**), **gōs** 'goose' (nominative plural **gēs**), **mūs** 'mouse' (nominative plural **mȳs**). Variant forms also appear in several OE texts, often derived from other paradigms by analogy, e.g. **tōþas** 'teeth', **fōtas** 'feet' (see Campbell 1959: 252). The forms in **fēt, menn** etc. derive from the operation of the sound-change i-mutation, cf. Proto-Germanic *****fōtiz**, *****manniz**; forms such as **fōtes** (genitive singular) seem to derive by analogy with the general masculine declension, while variants such as **bōce** (genitive singular) are taken analogously from the general feminine declension. There are no neuter mutation plurals.

A special set of mutation plurals consists of two masculine nouns ending in -nd, namely **frēond** 'friend' (nominative plural **frīend**), **fēond** 'enemy' (nominative plural **fīend**, cf. PDE **fiend**).

A few nouns have *irregular paradigms*, through the operation of analogy or as relics of Proto-Germanic paradigms otherwise extinct by OE times. One set of neuters decline like the general neuter declension in the singular, but add an intrusive -r- in the plural, e.g. **lamb** 'lamb', **lambru** (nominative/accusative plural), **lambra** (genitive plural), **lambrum** (dative plural). Other neuters with similar paradigms include **cealf** 'calf', **ǣg** 'egg', while **cild** 'child' can be declined like **word**, in the general neuter declension, throughout but also appears with -r- forms, e.g. **cildru** (nominative/accusative plural). Another small group of nouns display relics of the Proto-Indo-European t-declension, e.g. **mōnaþ** 'month' (see chapter 5, section 1).

## 7.2 Inflexional morphology II: pronouns and determiners

Prototypically, *pronouns* function in place of nouns or noun phrases; *determiners* function as the modifiers within noun phrases. However, the distinction between the categories is fuzzy. Thus words which are generally described in the handbooks as determiners, for example PDE **this, that,** can be used pronominally, as in **That was a good meal** beside **It was a good meal**. Similar usages are found in OE, e.g. **þæt wæs gōd cyning** 'That was a good king' beside **Hē wæs gōd cyning** 'He was a good king'. Similarly, possessives such as PDE **his, her, its, their,** which form part of PDE pronoun-paradigms, prototypically appear as modifiers within noun phrases, e.g. **his books, her pony, its colour, their house**. Similar usages appear in OE. This fuzzy distinction between categories derives from the origins of the forms concerned; as Roger Lass has pointed out, 'Proto-Germanic did not inherit a fully coherent pronoun or determiner system ... Rather the collections labelled "pronouns" or "articles" or "demonstratives" in the handbooks represent dialect-specific selections out of a mass of inherited forms and systems' (1994: 139).

OE pronouns, like nouns, are inflected for number and case, and, in the 3rd person singular, for gender. As in PDE, they are also inflected for person (1st, 2nd, 3rd); unlike PDE, however, there are also special 1st and 2nd person dual pronouns, equivalent to PDE 'we two', 'us two', 'you two'; these dual pronouns survive into the Early Middle English period but have since died out. Like nouns, pronouns *decline*. One helpful feature for the beginning student is that some of the equivalent forms in OE (though not all) resemble those forms used in PDE, for instance **mē** 'me', **hē** 'he', **wē** 'we', **ūs** 'us'.

The pronoun-paradigms are as follows:

*1st person*
Singular:
**ic** (nominative)
**mē** (accusative)
**mīn** (genitive)
**mē** (dative)
Plural:
**wē** (nominative)
**ūs** (accusative)
**ūre** (genitive)
**ūs** (dative)
Dual:
**wit** (nominative)
**unc** (accusative)
**uncer** (genitive)
**unc** (dative)

*2nd person*
Singular:
**þū** (nominative)
**þē** (accusative)
**þīn** (genitive)
**þē** (dative)
Plural:
**gē** (nominative)
**ēow** (accusative)
**ēower** (genitive)
**ēow** (dative)

Dual:
**git** (nominative)
**inc** (accusative)
**incer** (genitive)
**inc** (dative)

*3rd person*
Masculine singular:
**hē** (nominative)
**hine** (accusative)
**his** (genitive)
**him** (dative)
Feminine singular:
**hēo** (nominative)
**hīe** (accusative)
**hiere** (genitive, dative)
Neuter singular:
**hit** (nominative, accusative)
**his** (genitive)
**him** (dative)
Plural:
**hīe** (nominative, accusative)
**hiera** (genitive)
**him** (dative)

As modifying elements within a noun phrase, and in keeping with their fuzzy categorisation on the boundary between pronouns and determiners, the genitives **mīn, þīn, ūre, ēower** may be declined like strong adjectives (see section 7.3 below); **his, hiere** and **hiera** are, however, indeclinable. It will be noted that, in the 1st and 2nd persons, the accusative and dative forms are identical; in the earliest varieties of OE, distinctive forms of the accusative are found, e.g. **mec** 'me' (see section 7.5 below).

As well as these *personal pronouns*, there are also other words in OE which fall into the pronominal group. Distinctive *relative pronouns* (like PDE **who (m), which, that**) are not found in OE, though the indeclinable *subordinating particle* **þe** is often used in their place. There are also *interrogative pronouns* used in questions, i.e. **hwā** 'who', **hwelc** 'which'. **Hwelc** is declined like a strong adjective. The paradigm of **hwā**, which includes a distinctive instrumental form (dealing with the means or manner of an action), is as follows (singular only):

Masculine/feminine:
**hwā** (nominative)
**hwone** (accusative)

**hwæs** (genitive)
**hwǣm** (dative)
**hwȳ** (instrumental)
Neuter:
**hwæt** (nominative, accusative)
**hwæs** (genitive)
**hwǣm** (dative)
**hwȳ** (instrumental)

An alternative instrumental of the interrogative pronoun is **hwon**, used only in the phrase **for hwon** 'Why?' The *indefinite pronoun* **man** 'one' is used, often where a passive construction would be usual in PDE, e.g. **man Horsan ofslōg** 'Horsa was killed' (literally 'one killed Horsa'). The interrogative pronouns can also be used as indefinite pronouns, thus **hwā** can also mean 'anyone, someone'.

In PDE, determiners include the *definite* and *indefinite articles*, i.e. **the**, **a(n)**, and *demonstratives*, i.e. **this/these** and **that/those**. The OE system differed. There was no indefinite article as such, though **sum** 'a certain' and **ān** 'one' performed some of its functions; and there was no distinctive definite article. Rather, OE distinguished two sets of demonstratives: **þes** etc., equivalent to 'this, these', and **se** etc., which was used both for 'that, those' and in contexts where PDE would use the definite article. It seems that the OE demonstrative system differed semantically from that of PDE, with **se** etc. being less emphatic and **þes** etc. more so, rather like the distinction found in many PDE non-standard varieties between **them** and **them there**, as in **them boys, them there boys**. OE demonstratives were inflected for case, gender and number, agreeing with the noun which they modified. [1]

The paradigm of the **se**-type demonstrative is as follows:

Singular masculine:
**se** (nominative)
**þone** (accusative)
**þæs** (genitive)
**þǣm** (dative)
Singular feminine:
**sēo** (nominative)
**þā** (accusative)
**þǣre** (genitive, dative)
Singular neuter:
**þæt** (nominative, accusative)
**þæs** (genitive)
**þǣm** (dative)

Plural (all genders):
þā (nominative, accusative)
þāra (genitive)
þǣm (dative)

The paradigm of the þes-type demonstrative is as follows:

Singular masculine:
þes (nominative)
þisne (accusative)
þisses (genitive)
þissum (dative)
Singular feminine:
þēos (nominative)
þās (accusative)
þisse (genitive, dative)
Singular neuter:
þis (nominative, accusative)
þisses (genitive)
þissum (dative)
Plural (all genders):
þās (nominative, accusative)
þissa (genitive)
þissum (dative)

## 7.3 Inflexional morphology III: adjectives, adverbs and numerals

OE *adjectives* share many features of their morphology with nouns, and indeed the category 'adjective' was in Proto-Indo-European closely linked with that of the noun; adjectives were distinguished from nouns through their functions as qualitative modifiers. Adjectival inflexions distinguished case, number and gender, and were selected to agree with the case, number and gender of the noun the adjective modified. In common with other Germanic languages, adjectives in OE have two distinct paradigms, *strong* and *weak*. Weak adjectives appear after determiners; strong adjectives appear elsewhere.

Two paradigms for a model adjective, **gōd** 'good', follow here. Many of the endings of the strong and weak adjectives are identical with those of the strong and weak nouns respectively, though the endings of the strong adjective have been transferred from those of determiners rather than from nominal paradigms.

*Weak Singular*
Masculine:
**gōda** (nominative)
**gōdan** (accusative, genitive, dative)
Feminine:
**gōde** (nominative)
**gōdan** (accusative, genitive, dative)
Neuter:
**gōde** (nominative, accusative)
**gōdan** (genitive, dative)
*Weak Plural*
All genders:
**gōdan** (nominative, accusative)
**gōdra/gōdena** (genitive)
**gōdum** (dative)

*Strong Singular*
Masculine:
**gōd** (nominative)
**gōdne** (accusative)
**gōdes** (genitive)
**gōdum** (dative)
Feminine:
**gōd** (nominative)
**gōde** (accusative)
**gōdre** (genitive, dative)
Neuter:
**gōd** (nominative, accusative)
**gōdes** (genitive)
**gōdum** (dative)
*Strong Plural*
Masculine/Feminine:
**gōde** (nominative, accusative)
**gōdra** (genitive)
**gōdum** (dative)
Neuter:
**gōd** (nominative, accusative)
**gōdra** (genitive)
**gōdum** (dative)

Most adjectives behave inflexionally like **gōd**. The main group of exceptions consist of adjectives like **cwic** 'alive', which differ from **gōd** in the strong nominative singular and plural thus:

Masculine/neuter singular: **cwic**
Feminine singular: **cwicu**
Masculine plural: **cwice**
Feminine plural: **cwice/cwica**
Neuter plural: **cwicu**

As with nouns, there are certain variant forms and patterns. A few adjectives are indeclinable, e.g. **fela** 'many', which simply causes the noun it modifies to appear in the genitive case. Some adjectives vary their stressed vowel according to prehistoric sound-changes, thus **hwæt** 'active' (masculine nominative singular), **hwatum** (dative plural); compare the variation between **dæg** 'day', **dagum** (dative plural). Others lose final **-h** in inflected forms, e.g. **hēah** 'high', **hēane** (masculine accusative singular), while others have syncopation of a medial vowel, e.g. **hālig** 'holy', **hālge** (masculine nominative/accusative plural). Most adjectives, like nouns, derive from forms with **a-** or **ō-** themes in Proto-Germanic, but an important group derive from those with **ja-** and **jō-** themes; in OE, these lexemes generally have masculine/neuter nominative singular in **-e**, e.g. **wilde** 'wild', **clǣne** 'clean', **grēne** 'green', though in a few cases this **-e** has disappeared, e.g. **midd** 'middle', cf. Proto-Germanic *****miðja-**. Other thematic variation in Proto-Germanic is only sporadically reflected in OE, e.g. variation in the paradigms of *****wa-/wo-**lexemes like **gearu** 'ready', **gearwes** (masculine genitive singular). Historic i-adjectives, e.g. **blīþe** 'happy' (cf. Proto-Germanic **blīþiz**), have merged with the **ja-**group, while there are only fragmentary relics of the **u-**group, with forms such as **cwicu** 'alive' (masculine nominative singular) alongside **cwic**, and **wlacu** 'tepid' alongside **wlæc**. Most **u-**adjectives have been transferred to other paradigms, e.g. **heard** 'hard' (proto-Germanic *****xarðuz**), which follows the same paradigmatic pattern as **gōd**.

There are three degrees of *comparison of adjectives* in PDE: *absolute* (**dear**), *comparative*, used for comparisons between two entities (**dearer/ more dear**), and *superlative*, used for comparisons when more than two entities are involved (**dearest/most dear**). In OE, these degrees of comparison were expressed by endings added to the stem of the lexeme: **-ra** for comparative, **-ost** for superlative, e.g. **lēof** 'dear', **lēofra** 'dearer', **lēofost** 'dearest'; **blīþe** 'happy', **blīþra** 'happier', **blīþost** 'happiest'. Comparatives in OE always decline in accordance with the weak paradigm whether or not preceded by a determiner; superlatives decline according to either the weak or the strong paradigm, on the basis of the same criteria as for the absolute adjective.

As in PDE, there are irregular comparative and superlative forms. These fall into two groups: (a) those affected by i-mutation of the root vowel, and (b) those where the comparative and superlative derive from another lexeme altogether (i.e. *suppletive comparison*). Examples are as follows:

(a)　eald 'old', ieldra, ieldest
　　　geong 'young', gingra, gingest
　　　lang 'long', lengra, lengest
　　　strang 'strong', strengra, strengest
　　　hēah 'high', hīerra, hīehst

(b)　gōd 'good', betera/betra/sēlra, betst/sēlest
　　　yfel 'evil', wiersa, wier(re)st
　　　micel 'big', māra, mǣst
　　　lȳtel 'little', lǣssa, lǣst

For group (a), the unstressed element causing i-mutation was lost in pre-OE; however, it survives in Gothic, e.g. **hauhs** 'high', **hauhiza, hauhists**.

Many OE *adverbs* are related to adjectives and were formed from them by the addition of suffixes (*adjectival adverbs*). The most common ending is **-e**, yielding **hearde** 'harshly', cf. the adjective **heard** 'harsh, hard'. Many adjectives were themselves derived from nouns through the addition of the ending **-lic**, e.g. **cræftlic** 'skilful', and adverbs were formed from these adjectives through the addition of -e, e.g. **craeftlice** 'skilfully'. This process became so common that the ending **-lice** was extended to other words by analogy, yielding **heardlice** 'harshly' alongside **hearde**.

Adjectival adverbs in OE are indeclinable, of course, but are subject, like adjectives, to *comparison*. Comparative and superlative adverbs in OE were formed by the addition of the endings **-or, -ost**, e.g. **heardor** 'more harshly', **heardost** 'most harshly' alongside **heardlicor, heardlicost**. Some non-adjectival adverbs in OE also developed comparative and superlative forms, e.g. **oftor** 'more often' (cf. **oft** 'often'), **ǣrest** 'earliest' (cf. **ǣr** 'before').

*Numerals* in PDE are divided into *cardinal* (**one, two, three** etc.) and *ordinal* (**first, second, third** etc.) types. The following are the OE cardinal numbers 1–10, 20, 50, 100 and 1000, and equivalent ordinal numbers for 1–10:

Cardinal:
**ān, twā, þrēo, fēower, fīf, siex, seofon, eahta, nigon, tīen**
**twentig, fīftig, hund/hundred/hundtēontig, þūsend**
Ordinal:
**forma, ōþer, þridda, fēorþa, fīfta, siexta, seofoþa, eahtoþa, nigoþa, tēoþa**

Cardinal **ān** 'one' is declined like adjectives, strong and weak (weak forms are usually used in the sense 'alone'). **Twā** 'two' declines thus:

Masculine:
**twēgen** (nominative, accusative), **twēgra/twēg(e)a** (genitive), **twǣm** (dative)

Feminine:
**twā** (nominative, accusative), **twēgra/twēg(e)a** (genitive), **twǣm** (dative)
Neuter:
**twā/tū** (nominative, accusative), **twēgra/twēg(e)a** (genitive), **twǣm** (dative)

**þrēo** 'three' declines thus:

Masculine:
**þrīe** (nominative, accusative), **þrēora** (genitive), **þrim** (dative)
Feminine/Neuter:
**þrēo** (nominative, accusative), **þrēora** (genitive), **þrim** (dative)

All other cardinal numbers are generally undeclinable. Ordinal numbers are always declined according to the weak adjective paradigm, except for **ōþer** 'second', which is always declined strong.

# 7.4 Inflexional morphology IV: verbs

In PDE there are three types of verb, distinguished by their manner of forming the preterite: *strong* (e.g. **sing, sang**), *weak* (e.g. **love, loved**) and *irregular* (e.g. **go, went**). OE similarly distinguishes between strong, weak and irregular verbs, which may be differentiated by their manner of forming various tenses. Thus **bindan** 'to bind' is a typical strong verb: **hē band** 'he bound', **hē bindeþ/bint*** 'he binds'; **lufian** 'to love' is a typical weak verb: **hē lufode** 'he loved', **hē lufaþ** 'he loves'; irregular verbs include **wesan** 'to be': **ic wæs** 'I was', **ic eom** 'I am'. [2]

Both strong and weak verbs follow regular patterns or paradigms, called *conjugations*. All verbs conjugate to take account of the categories person, number, tense and mood.

Here are four model conjugations: **bindan** 'to bind', a typical strong verb; **lufian** 'to love' and **fremman** 'to perform', typical weak verbs; and the most important irregular verb, **wesan** 'to be'. The **ge-**prefix might be noted in past participles.

Infinitive: **bindan** 'to bind'
Indicative mood, present tense:
Singular:
**binde** (1st person)
**bindest/bintst** (2nd person)
**bindeþ/bint** (3rd person)
(**bintst, bint** are 'syncopated' forms of the **bindeþ**, commonly found in West Saxon.)

Plural:
**bindaþ** (all persons)

Subjunctive mood, present tense:
Singular:
**binde** (all persons)
Plural:
**binden** (all persons)

Indicative mood, preterite tense:
Singular:
**band** (1st person)
**bunde** (2nd person)
**band** (3rd person)
Plural:
**bundon** (all persons)

Subjunctive mood, preterite tense:
Singular:
**bunde** (all persons)
Plural:
**bunden** (all persons)

Imperative:
**bind** (2nd person singular = one person is commanded)
**bindaþ** (2nd person plural = more than one person is commanded)

Participles:
**bindende** (present)
**(ge)bunden** (past)

Infinitive: **lufian** 'to love'
Indicative mood, present tense:
Singular:
**lufi(g)e** (1st person)
**lufast** (2nd person)
**lufaþ** (3rd person)
Plural:
**lufiaþ** (all persons)

Subjunctive mood, present tense:
Singular:
**lufi(g)e** (all persons)
Plural:
**lufi(g)en** (all persons)

Indicative mood, preterite tense:
Singular:
**lufode** (1st person)
**lufodest** (2nd person)
**lufode** (3rd person)
Plural:
**lufodon** (all persons)

Subjunctive mood, preterite tense:
Singular:
**lufode** (all persons)
Plural:
**lufoden** (all persons)

Imperative:
**lufa** (2nd person singular = one person is commanded)
**lufiaþ** (2nd person plural = more than one person is commanded)

Participles:
**lufiende** (present)
**(ge)lufod** (past)

Infinitive: **fremman** 'to perform'
Indicative mood, present tense:
Singular:
**fremme** (1st person)
**fremest** (2nd person)
**fremeþ** (3rd person)
Plural:
**fremmaþ** (all persons)

Subjunctive mood, present tense:
Singular:
**fremme** (all persons)
Plural:
**fremmen** (all persons)

Indicative mood, preterite tense:
Singular:
**fremede** (1st person)
**fremedest** (2nd person)
**fremede** (3rd person)
Plural:
**fremedon** (all persons)

Subjunctive mood, preterite tense:
Singular:
**fremede** (all persons)
Plural:
**fremeden** (all persons)

Imperative:
**freme** (2nd person singular = one person is commanded)
**fremmaþ** (2nd person plural = more than one person is commanded)

Participles:
**fremmende** (present)
**(ge)fremed** (past)

Infinitive: **wesan/bēon** 'to be'
(This paradigm is a blend of verbs which were of distinct Proto-Indo-European origins; such blending is known as *suppletion*.)
Indicative mood, present tense:
Singular:
**eom/bēo** (1st person)
**eart/bist** (2nd person)
**is/biþ** (3rd person)
Plural:
**sind(on)/bēoþ** (all persons)

Subjunctive mood, present tense:
Singular:
**sīe/bēo** (all persons)
Plural:
**sīen/bēon** (all persons)

Indicative mood, preterite tense:
Singular:
**wæs** (1st person)
**wǣre** (2nd person)
**wæs** (3rd person)
Plural:
**wǣron** (all persons)

Subjunctive mood, preterite tense:
Singular:
**wǣre** (all persons)
Plural:
**wǣren** (all persons)

Imperative:

**wes/bēo** (2nd person singular = one person is commanded)

**wesaþ/bēoþ** (2nd person plural = more than one person is commanded)

Participles:

**wesende** (present)

**(ge)bēon** (preterite)

The inflexional endings listed above are more distinctive than those of PDE, but were already reduced from the variety of endings to be found in earlier forms of Germanic. Gothic, for instance, had distinctive endings for most persons in the present indicative, and also two distinct dual forms, thus:

Infinitive: **bindan** 'to bind'

Indicative mood, present tense:

Singular:

**binda** (1st person)

**bindis** (2nd person)

**bindiþ** (3rd person)

Dual:

**bindōs** (1st person, i.e. 'we two')

**bindats** (2nd person, i.e. 'you two')

Plural:

**bindam** (1st person)

**bindiþ** (2nd person)

**bindand** (3rd person)

The OE endings were derived from a selection of those found in Proto-Germanic; thus the present indicative plural ending for all persons in OE was derived from the 3rd person plural ending in Proto-Germanic, *-anþi (cf. Gothic -and), while the preterite indicative plural ending for all persons was derived from the 3rd person plural ending in Proto-Germanic, -unþ (cf. Gothic -un), for example, in **eis bundun** 'they (masculine, emphatic) bound'. (See further Campbell 1959: 296–9. For other parts of the Gothic paradigm, see Wright 1954.)

**Bindan** can act as the general model for all strong verbs, since the same inflexions appear in all of them. However, the defining characteristic of the strong verb is *Ablaut variation* in the root, and a series of patterns are traditionally distinguished by linguists, compare PDE **rise, rose, risen; choose, chose, chosen; drink, drank, drunken; come, came; shake, shook, shaken** etc. These different sets of variations are categorised as *classes* of strong verb, of which there are seven distinguished in the Germanic languages: see Classes I–VII on the following pages. The range of possible alternations in strong verbs is indicated by the forms of (1) the infinitive, (2) the 3rd person present singular indicative, (3) the 1st person preterite indicative, (4) the preterite plural, and (5) the past participle. These forms are traditionally known as the *principal parts* of the strong verb, since from them a complete verb-paradigm can be generated. Of these forms, (1) and (3)–(4) are derived from Proto-Indo-European Ablaut variation. Form (2) is distinct; it is a later development, derived through mutation. The relevant inflexions for the production of form (2) were *-isi (2nd person singular), *-iþi (3rd person singular), and the unstressed *-i- caused the preceding vowel, when back, to undergo mutation.

Here are some examples of the seven classes of strong verb distinguished by their principal parts. Classes of strong verb can generally be recognised by their infinitive form (e.g. Class I verbs have ī as the stressed vowel followed by a single consonant), but Classes III and VII present special difficulties, and there are some exceptions elsewhere in the system. Where syncopated forms of the 3rd person present singular indicative existed, they are cited here.

## Class I

scīnan 'shine' **scīnþ scān scinon (ge)scinen**

Other verbs belonging to this class include: **bītan** 'bite', **drīfan** 'drive', **(ā) rīsan** '(a)rise', **stīgan** 'ascend', **rīdan** 'ride', **(ge)wītan** 'depart'. Soundchanges have affected some verbs assigned to this class. One variant form is:

wrēon 'cover' **wrīehþ wrāh wrigon (ge)wrigen**

The form **wrīehþ** is the outcome of mutation on **ēo**. The form **wrēon** derives from an earlier *wrīon, itself derived, with breaking and loss of -h-, from *wrīhan. The <g> in **wrigon, (ge)wrigen** represents a voiced sound, and is the outcome of Verner's Law, a sound-change which took place before the stress in the ancestors of the OE preterite plural and past participle was shifted from inflexion to root syllable. (The effects of Verner's Law within the verb system are sometimes referred to in the scholarly literature as 'grammatical change'; in German, *grammatischer Wechsel*.) Verner's Law has also affected the paradigm of the following verb, indicated by <d> in the preterite plural and past participle:

snīþan 'cut' **snīþ snāþ snidon sniden**

## Class II

crēopan 'creep' **crīepþ crēap crupon (ge)cropen**

A variant paradigm for this class is represented by:

**brūcan** 'enjoy' **brȳcþ brēac brucon (ge)brocen**

The 3rd person singular present forms of both verbs display the effects of mutation, with **ēo > īe, ū > ȳ**. Other verbs belonging to this class include **bēodan** 'offer', **flēogan** 'fly', **scēotan** 'shoot', **būgan** 'bow', **scūfan** 'push'.

Sound changes other than mutation have produced further variations. A contracted verb of this class is:

**flēon** 'flee' **flīehþ flēah flugon (ge)flogen**

with **flēon** derived from an earlier *****flēohan**; <h> is retained in **flīehþ**, but voiced to <g> in accordance with Verner's Law in **flugon, (ge)flogen**. Some verbs of this class change the medial -s- to -r- in parts of their paradigm (*rhotacism*), another outcome of the operation of Verner's Law whereby a voiceless *-s- developed to -r- via a sound noted conventionally as -*ʀ-:

**cēosan** 'choose' **cīest cēas curon (ge)coren**

Like **cēosan** are **hrēosan** 'fall', **(for)lēosan** 'lose'.

Verner's Law has also affected the paradigm of the following verb, yielding -d- for -þ- in preterite plural and past participle:

**sēoþan** 'boil' **sīeþ sēaþ sudon (ge)soden**

## Class III

Class III strong verbs form a complex group, and sound-changes have obscured their relationship in Proto-Germanic. The original pattern of the infinitive, with root-vowel in -e- followed by two consonants, is exemplified by:

**bregdan** 'pull' **brītt brægd brugdon (ge)brogden**

The form **brītt** is rare, but demonstrates the effects of mutation. Breaking has produced a range of variant forms. Breaking of e, æ before -h- and -r- is particularly widespread in this class of verb, yielding:

**feohtan** 'fight' **fieht feaht fuhton (ge)fohten**
**weorpan** 'throw' **wierpþ wearp wurpon (ge)worpen**

Mutation has produced **ie** in **fieht, wierpþ**. Breaking did not affect e followed by l + consonant (other than h), but it did so affect æ, yielding **ea**, thus having a more limited effect on the paradigm of the following verb:

**helpan** 'help' **hilpþ healp hulpon (ge)holpen**

Palatal diphthongisation produces the following:

**gieldan** 'pay' **gielt geald guldon (ge)golden**

The form **geald** could be the outcome of either breaking or palatal diphthongisation.

Finally, nasal consonants have affected the original paradigm, yielding **i** for **e** and **u** for **o**, changes which affected all the Germanic languages, and causing the retention of **a** in place of **æ**, a feature which affected only English and Frisian. The following paradigm is a good example of the outcome:

**bindan** 'bind' **bint band bundon (ge)bunden**

## Class IV

**beran** 'bear' **bi(e)rþ bær bǣron (ge)boren**

**Beran** is typical, and this class also includes **brecan** 'break', **stelan** 'steal', **teran** 'tear'. Also of this class, but with a different paradigm resulting from the operation of palatal diphthongisation, is:

**scieran** 'cut' **scierþ scear scēaron (ge)score**.

The verbs **niman** 'take' and **cuman** 'come' also belong to this class:

**niman** 'take' **nimþ nam/nōm nōmon/nāmon (ge)numen**
**cuman** 'come' **cymþ c(w)ōm c(w)ōmon (ge)cumen**

The paradigm of **niman** has been affected by the influence of nasals in the Pre-Germanic and Ingvæonic periods, and by analogical processes. Gothic, for comparison, has the paradigm:

**niman** 'take' **nimiþ nam nēmum numans**

The paradigm of **cuman** is similarly irregular; -**y**- in **cymþ** is the result of mutation, while -**ō**- in the 3rd person preterite singular and preterite plural, in **cuman** and in variants of the paradigm for **niman**, represents the beginnings of a process whereby, as in PDE, there is no longer any distinction between the singular and plural forms of the preterite. The infinitive in -**u**- represents the extension of the vowel of the past participle to the present tense, a phenomenon found in some other (but not all) Germanic cognates of this verb, e.g. Old Saxon **kuman**, Old Norse **koma**, but cf. Gothic **qiman**, like **niman**, with the vowel to be expected in the environment of a following nasal. Old High German had both forms, and seems originally to have differentiated them in meaning: **queman** 'to be coming', **quomen** 'to arrive'.

## Class V

> **tredan** 'tread' **tritt træd trǣdon (ge)treden**

Similar are **etan** 'eat', **sprecan** 'speak', **wrecan** 'avenge'. A few verbs of this class have different stem-vowels in the infinitive, e.g. **sittan** 'sit', **licgan** 'lie', **biddan** 'pray', but are otherwise the same; in these cases, the present tense of the verb has been assimilated to that of weak verbs. **Giefan** 'give' belongs to this class, but its paradigm has been affected by palatal diphthongisation, yielding:

> **giefan** 'give' **giefþ geaf geafon (ge)giefen**

The contracted verb **sēon** 'see' belongs to this class, being derived from the sequence *sehan > *seohan (with breaking) > **sēon** (with loss of -h- and compensatory lengthening).

## Class VI

> **faran** 'go' **færþ fōr fōron (ge)faren**

is typical; others conjugated similarly are **scacan** 'shake', **sacan** 'quarrel'. **Standan** follows the same pattern, except that it drops -n- in the preterite tense (**stōd, stōdon**). The following have weak presents, but otherwise follow this pattern: **hebban** 'lift', **swerian** 'swear'.

Although most of its paradigm belongs to this class, the lexeme **scieppan** 'create' has a weak infinitive and present tense. The infinitive derives from Proto-Germanic *skapjan, with the stressed vowel *-a- subjected to palatal diphthongisation followed by i-mutation. The form also demonstrates the doubling of the consonant *-p- when forming the coda of a short syllable preceding -j-, a doubling found in all the West Germanic languages and particularly marked in Class I weak verbs (*gemination*). *-j- was lost in such positions in pre-OE and in most other West Germanic varieties, but was retained in Old Saxon, cf. Old Saxon **skeppian**.

Contracted forms include **slēan** 'strike', which is generally taken to derive from the sequence *slahan > *slæhan (with first fronting) > *sleahan (with breaking) > **slēan** (with loss of -h- and compensatory lengthening). For an interesting discussion relevant to the evolution of this last form, see Hogg 1992: 99–100. The paradigm of **slēan** demonstrates the operation of Verner's Law voicing, with -g- for -h- in **slōg** (3rd person preterite singular), **slōgon** (preterite plural), **slagen** (past participle) beside **sliehþ** (3rd person present singular, with -ie- through the operation of mutation).

## Class VII

Class VII contains a very varied group of verbs, but they have two common characteristics: (1) the same root-vowel appears in the 3rd person preterite singular and in the preterite plural, and (2) the same root vowel appears in the infinitive and the past participle (though see **wēpan** 'weep' below for an apparent exception). Some common verbs of this class are:

| | | | | |
|---|---|---|---|---|
| healdan 'hold' | hielt | hēold | hēoldon | (ge)healden |
| feallan 'fall' | fielþ | fēoll | fēollon | (ge)feallen |
| cnāwan 'know' | cnǣwþ | cnēow | cnēowon | (ge)cnāwen |
| slǣpan 'sleep' | slǣpþ | slēp | slēpon | (ge)slǣpen |
| hātan 'call' | hǣtt | hēt | hēton | (ge)hāten |

An apparent exception to this pattern is **wēpan** 'weep', which has a different root-vowel in infinitive and past participle:

**wēpan** 'weep' **wēpþ wēop wēopon (ge)wōpen**

However, this verb had a weak present tense, and the **-ē-** in **wēpan** is the mutation of an earlier ***wōpijan** via ***wōēpan**; thus the alternation **wēpan**, **(ge)wōpen** is only an apparent exception to the group. The verb appears in Gothic as **wōpjan**.

One group of these verbs, notably **hātan** 'call', is often referred to as *reduplicating*, and Class VII strong verbs are sometimes described as forming the 'reduplicating class'. Reduplication is a phenomenon whereby the root of a lexeme is repeated either in whole (*total*) or in part (*symbolic*); partial reduplication was common in Sanskrit and Greek to signal present/past differences, e.g. Greek **pempō** 'I send', **pepompha** 'I have sent', and is occasionally found in Latin, e.g. **tetigi** 'I have covered', cf. **tegō** 'I cover'. Among the Germanic languages, Gothic is the most regular in using reduplication to signal preterite tense in Class VII strong verbs, yielding such pairs as **haldan** 'hold', **haihald** (3rd person preterite singular), cf. OE **healdan**, **hēold** above. Reduplication was much less common in the other Germanic languages, but there are relics in OE, found in a few texts, e.g. **heht** 'called' (3rd person preterite) beside **hēt**, cf. Gothic **haihait**; reduplication sporadically appears in verbs of this class in other Germanic varieties, e.g. Old Norse **rōa** 'row', **røru** (3rd person plural preterite). [3]

Contracted forms of these verbs are also recorded, and again there is a distinction between the vowel of the infinitive and that of the past participle:

**fōn** 'seize' **fēhþ fēng fēngon (ge)fangen**

Compare also **hōn** 'hang'. The form **fōn** seems to arise from an earlier ***fāhan**; the inflected forms **fēngon**, **gefangen** show the impact of Verner's Law on ***h**, with retention of the nasal infix when the final sound underwent voicing, but loss of the nasal when followed by the voiceless ***h** /x/; the presence of **-n-** in **fēng** seems to be the result of analogy, probably in the early

West Germanic period, since Old High German has **fiang, feng** (see Prokosch 1938: 86, 185).

Weak verbs are distinguished from strong verbs by their use of a -d-element in forming their preterites, a Germanic peculiarity whose origins have been much disputed. Most scholars are of the opinion that the dental suffix derives from a compounding of the root lexeme with the verb 'do', (OE **dōn**); see Lass 1994: 164, also Ball 1968.

Weak verbs in OE fall into three classes: Class I, which conjugates like **fremman**, Class II, which conjugates like **lufian**, and Class III, consisting of the verbs **habban** 'have', **libban** 'live', **secgan** 'say' and **hycgan** 'think'. Weak Class II verbs can be recognised by their ending in **-ian** in the infinitive after consonants other than **r**; **nerian** 'save', **herian** 'praise', **werian** 'defend' etc. are, therefore, Class I verbs. However, **andswarian** 'answer', **gaderian** 'gather' and **timbrian** 'build' are exceptions to this rule; they belong to Class II. The forms of weak Class III verbs are much like those in Classes I and II, but they also show certain variations in the stressed vowels which can lead the beginner to suppose them to be strong verbs. Their principal parts are as follows:

| | | | | |
|---|---|---|---|---|
| habban 'have' | hæfþ | hæfde | hæfdon | (ge)hæfd |
| libban 'live' | leofaþ | leofode, lifde | leofode, lifde | (ge)leofod/-lifd |
| secgan 'say' | sægþ | sægde | sægdon | (ge)sægd |
| hycgan 'think' | hogaþ | hog(o)de | hog(o)don | (ge)hogod |

The OE weak verbs are in general 'derived' verbs, with stems consisting of roots from other lexemes with a following theme, to which endings may be added. Class I verbs had originally a theme in -i-, -j-, causing mutation of the stressed vowel in the present tense; this theme survives as -i- in (e.g.) **nerian** 'save' (cf. Gothic **nasjan**), but in lexemes with a short root-syllable when the consonant is other than -r- (and -r- derived from *s/z) there was loss of -j-and doubling of the consonant in West Germanic, thus OE **settan** 'set' (cf. Gothic **satjan**). The form **fremman** 'perform' therefore derives from an earlier *framjan. Singular forms in **fremeþ** with single consonants derive from forms where -j- was lost before the doubling process took place, when followed by the inflexion *-iþi, thus *framjiþi > *framiþ > *fremiþ (with mutation) > recorded OE **fremeþ**. When the root-syllable was long, the doubling process did not take place, thus OE **sēcan** 'seek', where ē is again the product of mutation (cf. Gothic **sōkjan**); mutation has not taken place in the preterite, thus **sōhte** (3rd person singular preterite) 'sought'. Other sound-changes could also affect weak Class I verbs, e.g. breaking produced the variation **cwellan** 'kill', cf. **cwealde** (3rd person preterite singular), **reccan** 'tell', cf. **reahte** (3rd person preterite singular).

Class II verbs consisted of a root followed by thematic -ō- sometimes followed by -j- as in Class I. In Gothic, -ō- was extended to all parts of the verb, cf. Gothic **lustōn** 'desire', 3rd person preterite singular **lustōda**, but in OE present-tense forms had -j-, thus the distinction between **lufian** 'love' (infinitive), **lufode** (3rd person preterite singular). Thematic -ō- blocked the operation of mutation, so back vowels can appear in the root, e.g. **lufian**, **bodian** 'announce', **lofian** 'praise' etc.

Class III verbs had generally become athematic in most West Germanic varieties, though a theme in -ē- is recorded in Old High German, e.g. **habēta** 'had' (3rd person singular preterite), cf. OE **hæfde**; Gothic has thematic -ai-, cf. **habaida**. Remnants of this theme, however, appear in variant forms of the 2nd and 3rd person present singular indicative, e.g. **hæfeþ** beside more regular **hæfþ**; failure of mutation (which would produce *e in the root-vowel) would indicate a theme distinct from that in Class I. [4]

*Irregular verbs* in OE are few in number of paradigms, but very common in occurrence. They fall into two groups: *preterite-present verbs*, whose present tense is formed from an old strong preterite paradigm and whose new preterite is formed on the weak model; and so-called *anomalous verbs*. Common preterite-present verbs are: **witan** 'know', **āgan** 'own', **cunnan** 'know', **magan** 'be able to', **sculan** 'be obliged to', 'have to', **mōtan** 'be allowed', **þurfan** 'need'; common anomalous verbs are **wesan/bēon** 'be', **willan** 'want to', **nyllan** 'not want to', **dōn** 'do' and **gān** 'go'. These verbs are very common in OE. The full paradigm of **wesan/bēon** is given in section 7.4 above. Here are the principal parts of other common irregular verbs (nb. 'no pp.' = no recorded past participle):

*Preterite-present verbs*

| witan 'know' | **wāt** | wiste | wiston | (ge)witen |
|---|---|---|---|---|
| āgan 'own' | **āh** | āhte | āhton | ǣgen |
| cunnan 'know' | **can(n)** | cūþe | cūþon | (ge)cunnen |
| magan 'be able to' | **mæg** | meahte, mihte | meahton, mihton | no pp. |
| sculan 'have to' | **sceal** | sc(e)olde | sc(e)oldon | no pp. |
| mōtan 'be allowed' | **mōt** | mōste | mōston | no pp. |
| þurfan 'need' | **þearf** | þorfte | þorfton | no pp. |

*Anomalous verbs*

| willan 'want to' | **wil(l)e** | wolde | woldon | no pp. |
|---|---|---|---|---|
| nyllan 'not want to' | **nyle** | nolde | noldon | no pp. |
| dōn 'do' | **dēþ** | dyde | dydon | (ge)dōn |
| gān 'go' | **gāþ** | ēode | ēodon | (ge)gān |

Preterite-present verbs can be classed among the strong verbs according to the form of their present tense; thus **witan**, **āgan** are Class I verbs, **cunnan**, þurfan are Class III, **sculan** is Class IV and **mōtan** Class VI. It is not possible to classify **magan** in OE (the traditional classification is with those verbs of Class VI, but there are difficulties with this assignment); the variation **meahte, mihte** seems to be the result of analogy with the noun **miht** 'power'. The verbs **cunnan, magan, sculan** are the ancestors of some PDE 'modal auxiliaries'; although in OE they seem still to have been lexical verbs, their unusual paradigms made them ripe for transfer to the closed-class set of 'grammatical words', i.e. for *grammaticalisation*. The anomalous verbs raise many complexities, and are subject to suppletion, especially 'to be' which is, in Roger Lass's description, 'not a single "verb", but a collection of semantically related paradigm-fragments – in the rest of Germanic as well as in OE' (1994: 170). As we will see in section 7.5 below, there is a good deal of dialectal variation in these verbs.

## 7.5 Diachronic and dialectal variation

So far in this chapter, the emphasis has been on the EWS variety. Inflexional variation, however, is an important characteristic of surviving OE, and this chapter concludes with some notes on some common or interesting dialectal and/or diachronic differences. It is not in any way comprehensive, and the standard authorities (e.g. Campbell 1959) should be consulted for further details.

As noted in chapter 2, section 4 and chapter 4, section 5, towards the end of the OE period vowels in unstressed syllables seem to have become indistinct in pronunciation, a development which seems to be related to the general synthetic–analytic shift in grammar. This spoken-language development is reflected in the written mode by inflexional loss and/or the interchangeability of inflexional endings such as -**an**, -**en**, -**on** etc. For instance, in LWS texts the ending -**an** on verbs, in EWS an infinitive inflexion, could function as a preterite plural indicative marker, while -**en** could function as an indicative as well as a subjunctive inflexion. Specific notes on parts of speech follow below.

*Nouns* show some variation of endings at different points in the history of OE. In early texts, for instance, -**æs** appears in place of -**es** for the genitive singular of general masculine and general neuter nouns, while in late texts -**um** tends to be replaced by -**an**/-**on**. Loss of final -**n** is common in the paradigm of weak nouns in Late Northumbrian. The mutated forms of **fōt** 'foot' etc. often have -**ōē**- in place of -**ē**- in early or Anglian texts, e.g. **fōēt**; analogous forms of plurals, based on the strong masculine and neuter declensions, are also recorded, e.g. **tōþas** 'teeth'.

In *pronouns* the accusative forms **mec** 'me', **þec** 'you' (singular), **ūsic** 'us' and **ēowic** 'you' (plural) appear quite regularly in non-WS texts, and in poetry (including that recorded in WS). The form **mec** appears in the Alfred Jewel inscription (see *Appendix 1*). There is a good deal of variation in the plural forms of the 3rd person pronoun; in WS texts, for instance, **hī** and **hēo** appear alongside **hīe**, while **hira** and **heora** appear commonly in place of **hiera**. The form **heom** is quite common in place of dative plural **him**. Forms ending in -**æ** are common in early texts, e.g. **hinæ** (accusative singular masculine) in the Ruthwell Cross inscription (see *Appendix 1*). In determiners, **þām** is common in place of **þǣm** (dative plural, dative masculine/neuter singular).

In *adjectives*, the ending -**æ** can appear in place of -**e** in early texts, thus **riicnæ** 'powerful' in the Ruthwell Cross inscription for the masculine accusative singular, cf. WS **rīcne**.

*Verbs* show a good deal of dialectal variation. Syncopated forms of the present singular (e.g. **bint** 'binds' as opposed to **bindeþ**) seem to be commoner in WS and in Late Old Kentish than in other varieties. Particularly significant for the later history of English is the occurrence of -**as** etc. in many Old Northumbrian texts as the general ending in the present tense, both singular and plural. Whereas WS has **sind(on)**, **bēoþ** 'are', other forms are recorded in non-WS dialects; Mercian, for instance, has **earun** (beside **sind (un)**), and **aron** occurs in some Northumbrian texts. These forms are the ancestors of PDE **are**, and derive from a distinct Germanic root which is also the ancestor of Old Norse **eru**, as opposed to **sind(on)**, which is cognate with PD German **sind**. These similarities between Anglian and North Germanic varieties are interesting for the typological relationship between OE and Old Norse on the one hand and OE and the other West Germanic dialects on the other (see further Nielsen 1981). For loss of inflexional distinctiveness over time, see chapter 5, section 1.

## Notes

1. Germanic languages inherited two demonstratives, reconstructed for Proto-Indo-European as *so- and *to- respectively. It seems that the former was more emphatic in meaning than the latter, and it is therefore no coincidence that *so-type demonstratives appear in the earliest Germanic varieties prototypically in the nominative case, which, as the subject case, tends to occupy what is known as *thematic position* in a clause. It is also an interesting fact, which may be related to the non-standard usage in PDE cited in chapter 7, section 2, that **þes**-type demonstratives derive from an ancient compounding of *to-type and *so-type demonstratives; for that reason, **þes** etc. is sometimes referred to by scholars as the *compound demonstrative*, as opposed to the **se**-type, known as the *simple demonstrative*.

2. The terms *strong* and *weak*, as applied to the verb, were first developed by Jacob Grimm; see Prokosch 1938: 159–60.

3. Classical Greek distinguished two kinds of past tense, *aorist* and *perfect*, these being traditionally translated as 'I loved' (aorist), 'I have loved' (perfect).

The distinction seems to have been aspectual; aorist was used when the action was completed, thus *perfective*, while the perfect was used to refer to a state resulting from the completed action, thus *stative*. The aorist–perfect distinction seems to derive from Proto-Indo-European. Some varieties of IE retained this functional distinction, e.g. Sanskrit and Greek, but in others it disappeared, some (such as Gothic) retaining the reduplicated perfect form as the basis of their preterite paradigms, with others (e.g. Celtic, OE) generally choosing the aorist form which was derived through Ablaut. For further discussion, see Prokosch 1938: 145–6, 176–8.

4. A fourth class of weak verb is recorded in Gothic, e.g. **fullnan** 'to become full', **fullnōda** (3rd person preterite singular). The -n- may remain in other Germanic varieties, but the verb otherwise falls in with other classes of weak verb; thus the OE cognate of Gothic **gawaknan** 'to awake' is **wæcnian**, a Class II weak verb.

The four classes of weak verb recorded in Germanic were originally distinguished on formal and/or semantic grounds. Class I verbs thus included many *causatives* with roots derived from strong verbs (thus *deverbative*); Class II verbs were generally derived from nouns (thus *denominative*); Class III verbs, which were much more common in Germanic varieties other than OE, were often *durative* (to do with continuing action) or *inchoative* (to do with the beginning of an action). Class III verbs were deverbative and derived from adjectives. Class IV verbs seem to have been both inchoative and causative.

## Exercises

Exercise 7a   List the principal parts of the following verbs, and discuss the sound-changes responsible for their morphological alternation: **bindan, gieldan, cēosan**

Exercise 7b   Write on the morphological implications of Ablaut and Umlaut during the OE period.

**Key terms introduced in this chapter:**
declension
syncretism
suppletion
comparison of adjectives
conjugation
principal parts
grammaticalisation

# Texts

## 1. Inscriptions: Runic

### (a) Fuþarks and fuþorcs (Kylver Stone, Rök Stone, Thames scramasax)

Standard runic sequences are known as *fuþarks* (when referring to the common Germanic usage, or the usage found in non-OE texts) or as *fuþorcs* (when referring to the OE sequence). The name derives from the first six letters in the sequence, just as the term alphabet, used for the Greek-/Latin-based sequence, derives from the first two letters of the Greek alphabet (*alpha*, *beta*). A fair number of such sequences survive; 'runemasters' seem to have liked making such lists, either because of the decorative possibilities of the sequence or for some other purpose – perhaps magical or (a more pedestrian explanation) for mnemonic or pedagogic purposes.

The earliest Germanic fuþark is that on the Kylver stone, Gotland, which is usually dated to the early fifth century. Gotland, as its name suggests, was the Gothic *Heimat*, from where the Goths spread down the Vistula to the Black Sea and Mediterranean. It may be taken as an example of the application of the runes to Gothic. The Rök inscription from Östergötland, Sweden, dates from c. 800 AD and is the longest runic inscription recorded, with over 700 characters; it records a North Germanic usage. The Thames inscription is on a *scramasax*, or single-sided sword, found in 1857 in the River Thames; it is now in the British Museum. It dates from the late eighth/ninth century, and is one of the earliest complete OE fuþorcs.

Kylver

ᚠ 'f' ᚺ 'u' ᚦ 'þ' ᛁ 'a' ᚱ 'r' ᚲ 'k' ᚷ 'g'
ᛈ 'w' ᚺ 'h' ᛏ 'n' ᛁ 'i' ᛊ 'j' ᛇ 'p' ᛉ 'ẹ'
ᛏ 'z' ᛋ 's' ᛏ 't' ᛒ 'ᵬ' ᛗ 'e' ᛗ 'm' ᛚ 'ᴉ'
□ 'ŋ=ng' ᛗ 'đ' ᛟ 'o'

Rök

ᚠ 'f' ᚺ 'u' ᚦ 'þ' ᛁ 'ạ' ᚱ 'r' ᛣ 'k' ᚼ 'h'
ᛏ 'n' ᛁ 'ï' ᛘ 'a' ᛋ 's' ᛏ 't' ᛒ 'b' ᛘ 'm' ᛚ 'ᴉ' 'ᴿ'

Thames

ᚠ 'f' ᚢ 'u' ᚦ 'q' ᚠ 'o' R 'r' ᚺ 'c' ᚷ 'g' ᛈ 'w'
ᚺ 'h' ᛏ 'n' I 'ï' ᛀ 'j' ᚴ 'ë' ᚲ 'p' Y 'x' ᛉ 's' ᛏ 't'
ᛒ 'b' ᛗ 'e' ᛣ 'ŋ=ng' ᚼ 'd' ᛁ 'l' ᛗ 'm' ᛁ 'œ'
ᚠ 'a' ᚨ 'æ' ᛣ 'y' ᛏ 'ea'

## (b)  The Negau helmet

In 1812, a cache of twenty-six bronze helmets were found at Negau, on the border between Austria and the former republic of Yugoslavia, in modern Slovenia. On one of these helmets, helmet 'B' or '22', appeared a short inscription which may be transliterated as **'hariXasti teiva'**, usually interpreted as a Germanic phrase meaning 'to the god Herigast' (Elliott 1959: 9; for an illustration, see Elliott 1959: Plate I).

The Negau helmet inscription is often taken as evidence for the operation of Grimm's Law. The form **teiva**, it has been argued, is cognate with Latin **divus** 'godlike' (cf. **deus** 'god') and would thus indicate a sound-shift **d > t**. Most scholars date the Negau helmets to the third or second century BC, and thus the Law can be seen as having taken place by that time.

There are, however, major problems with seeing the Negau helmet as conclusive evidence for such a development. The dating and the interpretation of the inscription have both proved controversial; it has been argued that **teiva** is a second name in apposition with **hariXasti** (the transliteration X is used to represent what seems to be a velar fricative), though it may be a copying of, or a parallel to, the Roman habit of linking divinity with their leaders, e.g. 'the divine Augustus', on the model of the heroic epithet (cf. **pius Aeneas**). Moreover, there is evidence that Germanic peoples tended not to wear metal helmets, preferring lighter leather caps in order to sustain their mobility, their chief advantage in battle. However, the Germanic habit of acting as mercenaries for others – first for the Celts, later for the Romans – make it probable that some adopted from the Celts the habit of wearing metal helmets, as recorded by Diodorus Siculus, whose historical compilation dates from the end of the first century BC, and there is later evidence that individuals who were prominent in Germanic society, at any rate, adopted helmets as a sign of their status (see further Wilson 1981: 128).

The lettering of the Negau inscription is not runic, but North Italic, a writing system current in the Roman provinces of Rhaetia, Noricum, Venetia and Pannonia, i.e. spanning the southern Alps. The North Italic system seems to derive from that used by the ancient Etruscans, a somewhat mysterious people who lived in Italy before the rise of Rome. North Italic lettering is seen by many scholars as a source – possibly *the* source – of the Germanic fuþark, and there are certainly several parallels between the North Italic and runic systems, e.g. in certain North Italic forms for the letters conventionally transliterated as 'a', 'k', 'l', 'd', 'o':

| North Italic | Runic |
|---|---|
| ᚠ∧ᚠ∧ | ᚠ 'a' |
| <CKᚴ | < 'k' |
| ᛙ⅃ᛚ | ᛚ 'l' |
| ᛉ | ᛉ 'd' |
| ᛚᛤᚾᛞᛜ◇ | ◇ 'o' |

A reproduction of the inscription, with parallel transliteration, appears below:

ᚺᚨᚲᛁ ᚤᚨᛉᛏᛁ ᛏᛖᛁᚤᚨ

'h a r i    X a s t i    t e i v a'

[The Italic letters appear in reverse sequence in the inscription, i.e. reading from right to left. The interpretation 'teiva' is controversial.]

## (c)  The Gallehus horn

In 1734, a fifth-century golden drinking-horn was discovered at Gallehus in Schleswig, in modern Denmark. Unfortunately, this horn was stolen and melted down in 1802, but a reliable reproduction survives of the runic inscription which was written on its rim: **'ek hlewagastiR holtijaR horna tawido'** 'I, Hlewagast, Holt's son, made the horn', i.e. a maker's inscription of a kind which is fairly common on weapons and other ornaments. It is written in the Germanic fuþark. The linguistic interest of the Gallehus inscription is considerable, demonstrating not only inflexional patterns in an ancient form of North/West Germanic but also verb-final element order, which seems to be the oldest prototypical Germanic pattern (cf. Latin usage).

A reproduction of the inscription, with parallel transliteration, appears below:

ᛖᚲᚺᛚᛖᚹᚨᚷᚨᛋᛏᛁᚣᚼᛟᛚᛏᛁᛇᚨᚣ
'e k h l e w a g a s t i R    h o l t i j a R
ᚺᛟᚱᚾᚨᚣ ᛏᚨᚹᛁᛗᛟ
h o r n a    t a w i d o'

[The transliteration R is usually used to represent the earliest rhotacised outcome of Verner's Law, possibly pronounced something like the <ř> in the name of the composer *Dvořák*.]

## (d)  The Arum 'sword'

In 1895, a wooden object was found at Arum in west Friesland in the Netherlands. It is usually described as a 'sword', but it may be a ritual or ceremonial object, a teaching tool, or even a toy. This 'sword' carries an inscription in Frisian runes, viz. **'edæboda'**, usually interpreted as either a personal name or as meaning 'return-messenger'. The Arum inscription is interesting as an example of an Ingvaeonic inscription to be placed alongside those in OE; like OE, it has fuþorc-style runes for 'o', 'a' and 'æ'. A reproduction of the inscription, with parallel transliteration, appears below:

ᛖ ᛗ ᚠ ᛒ ᚠ ᛗ ᚠ
'e d æ b o d a'

## (e)  The Caistor-by-Norwich astragalus bone

Caistor-by-Norwich is a Romano-British walled town in Norfolk that, by the fifth century AD, seems to have become home for a community of Germanic settlers, possibly mercenaries employed by the declining Roman Empire. Just outside the walls of the town is an important Anglo-Saxon cemetery that seems to have been in use for the whole of the pagan period (i.e. from the *Adventus Saxonum* to the coming of Christianity in the sixth century). Amongst many important finds made by archaeologists in this cemetery was an urn containing a set of between 35 and 38 knucklebones that seem to have been used as gaming pieces. Most of these bones were of sheep, but one was of a roe-deer, on which a runic inscription appeared:

ᚱ ᚠ ᛌ ᚺ ᚠ ᛏ
'r a ï h a n'

This form clearly relates to OE **rā** 'roe', which appears in the eighth-century Mercian Corpus Glossary as **raha**. It may be an inflected form of a proto-Germanic *****raiho**, with retention of **ai** (see chapter 4, section 5). The Corpus and Caistor forms both display medial -**h**-; this feature is archaic, and clearly predates loss of **h** and compensatory lengthening (see chapter 4, section 5).

Why the name of the material should appear on this item is unclear, but it does seem to be a comparatively common Germanic practice; the Franks Casket, for instance, has **'hronæsban'** 'whalebone'; see (f) below.

## (f) The Franks (Auzon) Casket inscription

Three sides and the lid of the Franks Casket were discovered at the beginning of the nineteenth century in the possession of a French family in the town of Auzon, in the Haute-Loire. One side of the object ended up in the Museo Nazionale, Florence, where it was rediscovered in 1890. A plaster cast of this side was made, and attached to the other three sides and lid, which had been acquired by Sir Augustus Franks (whence its usual name) and gifted by him to the British Museum in 1867.

The casket is made of whalebone, and is usually dated to the early eighth century. It is localised by its language to Northumbria. It is carved with inscriptions in runes and Latin lettering, and with scenes from Germanic myth and classical narrative. On the lid and the front of the casket are depictions of incidents from the story of Wayland, the legendary Germanic smith; on the back is a representation of the sack of Jerusalem by the emperor Titus; on the left side appears the suckling of Romulus and Remus by the she-wolf. The right side, the original of which is still in Florence, is usually interpreted as a representation of part of the legend of Sigurd the Volsung. (For further discussion, see Elliott 1959: 96–109.)

The passage below is from the front of the casket:

ᚠᛁᛋᛕ   ᚠᛚᚠᛗᚢ   ᚠᚻᚠᚠ   ᚠᛏ   ᚠᛗᚱᚷᛗᛏᛒᛗᚱᛁᚷ
'f isc  flo d u   a h o f  on  f e r g e n b e r i g

ᚠᚠᚱᚦ   ᚷᚠᚺᚱᛁᛕ   ᚷᚱᚠᚱᛏ   ᚦᚠᚱ   ᚺᛗ   ᚠᛏ
w a r þ  gas ric   gror n   þær  he  o n

ᚷᚱᛗᚢᛏ   ᚷᛁᚺᚠᚠᛗ   ᚺᚱᚠᛏᚠᚺ   ᛒᚠᛏ
g r e u t  giswom  hron æs ban'

'The flood lifted up the fish on to the cliff-bank; the whale became sad, where he swam on the shingle. Whale's bone.' *(after Elliott 1959:99)*

## (g) The Ruthwell Cross inscription

For further details, see chapter 3, section 3.3. Part of the runic inscription, with parallel transliteration, appears below:

ᛁᚳ   ᚱᛁᛁᚳᚾᚫ   ᚷᚪᛏᛁᚷᚳ   ᚻᚣᚾᛏᚫᛋ

'ic  riicnæ  k̄yniŋc  heafunæs

ᚻᛚᚠᚠᚪᚱᚻ   ᚻᚪᛚᚻᚠ   ᛁᚳ   ᛏᛁ   ᚻᚠᚱᚳᛏᚠ

hlafard   hælda  ic  ni  dorstæ

ᛒᛁᚳᚻᚠᚱᚠᚻᚾ   ᚾᚷᚷᚳᛏ   ᚻᚻᛏ   ᛒᚷ

bismærædu  uŋk̄et   men  ba

ᚠᛏᚷᚠᚻ..   ᛁᚳ   ...   ᚻᛁᚦ   ᛒᛁᚠᚻᚠ .  ᛁᚳᛏᚻᚻᛁ.

ætḡad[ræ]  ic  [wæs]  miþ  blodæ[b]  istemi[d]'   *(after Elliott 1959:91)*

## 2. **Inscriptions: Non-runic**

The following are both non-runic inscriptions, i.e. written in the Latin-based alphabet adopted in Anglo-Saxon England. Further details of all the inscriptions studied here are to be found in Okasha 1971.

## (a) The Alfred Jewel inscription (see Okasha 1971: 48–9)

The 'Alfred Jewel', one of the most famous items of Anglo-Saxon jewellery, was discovered in 1693 at Athelney in Somerset. Its use is uncertain, though many scholars consider it to be the head of an **æstel** or 'bookmark', an object rather like the *yad* pointer used in the Jewish tradition to indicate the text of the day to be read from the Torah. The following inscription appears in Anglo-Saxon capital letters:

**ÆLFRED MEC HEHT GEVVYRCAN**
'Alfred commanded me to be made'.

The forms **mec** and **heht** are archaic, while **VV** for **w** (usually, though not invariably, 'wynn' in OE manuscripts) is also interesting.

The area where the jewel was found has many associations with King Alfred 'the Great' (*c*.849–899). It was at Athelney in 879, at that time a raised area of land within a swamp, that Alfred took refuge and rallied an army before defeating Guthrum's Danes at the battle of Edington. That **AELFRED** is therefore Alfred the Great is an attractive interpretation, though obviously not capable of definite proof.

A passage from the *Anglo-Saxon Chronicle* referring to Alfred's period in Athelney, and the subsequent battle of Edington, appears as Text 3(a) below.

## (b) The Brussels Reliquary Cross inscription
### (see Okasha 1971: 57–8)

In 1650, a relic, supposedly of the True Cross, was deposited in the church of saints Michael and Gudele in Brussels, Belgium. The relic was covered with silver laminate, on which texts were carved. The object is usually dated to the tenth/eleventh centuries, possibly *c.* 1000.

Text I consists of the simple Latin formula **AGNVS D[E]I** 'lamb of God', but texts II and III are in OE. Text II is a maker's formula, 'Drahmal made me' (the name **Drahmal** may be of Norse origin); text III is a verse text, possibly related to *The Dream of the Rood* and the Ruthwell Cross inscription, followed by a reference to the commissioners of the object and its dedicatees.

Text I

   **AGNVS DI**

Text II

   **DRAHMAL ME WORHTE:**

Text III

   **ROD IS MIN NAMA**    **GEO IC RICNE CYNING**
   **BÆR BYFIGYNDE**     **BLODE BESTEMED**

   **ÞAS RODE HET ÆÞLMÆR WYRICAN & AÐELWOLD HYS BEROÞO[R] CRISTE TO LOFE FOR ÆLFRCES SAVLE HYRA BEROÞOR**

   'Cross is my name; once, trembling (and) drenched with blood, I bore the powerful king. Æþelmær and Aðelwold his brother ordered this cross to be made to the glory of Christ (and) for the soul of Ælfric their brother.'

## 3. **West Saxon Texts**

### (a) From the *Anglo-Saxon Chronicle*

The following passage is taken from the *Parker Chronicle*, now MS Cambridge, Corpus Christi College 173, which dates from the ninth/tenth centuries and is (in this instance) roughly contemporary with the dates it describes (see further Ker 1957: 57–9). The *Parker Chronicle*, so-called because it was one of Archbishop Matthew Parker's sixteenth-century donations to Corpus Christi College, is the earliest text of the *Anglo-Saxon Chronicle* to have survived.

The *Anglo-Saxon Chronicle* seems to have been begun in the time of King Alfred, possibly (though not certainly) as part of Alfred's programme of vernacular learning, for which see Text 3(b). The passage below is a good example of the language of Alfred's period, Early West Saxon, though there are some variations from the 'canonical' EWS found in textbooks, e.g. **was** for **wæs**, **wærun** for **wæron**, and **kyning** alongside **cyning**. As in the remaining texts in this *Appendix*, the letter þ is here represented by **w**, but note **tuelftan** 'twelfth', and **uu** in **uuoldon** alongside wolde, and the 'insular' ʒ is represented by g. In all the following texts, the other special letters (æ, þ, ð) are retained.

Anno [878]. Hēr hiene bestæl se here on midne winter ofer tuelftan niht tō Cippanhamme ond geridon Wesseaxna lond ond gesǣton, ond micel þæs folces ofer sǣ ādrǣfdon ond þæs ōþres þone mǣstan dǣl hīe geridon ond him tō gecirdon būton þām cyninge Ælfrede, ond hē lȳtle werede unīeþelīce æfter wudum fōr ond on mōrfæstenum. Ond þæs ilcan wintra wæs Inwæres brōþur ond Healfdenes on Westseaxum on Defenascīre mid xxiii scipum ond hiene mon þǣr ofslōg ond dccc monna mid him ond xl monna his heres. Ond þæs on ēastron worhte Ælfred cyning lȳtle werede geweorc aet Æþelingaēigge ond of þām geweorce was winnende wiþ þone here ond Sumersǣtna se dǣl sē þǣr nīehst wæs. Þā on þǣre seofoðan wiecan ofer ēastron hē gerād to Ecgbryhtesstāne be ēastan Sealwyda ond him tō cōmon þǣr ongēn Sumorsǣte alle ond Wilsǣtan ond Hamtūnscīr, se dǣl se hiere behinon sǣ was, ond his gefægene wǣrun. Ond hē fōr ymb āne niht of þām wicum tō Iglēa ond þæs ymb āne to Eþandūne ond þǣr gefeaht wiþ alne þone here ond hiene geflīemde ond him æfter rād oþ þæt geweorc ond þǣr sæt xiiii niht; ond þā salde se here him foregīslas ond micle āþas, þæt hīe of his rīce uuoldon, ond him ēac gehēton þæt hiera kyning fulwihte onfōn wolde ond hīe þæt gelǣston swā. Ond þæs ymb iii wiecan cōm se cyning tō him Godrum, þrītiga sum þāra monna, þe in þām here weorþuste wǣron, æt Alre, and þæt is wiþ Æþelinggaēige; ond his se cyning þǣr onfēng æt fulwihte and his crismlīsing was æt Weþmor ond hē was xii niht mid þām cyninge ond hē hine miclum ond his gefēran mid fēo weorðude.

'In this year the raiding army moved stealthily in midwinter after Twelfth Night to Chippenham, and overran and occupied the land of the West Saxons, and drove a great [number] of people over sea, and they overran and made subject the greatest part of the remainder except for the king Alfred; and he with a small troop travelled with difficulty through woods and into fen-strongholds. And in that same year the brother of Ivarr and Halfdane was in Devonshire with twenty-three ships; and he was slain there, and 800 men with him, and 40 men of his raiding army.[1] And from that time at Easter King Alfred with a small troop built a fortress at Athelney; and from that fortress [he], and the part of the men of Somerset that was nearest there, were striving against the raiding army. Then on the seventh week after Easter he rode to 'Ecgbryht's stone' east of Selwood. And all the men of Somerset, and Wiltshire, and Hampshire (the part of it which was on this side of the sea)[2] came to meet him there, and were glad of him. And he went after one night from the camp to Iley Oak, and one day later to Edington; and there he fought against all the raiding army and put them to flight, and rode after them to the [= their] fortress, and there surrounded it [literally = sat] for fourteen nights. And then the raiding army gave him preliminary hostage and great oaths that they would [go] from his kingdom; and they also promised him that their king would receive baptism; and they carried it out thus. And after three weeks Godrum the king came to him, along with twenty-nine of the men who were most noble in the raiding army,[3] at Aller, and that is near Athelney; and the king received him there in baptism, and the removal of his baptismal robes took place at Wedmore. And he was twelve nights with the king; and he and his companions honoured him greatly with money.'

## Notes
1. i.e. 840 men. The expression is odd; it is possible that **heres** is an error for **hiredes** 'of his retinue' (and thus especially devoted to their lord).
2. I have interpreted the text territorially, meaning 'men from that part of Hampshire which is to the west of Southampton Water'.
3. A curious expression, though paralleled in other OE and Old Norse texts; Godrum is **þrītiga sum** 'one of thirty', and thus he has twenty-nine companions.

## (b) From Alfred's Preface to the *Pastoral Care*

The following passage is from a letter by King Alfred prefixed to the English translation of Pope Gregory the Great's *Pastoral Care* (*Cura Pastoralis*), in the version of the text that survives in MS Oxford, Bodleian Library Hatton 20. The Hatton manuscript dates from the ninth century, and is thus contemporary with King Alfred. The inscription on folio 1, **ÐEOS BOC SCEAL TO WIOGORA CEASTRE** 'This book must [be sent] to Worcester', combined with various marginalia, indicates its provenance; the king evidently arranged for copies to be sent to major centres in his kingdom (see further Ker 1957: 384–6).

The letter describes Alfred's ambitious programme of vernacular education, whereby those books **ðe nīedbeðearfosta sīen eallum monnum tō wiotonne** 'which may be most necessary for all men to know' were to be translated for the improvement of ecclesiastical education, which the king considered to be in a sad state of decline because (most notably) of the ravages of the Danes. Recent research suggests that the king's programme was not quite as successful as has traditionally, rather romantically, been suggested.

The following passage is from the middle of the letter. Like passage 3(a), it is a fair representative of Early West Saxon. Notable features are the use of **io** instead of **eo** in (e.g.) **giond** etc., **hiora** for **hiera** 'their', **meahton** 'could' rather than **mihton**, and an inflexion in **-ae** in **gefyldae** beside more common **-e**. Early West Saxon **ie, īe** appear in place of Late West Saxon **y, ȳ** in **ieldran** 'elders' (cf. Late West Saxon **yldran**), **gīet** 'still' (cf. Late West Saxon **gȳt**, PDE **yet**).

> **Ðā ic ðā ðis eall gemunde, ðā gemunde ic ēac hū ic geseah, ǣr ðǣm ðe hit eall forhergod wǣre ond forbǣrned, hū ðā ciricean giond eall Angelcynn stōdon māðma ond bōca gefyldae, ond ēac micel mengeo Godes ðīowa; ond ðā swīðe lȳtle fiorme ðāra bōca wiston, for ðǣm ðe hīe hiora nānwuht ongiotan ne meahton, for ðǣm ðe hīe nǣron on hiora āgen geðiode āwritene. Swelce hīe cwǣden: 'Ure ieldran, ðā ðe ðās stōwa ǣr hīoldon, hīe lufodon wīsdōm, ond ðurh ðone hīe begēaton welan ond ūs lǣfdon. Hēr mon mæg gīet gesīon hiora swæð, ac wē him ne cunnon æfter spyrigean. For ðǣm wē habbað nū ǣgðer forlǣten ge ðone welan ge ðone wīsdōm, for ðǣm ðe wē noldon tō ðǣm spore mid ūre mōde onlūtan.'**

'When I remembered all this, then I remembered also how I saw, before it was all ravaged and burned, how the churches throughout all England stood filled with treasures and books, and also a great multitude of God's servants; and then they derived very little benefit from those books, because they could not understand any part of them, because they were not written in their own language. Such they may have said: "Our forefathers, who formerly held these places, they loved wisdom, and through that they acquired wealth and left [it] to us. Here one can still see their track, but we cannot follow after [them]. Therefore we have now lost both the wealth and the wisdom, because we bend with our spirit to that course."

## (c) From Ælfric's *Life of King Oswald*

Ælfric wrote his homilies and saints' lives in the last decade of the tenth century, for the instruction of the pious laity. He was at this time a monk at Cerne Abbas in Dorset; he later became abbot of Eynsham, Oxfordshire. Ælfric was a prolific author; some 160 homilies ascribed to him (not always convincingly) survive, plus various other pieces, including a much-copied vernacular *Grammar* for the teaching of Latin, a *Colloquy*, designed for teaching Latin conversation, and a work on astronomy and chronology, *De Temporibus Anni*, designed to help clergy calculate the date of Easter.

The following passage comes from one of *The Lives of the Saints*, Ælfric's third set of homilies, issued most probably by 998. The set survives in many manuscripts; the earliest, from which this text is taken, is MS London, British Library Cotton Julius E.vii, a MS which was acquired by Sir Robert Cotton, the Tudor antiquarian, from the collection of the suppressed monastery at Bury St Edmunds (see further Ker 1957: 206–10).

The passage here is the opening of the *Life of King Oswald*. Oswald ruled Northumbria from 633 to 641; his rule, and that of subsequent Northumbrian kings, is associated with the cult of the Cross, and the Ruthwell Cross was erected, it seems, while his memory was still fresh. This passage describes how Oswald's success in battle over the pagan king of the British, Ceadwalla, followed from an act of devotion expressed in the erection of a wooden cross. The material derives from Bede's Latin *Ecclesiastical History*, but it has been carefully selected and rearranged.

The passage is in Late West Saxon, with forms such as **fȳnd** 'enemies', **gelȳfed** 'believed' (cf. Early West Saxon **fīend, gelīefed**). Interesting variants include forms of the 3rd person plural pronouns, e.g. **hī** 'they', **heom** 'them', **heora** 'their' (cf. the textbook forms **hīe, him, hiera**), and forms such as **cynincg** 'king' (cf. more common **cyning**).

Æfter ðan ðe Augustīnus tō Engla lande becōm, wæs sum æðele cyning, Oswold gehāten, on Norðhymbra lande, gelȳfed swȳþe on God. Sē fērde on his iugoðe fram his frēondum and māgum tō Scotlande on sǣ, and þǣr sōna wearð gefullod, and his gefēran samod þe mid him sīþedon. Betwux þām wearð ofslagen Eadwine his ēam, Norðhymbra cynincg, on Crīst gelȳfed, fram Brytta cyninge, Ceadwalla gecīged, and twēgen his æftergengan binnan twām gēarum; and se Ceadwalla slōh and tō sceame tūcode þā Norðhymbran lēode æfter heora hlāfordes fylle, oð þæt Oswold se ēadiga his yfelnysse ādwǣscte. Oswold him cōm tō, and him cēnlīce wið feaht mid lȳtlum werode, ac his gelēafa hine getrymde, and Crīst gefylste tō his fēonda slege. Oswold þā ārærde āne rōde sōna Gode tō wurðmynte, ær þan þe hē tō ðām gewinne cōme, and clypode tō his gefērum: 'Uton feallan tō ðǣre rōde, and þone Ælmihtigan biddan þæt hē ūs āhredde wið þone mōdigan fēond þe ūs āfyllan wile. God sylf wāt geare þæt wē winnað rihtlīce wið þysne rēðan cyning tō āhreddenne ūre lēode.' Hī fēollon þā ealle mid Oswolde cyninge on gebedum; and syþþan on ǣrne mergen ēodon tō þām gefeohte, and gewunnon þǣr sige, swā swā se Eallwealdend heom ūðe for Oswoldes gelēafan; and ālēdon heora fȳnd, þone mōdigan Cedwallan mid his micclan werode, þe wēnde þaet him ne mihte nān werod wiðstandan.

'After Augustine came to England, there was a certain noble king, called Oswald, in the land of the Northumbrians, who believed very much in God. He travelled in his youth from his friends and kinsmen to Dalriada ("Scotland in sea"), and there at once was baptised, and his companions also who travelled with him. Meanwhile his uncle Edwin, king of the Northumbrians, who believed in Christ, was slain by the king of the Britons, named Ceadwalla, as were two of his successors within two years; and that Ceadwalla slew and humiliated the Northumbrian people after the death of their lord, until Oswald the blessed put an end to his evil-doing. Oswald came to him, and fought with him boldly with a small troop, but his faith strengthened him, and Christ assisted in the slaying of his enemies. Oswald then immediately raised up a cross in honour of God, before he came to the battle, and called to his companions: "Let us kneel to the cross, and pray to the Almighty that he rid us from the proud enemy who wishes to destroy us. God himself knows well that we strive rightly against this cruel king in order to redeem our people." They then all knelt with King Oswald in prayers; and then early on the morrow they went to the fight, and gained victory there, just as the All-powerful granted them because of Oswald's faith; and they laid low their enemies, the proud Ceadwalla with his great troop, who believed that no troop could withstand him.

## (d) From *Beowulf*

*Beowulf* survives in one manuscript, MS London, British Library Cotton Vitellius A.xv. The manuscript consists of two parts, originally separate books. The Beowulf Manuscript proper is the second part, containing in addition a homily on St Christopher, works known as *Marvels of the East* and *The Letter of Alexander to Aristotle*, and another fragmentary poem on a Biblical theme, *Judith*. Part II of the manuscript dates from *c*. 1000 AD; part I, though containing OE materials, dates from the middle of the twelfth century (see further, Ker 1957: 279–83).

*Beowulf*, an epic poem of some three thousand lines describing the hero's victories over three monsters – Grendel, Grendel's mother and a dragon, is the single most famous work of OE literature. The following passage (lines 1251–1264) comes at the moment when Grendel's mother, emerging from her lair beneath a nearby haunted lake, is about to enter the great hall of Heorot to avenge her son.

Two versions of this passage are given. Version (1) is a transcription of the text from the manuscript, reproducing the layout of the original and without editorial additions (e.g. modern punctuation, diacritic marks); it may be noted that OE poetry was written in the same way as OE prose. Version (2) is an edited text of the same passage, using modern editorial conventions of layout and punctuation.

The dating of *Beowulf* is a matter of considerable controversy. The text as it survives in the Vitellius manuscript is written in Late West Saxon, though there are occasional archaic and non-West Saxon features. Discussion of the poem's linguistic features is to be found in all the standard editions; particularly recommended are those by Jack (1994), Klaeber (1950) and Mitchell and Robinson (1998).

(1)  Transcribed text

### XVIIII.

Sigon þato slæpe sum sare angeald æfen
ræste swa him ful oft gelamp siþðan gold
sele grendel warode unriht æfnde oþ *þæt*
ende be cwom swylt æfter synnum *þæt* gesyne
wearþ wid cuþ werum *þæt* te wrecend þagyt lif
de æfter laþ*um* lange þrage æfter guð
ceare grendles modor ides aglæc wif yrm
þe gemunde seþe wæter egesan wunian
scolde cealde streamas siþðan cain wearð
to ecgbanan angan breþer fæderen mæge
heþa fag gewat morþre gemearcod

(2)  Equivalent edited text

Sigon þā tō slǣpe.   Sum sāre angeald
ǣfen-rǣste,   swā him ful oft gelamp
siþðan gold-sele   Grendel warode,
unriht ǣfnde,   oþ þæt ende becwōm,
swylt æfter synnum.   Þæt gesȳne wearþ,   1255
wīd-cūþ werum   þætte wrecend þā gȳt
lifde æfter lāþum,   lange þrāge,
æfter gūð-ceare.   Grendles mōdor,
ides, āglǣc-wīf   yrmþe gemunde,
sē þe wæter-egesan   wunian scolde,   1260
cealde strēamas,   siþðan Cāin wearð
tō ecgbanan   āngan brēþer,
fæderen-mǣge;   hē þā fāg gewāt,
morþre gemearcod ...

'Then they went to sleep. A certain one paid painfully for [his] evening-rest, just as very often happened when Grendel occupied the gold-hall, he performed evil-doing, until an end arrived [for him], death after sins. It became clear, widely known to men, that an avenger then still lived after [the] hostile [one], for a long time after the grievous fighting. Grendel's mother, a woman, a female warrior, brooded on misery, she[1] who had to occupy [the] terrible water cold currents, after Cain became the slayer of his only brother, his kinsman on his father's side; outlawed, he then departed, marked by murder ....'

**Note**
1. Translated as 'she', despite the form **sē** ; Grendel's mother is sporadically referred to by a masculine pronoun, a usage paralleled in other texts. See Jack 1994: 104 note, Klaeber 1950: 180, Mitchell and Robinson 1998: 90 note.

## (e) *Cædmon's Hymn* (WS Version)

This poem survives in many manuscripts as the centrepiece of Bede's account of the poet Cædmon (*Ecclesiastical History* IV, chapter 24). The following text, in West Saxon, is taken from MS Oxford, Bodleian Library Tanner 10, a tenth-century translation of Bede's history into OE (see further Ker 1957: 428–9).

The Tanner text is here collated with another version of the Hymn, that contained in MS Oxford, Bodleian Library Hatton 43, a copy of Bede's work in the original Latin dating from the beginning of the eleventh century (see further Ker 1957: 387–8). The Hatton and Tanner texts differ in several interesting respects, e.g. the Late West Saxon form **wurc** in Hatton corresponds to Early West Saxon **weorc** in Tanner (see Campbell 1959: 133, para. 320). Variant readings in Hatton (H) are recorded in the notes at the end of the text of the poem.

> Nū sculon herigean   heofonrīces weard,
> Meotodes meahte   and his mōdgeþanc,
> weorc wuldorfaeder,   swā hē wundra gehwæs,
> ēce drihten,   ōr onstealde;
> hē ǣrest scēop   eorðan bearnum     5
> heofon tō hrōfe,   hālig scyppend,
> þā middangeard   monncynnes weard;
> ēce drihten   æfter tēode
> fīrum foldan,   frēa ælmihtig.

line 1 **Nū sculon herigean**] H **Nū wē sculan herian**
line 2 **Meotodes meahte**] H metudes myhte
line 3 **weorc**] H wurc   **gehwæs**] H gehwil
line 4 **ōr onstealde**] H ord āstealde
line 5 **scēop**] H gesceop   **eorðan**] H ylda
line 6 **þā middangeard**] H middangearde   **monncynnes**] H mancynnes
line 7 **tēode** ] H tīda
line 8 **foldan**] H on foldum

'Now we must praise the guardian of the heavenly kingdom, the power of God and his conception, work of the father of glory, in that he, eternal lord, appointed the beginning of every marvel; he, holy creator, first created heaven as a roof for the children of men; eternal lord, lord almighty, afterwards adorned the earth for living beings.'

## 4. Non-West Saxon Texts

### (a) *Cædmon's Hymn* (Northumbrian version)

The following is a Northumbrian version of *Cædmon's Hymn*, surviving in MS Cambridge, University Library Kk 5.16, a Latin version of Bede's *Ecclesiastical History* dating from the early eighth century. The manuscript is sometimes referred to as the 'Moore Manuscript', since it came to Cambridge University in 1715, along with other books in the collection of John Moore, Bishop of Ely, who had acquired it at the end of the seventeenth century (see further Ker 1957: 38–9).

This text is good evidence for an early form of Northumbrian, and can be compared not only with West Saxon usages – see 3(d) above – but also with Late Northumbrian – see 4(b) below. Notable forms include: (1) **Uard** for WS **weard**, demonstrating failure of breaking; (2) **suē** (cf. WS **swā**); in this form the **ē** is the Anglian reflex of West Germanic **ā**, contrasting with the WS form which represents an unstressed form with subsequent lengthening on transference to stressed position (thus sporadic **swǣ** alongside more usual **swā** in WS texts); (3) the retention of spellings such as <b> for <f> in **heben** 'heaven', and <th> for <þ> in **Thā**; (4) **til** for WS **tō** (cf. Old Norse **til**); (5) <ae> for <æ> in (e.g.) **hefaenrīcaes Uard**, beside **moncynnæs Uard**.

Nū scylun hergan   hefaenrīcaes Uard,
Metudaes maecti   end his mōdgidanc,
werc Uuldurfadur,   suē hē uundra gihuaes,
ēci Dryctin,   ōr āstelidae.
Hē āērist scōp   aelda barnum     5
heben til hrōfe,   hāleg Scepen.
Thā middungeard   moncynnæs Uard,
ēci Dryctin,   aefter tīadae
fīrum foldu,   Frēa allmectig.

### (b) Gloss to the Lindisfarne Gospels (selection)

MS London, British Library Cotton Nero D.iv, the Lindisfarne Gospels, is one of the greatest treasures of the British Library. The Latin text was written by Eadfrið, bishop of Lindisfarne (698–721), and lavishly illuminated and decorated in a style transferred from the traditions of Anglo-Saxon metalwork. In the tenth century the Latin was given an interlinear English gloss by someone calling himself 'Aldred presbyter'. Aldred's gloss, probably added at Chester-le-Street in Co. Durham, is good evidence for Late Old Northumbrian (see further Ker 1957: 215–16).

The passage following is the gloss to the beginning of the Gospel of Matthew, chapter 7, verses 1–12. The Latin text appears interlineally; the scribe indicated alternative English glosses to Latin words by the Latin word **vel** 'or'. The

'Tyrrhenian' form of 'and', 7, is replaced by an ampersand, &, in this text; I have also added length-marks, but otherwise the text is as it appears in the manuscript. A translation of the equivalent passage from the New Revised Standard Version of the Bible appears underneath.

There are numerous features of linguistic interest, e.g. the spelling <oe>, used to represent a mid rounded front vowel; the 3rd person singular and plural verb endings in -as; the pronominal forms; and the form **aron** 'are' beside **biðon**.

**nellað gē dōēme** *þæt* **gē ne sē gedōēmed in ðǣm forðon**
1. nolite judicare, ut non judicemini. 2. in quo enim

**dōme gīe dōēmes gē biðon gedōēmed & in suā huelc wōēgas hrīpes**
judicio judicaberitis, judicabimini; et in qua mensura mensi

**gē biðon gewegen bið īuh huæt ðon*ne* gesiistu strē** *vel* **mot**
fueritis, metietur vobis. 3. quid autem vides festucam

**in ēge brōðres ðīnes & ðone bēam in ēge ðīn**
in oculo fratris tui, et trabem in oculo tuo

**ne gesiistu** *vel* **hū cueðestū brōēðer ðīnum būta ic**
non vides? 4. aut quomodo dicis fratri tuo, sine

**worpe mot** *vel* **strē of ēgo ðīn & heonu bēam is in ēgo ðīn ðū**
eiciam festucam de oculo tuo; et ecce trabes est in oculo tuo?

**ēsuica worp ǣrest ðone bēam of ēgo ðīn &**
5. hypocrita, eice primum trabem de oculo tuo; et

**ðon*ne* ðū gesiist geworpe ðone mot of ēgo**
tunc videbis eicere festucam de oculo

**brōðres ðīnes nellas gē sella hālig hundum ne sendas gē**
fratris tui 6. nolite dare sanctum canibus, neque mittatis

**meregrotta īurre be*fore* berg ðȳ lǣs hīa getrede ðā ilco**
margaritas vestras ante porcos; ne forte conculcent eas

**mið fōtu*m* hiora & gewoendo** *vel* **gecerdo tōslitas īuh**
pedibus suis, et conversi disrumpant

**giwias** *vel* **gebiddas gē & gesald bið īuh sōēcað gē & gē**
vos. 7. petite, et dabitur vobis; quaerite et

**infindes** *vel* **gē begeattas cnysað** *vel* **cnyllas gē & untȳned bið īuh ēghuelc**
invenietis; pulsate, et aperietur vobis. 8. omnis

**forðon sē ðe giuæð** *vel* **biddes onfōēð & sē ðe sōēcas infindes**
qui petit, accipit; et qui quaerit, invenit;

**& ðǣm cnysende** *vel* **cnyllende huā is fro*m* īuh**
**untūned bið** *vel*
et pulsanti aperietur. 9. aut quis est ex vobis

**monn ðene gif hē giuias sunu his hlāf cuidestū ðone**
homo quem si petierit filius suus panem numquid

**stān rāēceð** *vel* **gif ðone fisc wilniað** *vel* **giuias cuiðestū**
**seles him** *vel* **ðā nēdrie**
lapidem porriget ei? 10. aut si piscem petet numquid serpentem

**ræces him gif ðonne īuh mið ðȳ gē aron yflo wutas gē gōdo gesealla**
porriget ei? 11. si ergo vos cum sitis mali nostis bona dare
**sunum īurum māra wōēn is fader īuer sē ðe in heofnum is**
filiis vestris, quanto magis pater vester qui in caelis est
**geselleð gōdo biddendum *vel* giuiendum hine alle ðonne *vel***
dabit bona petentibus se! 12. Omnia ergo
**forðon suā huæt gīe welle *þæt* hēa gedōe īuh ðā menn & gee**
quaecumque vultis ut faciant vobis homines, et vos
**dōeð *vel* wyrcas him ðīus is forðon ǣ & wītgas *vel* wītgo**
facite eis; haec est enim lex et prophetae

'Do not judge, so that you may not be judged. For with the judgement you make you will be judged, and the measure you give will be the measure you get. Why do you see the speck in your neighbour's eye, but do not notice the log in your own eye? Or how can you say to your neighbour, "Let me take the speck out of your eye", while the log is in your own eye? You hypocrite, first take the log out of your own eye, and then you will see clearly to take the speck out of your neighbour's eye. Do not give what is holy to dogs; and do not throw your pearls before swine, or they will trample them under foot and turn and maul you. Ask, and it will be given to you; search, and you will find; knock, and the door will be opened for you. For everyone who asks receives, and for everyone who knocks, the door will be opened. Is there anyone among you who, if your child asks for bread, will give a stone? Or if the child asks for a fish, will give a snake? If you then, who are evil, know how to give good gifts to your children, how much more will your Father in heaven give good things to those who ask him! In everything do to others as you would have them do to you; for this is the law and the prophets.'

## (c) From the Vespasian Psalter Gloss

MS London, British Library Cotton Vespasian A.i is an eighth-century decorated Latin Psalter, which was given an interlinear gloss, in OE, in the ninth century. The manuscript was seen on the high altar of St Augustine's Canterbury, in the fifteenth century, and the hand of the main text is comparable with other hands known to have been active at St Augustine's at the period; it seems, therefore, that the manuscript was continuously in Kent until acquired by Sir Robert Cotton, from whose collection it subsequently passed to the British Museum (later the British Library) (see further Ker 1957: 266–7).

The OE gloss is, however, in Old Mercian, the language-variety current in the Midlands of England, and indeed is the principal witness for that dialect: note forms such as **feder** 'father' (cf. WS **faeder**), **daegas** 'days' (cf. WS **dagas**), **aeldran** 'elders' (cf. WS **ieldran**). There were important cultural/political connexions between Kent and Mercia, and it seems that a Mercian scribe, visiting or resident in Canterbury, was responsible for the gloss.

The Vespasian Psalter is a collection of psalms, canticles and hymns. The following passage is part of the canticle in Deuteronomy 32. The Latin text is given

interlineally; a translation from the equivalent passage in the New Revised Standard
Version of the Bible appears at the end.

Bihald, heofen, & spreocu, & gehēre eorðe word of
adtende caelum, et loquar, et audiat terra verba ex

mūðe mīnum. sīe ābiden swē sw [ē] regn gesprec mīn
ore meo expectetur sicut pluvia eloquium meum

& āstīgen swē swē dēaw word mīn, swē swē scūr
et descendant sicut ros verba mea, sicut imber

ofer grēd & swē swē snāw ofer hēg; forðon noma[n]
super gramen, et sicut nix super faenum, quia nomen

dryhtnes ic gecēgu; sellað micelnisse gode ūrum.
domini invocabo. date magnitudinem deo nostro

god, sōðe werc his, & alle wegas his dōmas.
deus, vera opera ejus, et omnes viae ejus judicia

god getrēowe & nis unrehtwīsnis in him; rehtwīs
deus fidelis, et non est iniquitas in eo; justus

& hālig dryhten. syngadun nales him bearn unwemme
et sanctus dominus. peccaverunt non ei filii immaculati

cnēoris ðweoru & forcerredu ðās dryhtne geedlēanades,
natio prava et perversa; haec domino retribuisti

swē folc dysig & nales snottur. ahne ðes illce ðū ear
sic plebs fatua et non sapiens. nonne hic ipse tuus

feder gesiteð ðec, dyde ðec, & gescōp ðec? in mōde
pater possedit te; fecit te, et creavit te? in mente

habbað dægas weorulde; ongeotað gēr cnēorisse cnēorissa.
habete dies saeculi; intellegite annos nationis nationum.

frign feder ðīnne & segeð ðē ældran
interroga patrem tuum: et adnuntiabit tibi seniores

ðīne & cweoðað ðē. ðonne tōdāēleð se hēa ðīode, tō
tuos et dicent tibi, cum dividerit excelsus gentes,

ðǣm gemete tōstrigdeð bearn Adāmes, sette endas
quemadmodum dispersit filios Adae. statuit terminos

ðīeda efter rīme eng[l]a godes. & geworden
gentium secundum numerum angelorum dei. et facta

wes dāēl dryhtnes folc his [Iācob] rāp erfewordnisse
est pars domini populus ejus, Jacob funiculum hereditatis

his [Israhēl]. genyhtsumiendne hine him dyde in
ejus Israhel. sufficientem eum sibi fecit in

wōēstenne in ðurs[t] hāētu ðēr ne wes weter. ymblāēdde
heremo in sitim caloris ubi non erat aqua. circumduxit

hine & gelǣrde hine & hēold hine swē swē
eum, et erudivit eum, et custodit eum sicut

sīan ēgan. swē swē earn ðeceð nest his &
pupillam oculi. sicut aquila tegit nidum suum, et

**ofer briddas his geset, āðenede fiðru his, & onfēng**
super pullos suos consedit. expandit alas suas, et accepit
**hīe & onfēng hīe ofer gescyldru his. dryhten āna**
eos, et suscepit eos super scapulas suas. dominus solus
**lǣrde hīe & ne wes mid him god fremðe.**
docebat eos, et non erat cum eis deus alienus.

'Give ear, O heavens, and I will speak: let the earth hear the words of my mouth. May my teaching drop like the rain, my speech condense like the dew; like gentle rain on grass, like showers on new growth. For I will proclaim the name of the Lord; ascribe greatness to our God! The Rock, his work is perfect, and all his ways are just. A faithful God, without deceit, just and upright is he: yet his degenerate children have dealt falsely with him, a perverse and crooked generation. Do you thus repay the Lord, O foolish and senseless people? Is not he your father, who created you, who made you and established you? Remember the days of old, consider the years long past; ask your father, and he will inform you, your elders, and they will tell you. When the Most High apportioned the nations, when he divided humankind, he fixed the boundaries of the peoples according to the number of the gods; the Lord's own portion was his people, Jacob his allotted share. He sustained him in a desert land, in a howling wilderness waste; he shielded him, cared for him, guarded him as the apple of his eye. As an eagle stirs up its nest, and hovers over its young; as it spreads its wings, takes them up, and bears them aloft on its pinions, the Lord alone guided him; no foreign god was with him.'

## (d) Kentish Psalm

MS London, British Library Cotton Vespasian D.vi is a miscellany of various texts in Latin and OE, dating from the middle of the tenth century. The manuscript has associations with St Augustine's Canterbury (see further Ker 1957: 268–9). OE items in the manuscript include glosses, a hymn, a note of the 'ages of the world' and a free paraphrase of Psalm 51 (= Vulgate Psalm 50). Part of this paraphrase follows; the equivalent lines in the *New Revised Standard Version* appear underneath, after a more literal translation.

Unlike the Vespasian Psalter Gloss, the Kentish Psalm is a good witness for written Kentish of its period. Characteristic forms include **efter** 'after' (cf. WS **æfter**), **sennum** 'sins' (dative plural; cf. WS **synnum**) and **geltas** 'guilts' (cf. WS **gyltas**), **on aldre** 'in life' (cf. WS **on ealdre**).

Miltsa ðū mē,   meahta Walden,
nū ðū wāst [ðā manigfaldan]   manna geðōhtas;
help ðū, Hǣlend mīn,   handgeweorces
þīnes ānes,   ælmehtig God,
efter þīnre ðāra miclan   mildhiornesse.   35
Ond ēac efter menio   miltsa ðīnra,
Dryhten weoruda,   ādīlga mīn unriht
tō forgefenesse   gāste mīnum.

Aðweah mē of sennum,    sāule fram wammum,
gāsta Sceppend,    geltas geclānsa,    40
þā ðe ic on aldre    ǣfre gefremede
ðurh līchaman    lēðre geðōhtas.

'Have mercy on me, Lord of powers, now you know the manifold thoughts of men; may you help me, my saviour, almighty God, through your handiwork alone in accordance with your great mercy. And also in accordance with the multitude of your mercies, Lord of hosts, erase my unrighteousness for forgiveness in my spirit. Wash me of sins, [my] soul from defilements, Creator of spirits, cleanse [my] sins, those which I ever performed in life through [the] body's wicked thoughts.'

Compare the *New Revised Standard Version*:

'Have mercy on me, O God, according to your steadfast love; according to your abundant mercy blot out my transgressions. Wash me thoroughly from my iniquity, and cleanse me from my sin.'

## 5. The transition to Middle English

### The *Peterborough Chronicle*

MS Oxford, Bodleian Library Laud Misc. 636 is a text of the *Anglo-Saxon Chronicle* which was copied in the early twelfth century. The manuscript was produced at the monastery of Peterborough, in East Anglia, and is thus known as the *Peterborough Chronicle*. Up until and including the annal for 1121, the text was copied by a single scribe (with occasional interpolations) from a version of the *Chronicle*, now lost, which was written in Late West Saxon. This scribe continued to make additions to the *Chronicle* until 1131; a second scribe added annals for the period 1132–1154. These two added sections are traditionally known as the First and Final Continuations (see further Ker 1957: 424–6).

The language of the *Peterborough Chronicle* Continuations famously represents the transition from Old to Middle English. The passage below is from the annal for the year 1140, within the Final Continuation, and several features characteristic of Middle English may be observed. Relics of OE usage include syntactic structures such as 'verb-second' constructions, e.g. **Þa ferde Eustace**, but the loss of distinctive determiners may be noted, as should the appearance of a new form of pronoun, **scæ** for 'she'. Norse loanwords may also be observed: **oc** 'and/but', **toc** 'took'; **castel** 'castle' may be a loanword from Norman French. The standard edition of the text is that by Cecily Clark (1970), which includes a valuable discussion of the language.

In accordance with the usual practice in editing ME, length-marks are not given. Tyrrhenian 7 'and' is replaced by an ampersand, &. Other contractions have been expanded silently. It should be noted that the scribe replaces insular <ʒ> with <g> throughout, transferring Latin usage to the vernacular; and although he often retains <þ, ð, p, æ>, he often replaces these forms with <th, uu> etc.

Þa ferde Eustace þe kinges sune to France & nam þe kinges suster of France to wife; wende to bigæton Normandi þaerþurh. Oc he spedde litel, & be gode rihte, for he was an yuel man; for warese he [com he d]ide mare yuel þanne god: he

reuede þe landes & læide mic[ele gelde]s on. He brohte his wif to Engleland, &
dide hire in þe caste[l on Can]tebyri. God wimman scæ wæs, oc scæ hedde litel
blisse mid him.

'Then Eustace the king's son travelled to France, and took the king of France's
sister as wife; he hoped to gain Normandy thereby. But he succeeded little, and
for a good reason, for he was an evil man; for wherever he came he did more evil
than good; he ravaged the lands and placed many taxes thereon. He brought his
wife to England, and put her in the castle in Canterbury. She was a good woman,
but she had little joy with him.'

# Discussion Questions and Further Reading

## Discussion questions

1. Consider the typological relationship of OE to the other Germanic languages.
2. Write on the relationship of EITHER writing and speech OR grammar and lexicon, with reference to the history of English during the pre-OE and OE periods.
3. What are the implications of the linguistic study of OE for EITHER (a) the general history of English, OR (b) the study of the principles of linguistic change?
4. How far, and for what reasons, is it important for historians of OE to have a wider knowledge of Anglo-Saxon archaeology and history?
5. 'Old English is the period of full inflexion; Present-Day English is the period of reduced inflexion.' Discuss the truth and/or implications of this statement.
6. Here is a short passage from the OE poem *The Wanderer*, in a modern edition by T. P. Dunning and A. J. Bliss published in 1969. The poem survives in the Exeter Book (MS Exeter, Cathedral 3501; see Ker 1957: 153); the readings of the manuscript, along with a selection of readings as presented in other modern editions, are also included. What were the linguistic reasons for the decisions made by Dunning and Bliss? Please note: the translation below is based on decisions taken by Dunning and Bliss.

TEXT:

| | | |
|---|---|---|
| … siþþan geāra iū | goldwine mīnne | |
| hrūsan heolstre biwrāh | ond ic hēan þonan | |
| wōd wintercearig | ofer waþema gebind, | |
| sōhte seledrēorig | sinces bryttan, | 25 |
| hwǣr ic feor oþþe nēah | findan meahte | |
| þone þe in meoduhealle | minne myne wisse, | |
| oþþe mec frēondlēasne | frēfran wolde … | |

Textual notes:
22 **minne**] *MS* **mine**
23 **heolstre**] *Sweet/Whitelock* 1967 **heolster**

[Dunning and Bliss interpret **hrūsan** as an example of 'levelling of endings in late Old English', and thus in the nominative singular despite the ending.]

24 waþema] *MS* waþena

25 seledrēorig] *Sweet/Whitelock* 1967 sele drēorig

26 minne myne] *MS* mine *Sweet/Whitelock* 1967 mīn mine

27 frēondlēasne] *MS* freondlease

'… since long ago earth covered my lord in darkness, and I journeyed thence, abject, winter-hearted, over the expanse of waves, sad at the loss of a hall, [I] sought one who gives treasure, where I far or near could find the one in meadhall who might know my thought, or would comfort my friendless self …'

## Recommended further reading

The following books, all in English, are recommended for further study.

On **reconstruction**, see further Fox 1995, Lehmann 1992. Lockwood 1969 is a useful introduction to Indo-European; much more advanced, with an extensive and authoritative bibliography and exhaustive in its coverage of most issues to do with the evolution of the Indo-European languages, is Szemerenyi 1996. The 'rules' of Indo-European are helpfully summarised, with full bibliographies to date, in Collinge 1992. On the Germanic languages in general, see Robinson 1992, which includes a helpful reader; more advanced are Prokosch 1938, van Coetsem and Kufner 1972. Wright 1954 is essential for Gothic. For German, see Keller 1978 for a comprehensive account, though Chambers and Wilkie 1970 is also useful. For Norse, see Haugen 1976; for Norse texts, see Gordon/Taylor 1957. On the relationship between language and archaeology, see (controversially) Renfrew 1987. Knowledge of the historical context of OE is important; standard historical accounts include Myres 1986 and Stenton 1971, and students will also benefit from Wilson 1981.

A useful **general history of English** is Barber 1993; more advanced is Strang 1970. Hogg and Denison 2006 and Mugglestone 2007 are useful, up-to-date collections; see also, for a comprehensive advanced survey, *The Cambridge History of the English Language (CHEL)*. Other good general histories include Baugh and Cable 2002, Fennell 2001, Millward 1989, Pyles and Algeo 1982. On language change in general, see Aitchison 1991 for a preliminary account; more advanced and theoretically challenging, but essential reading for any serious historical linguists, are Lass 1997, McMahon 1994, Samuels 1972. On the historical study of English, see Smith 1996. On the transition to ME, see relevant sections in Horobin and Smith 2003.

On **OE in general**, useful beginners' books with a linguistic focus include McCully and Hilles 2005, and Hogg 2002. Hough and Corbett 2006 takes a novel, and highly effective, 'communicative' approach, and makes a valuable supplement to this book. Smith 1999 (later edition 2005) places OE in relation to later stages of the language, and includes a 'describing language' chapter whose terminology is congruent with that used here. Sweet/Davis 1953 remains useful, though its approach may be considered old-fashioned by some. Mitchell and Robinson 1992 (and subsequent editions) combines a valuable reader with a useful outline of grammar; it is particularly good at linking sound-change with morphological variation, and has a good section on syntax. Hamer 1967, now hard to acquire, is an invaluable short account of OE sound-changes. Quirk and Wrenn 1955 is a useful intermediate-level grammar, covering all levels of language.

On **English runes**, see Elliott 1959 and Page 1999. For OE palaeography, see Roberts 2005. The standard advanced grammars include Campbell 1959 (for phonology and morphology), Hogg 1992 (for phonology) and Mitchell 1985a/1985b (for syntax). These standard works should be supplemented by broader historical surveys of the history of English phonology and grammar. *CHEL* is essential in this regard. Prins 1972 is a good general survey of phonology from a traditional viewpoint, while Jones 1989 and Smith 2007 give more theoretically oriented accounts. Inflexional morphology is less well-served; Welna 1996 is very useful, but not easily available, and is more of a resource than a narrative. On syntax, Denison 1993 is invaluable, as is Fischer *et al.* 2000.

The best single-volume **dictionary** is Clark-Hall 1960, while the standard dictionary remains Bosworth-Toller 1898–1921 (supplemented by Campbell 1972). The *Toronto Dictionary of OE* is still in progress; for an update, see <http://www.doe.utoronto.ca/>. Campbell 1959 gives an account of loanwords; for the Celtic–English relationship, see also Jackson 1953. For the investigation of OE semantics, the crucial resource is TOE, now online. A good, up-to-date overall study of OE semantics is currently lacking; however, exceptionally interesting work in this area is represented by Biggam (e.g. 1997, 1998); see also, for example, Hough 2001, Lowe 1993. An important sub-field of OE studies is onomastics, the study of names, for which the main resource is the series published by the English Place-Name Society; a general survey of place-names in relation to patterns of settlement appears in Myres 1986, and a useful account of name-studies, by R. Coates, appears in Hogg and Denison 2006.

*Appendix 1: Texts* supplied in this book is designed only for preliminary study, and students will want to secure their own **collections of texts**. Important student readers include Mitchell and Robinson (1992 and later editions) and Marsden 2004, but, for philological work, the best 'readers' remain those originally devised by Henry Sweet and now in their fifteenth and second editions respectively: Sweet/Whitelock 1967 and Sweet/Hoad 1978. These readers can be supplemented by standard editions, e.g. Sweet's own edition of early texts (Sweet 1885), Pheifer's edition of early glosses (Pheifer 1974) and the editions in the Methuen Old English series (many since republished by Exeter University Press). *The Anglo-Saxon Poetic Records (ASPR)* remains an important resource; many major editions of OE texts have been published by the Early English Text Society (EETS). For *Beowulf*, the major scholarly edition remains Klaeber 1950, though Mitchell and Robinson 1998 and, especially, Jack 1994 are also invaluable. The key transitional text, the *Peterborough Chronicle*, has been edited by Clark 1970; students will also find useful Bennett and Smithers 1974. There is no comprehensive corpus of OE runes, but Elliott 1959 and Page 1999 are the best accounts, with texts of the most important monuments. For non-runic inscriptions, see Okasha 1971. For the manuscript background, the major resource remains Ker 1957, supplemented by Ker 1976; see also Roberts 2005.

For **valuable insights into OE**, and for a 'follow-up' to many of the issues raised in the current book, see in the first instance Lass 1994. Individual problems, many of them still current, are discussed in an important 'agenda-setting' symposium held in the late 1980s (Kastovsky and Bauer 1988). OE in relation to wider Germanic issues is surveyed by Nielsen 1981 (see also Nielsen 1989); connexions with Norse are explored in Dance 2004 and Townend 2002. Current debates in OE philology appear in all the major symposia and journals on English historical linguistics. The two principal conferences relevant to the subject are the International Conference on English Historical Linguistics (ICEHL), which takes place in Europe, and Studies in the History of the English Language (SHEL), which is held in North America. Major journals in the field include *Anglia, Anglo-Saxon England, Diachronica, English Language and Linguistics, English Studies, Folia Linguistica Historica, Journal of Linguistics, Language, Lingua, Neophilologus, Neuphilologische Mitteilungen, Nomina, Notes and Queries, NOWELE, Review of English Studies, Studia Neophilologica, Transactions of the Philological Society, Word.*

# Glossary of Old English–Present-Day English

This glossary records all OE forms used in this book. Forms with **æ** appear after those with **ad**, and forms with **þ** and **ð** appear after those with **t**. **þ** and **ð** are not distinguished alphabetically. The following abbreviations are used: *N* (noun), *V* (verb), *Aj* (adjective), *Av* (adverb), *pn* (pronoun), *d* (determiner), *pr* (preposition), *cj* (conjunction), *num* (numeral), *st* (strong), *wk* (weak), *irreg* (irregular), *m* (masculine), *f* (feminine), *n* (neuter), *nom* (nominative), *acc* (accusative), *gen* (genitive), *dat* (dative). Where a noun is recorded as 'm, f' etc., this means that the noun is recorded as either masculine or feminine. Numbers refer to classes of strong verb, so '*V st 3*' means 'strong Class III verb'. Short and long vowels are not distinguished in ordering, except when two forms are distinguished by length, when the form with a short vowel precedes that with the long vowel; thus **God** precedes **gōd**. The prefix **ge-** is ignored; thus **gebed** appears under **b**. When two forms are linked by '=', they represent alternative spellings, e.g. '**scēop = scōp**'. The usage '**scōp**: *see* **scieppan**' relates an inflected form to a base form.

**abbod** *N m* abbot
**ābīdan** *V st 1* abide, wait
**ābīden**: *see* **ābīdan**
**ac** *cj* but
**āc** *N f* oak
**ācsian** *V wk* ask
**ādīlga**: *see* **ādīlgian**
**ādīlgian** *V wk* erase, destroy
**ādrǣfan** *V wk* drive away
**ādrǣfdon**: *see* **ādrǣfan**
**ādwǣscan** *V wk* put out, quench, blot out
**ādwǣscte**: *see* **ādwǣscan**
**ǣ** *N f* law, custom, faith
**ǣfenræst** *N f* evening rest
**ǣfenræste**: *see* **ǣfenræst**
**æfnan** *V wk* carry out, fulfil, endure
**æfnde**: see **æfnan**
**ǣfre** *Av* continually, ever
**aefter = æfter**
**æfter** *Av* afterwards; *pr + dat* after
**æfter þan/þǣm þe** *cj* after

æfter ðan ðe = æfter þan þe

æftergenga *N* follower

æftergengan: *see* æftergenga

ǣg *N n* egg

ǣgen: *see* āgan

ǣghwilc *Aj* each

ǣgðer ... ge *cj* either ... or; both ... and

ælda: *see* eald

ældran: *see* eald

ælmehtig = ælmihtig

ælmihtig *Aj* almighty

ǣr *Av* formerly; *Aj* early; ǣr (þan þe), ǣr þǣm þe, ǣr ðǣm ðe *cj* before

ǣrest *Av* earliest

āērist = ǣrest

ærn *N n* house

ǣrne: *see* ǣr *Aj*

æsc *N m* ash-tree

æstel *N m* bookmark, pointer

æþel *Aj* noble

æþela, æðele: *see* æþel

āfyllan *V wk* fill up; cause to fall

āgan *V irreg* own

āgen *Aj* own, proper

āglǣcwīf *N n* female monster

āgyltan *V wk* sin

āgyltaþ: *see* āgyltan

āh: *see* āgan

ahne *Av* = *Latin* nonne, not?

āhōf: *see* āhōn

āhōn *V st 7* lift up, hang, crucify

āhreddan *V wk* set free, rescue, save

āhredde: *see* āhreddan

āhreddenne, *in* tō āhreddenne to deliver (*inflected infinitive*); *see* āhreddan

āhte, āhton: *see* āgan

ālǣdan *V wk* lead (away), withdraw

ald: *see* eald

aldre: *see* ealdor

ālēdon: *see* ālǣdan

ālīes: *see* ālīesan

ālīesan *V wk* release, absolve

alle = ealle; *see* eall

allmectig, almegttig = ælmihtig

alne = ealne; *see* eall

alter *N m* altar

āmasian *V wk* amaze

ān *num* one

āna: *see* ān

ancora *N m* anchorite, religious recluse
and *cj* and
andswarian *V wk* answer
āne, ānes: *see* ān
ānga *Aj (wk only)* only
āngan: *see* ānga
angeald: *see* ongyldan
anmēdla *N m* pomp
ānmōd *Aj* unanimous
ānmōde: *see* ānmōd
ānrǣd *Aj* single-minded
ānrǣdum: *see* ānrǣd
ānum: *see* ān
ārǣran *V wk* lift up, raise
ārǣrde, ārǣred: *see* ārǣran
ārīsan *V st* arise
ārlēasa *Aj* cruel
aron: *see* bēon
āscian: *see* ācsian
āstealde, āstelidæ: *see* āstellan
āstellan *V wk* place, establish
āstīgan *V st 1* mount, ascend
āstīgen: see āstīgan
āþ *N m* oath
āþas: *see* āþ
āþenede: *see* āþenian
āþenian *V wk* extend
āðweah: *see* āþwēan
āþwēan *V st 6* wash
āwacian *V wk* awaken
āwācian *V wk* grow weak
āwrītan *V st 1* write, write down
āwritene: *see* āwrītan
āxian = ācsian
bā *Aj* both
bæcere *N m* baker
bæd: *see* biddan
bælc *N m* arrogance
bær, bǣron: *see* beran
bagga *N m* badger
bān *N n* bone
band: *see* bindan
bannuc *N m* bit, small piece
barn: *see* bearn
barnum: see bearn
bāt *N f, m* boat
be *pr + dat* by

**bealdnes** *N f* boldness

**bēam** *N m* beam, tree

**bearn** *N n* child

**bearnum:** *see* **bearn**

**bearu** *N m* grove

**bearwes:** *see* **bearu**

**bebūgan** *V st 2* surround

**bēc:** *see* **bōc**

**becōm:** see **becuman**

**becuman** *V st 4* come, approach, happen

**becwōm = becōm**

**gebed** *N n* prayer

**bedd** *N n* bed

**gebedum:** *see* **gebed**

**beforan** *Av; pr + dat* before

**begēaton:** *see* **begietan**

**begeattas:** *see* **begietan**

**begietan** *V st 5* acquire

**behēafdian** *V wk* behead

**behealdan** *V st 7* behold, see

**behinon** *Av, pr + dat* beside, close by

**benn** *N f* wound

**bēo** *N f* bee

**bēo:** *see* **bēon**

**bēodan** *V st 2* offer, command

**bēom, bēon, bēona:** *see* **bēo** *N*

**bēon** *V irreg* be; *see also* **wesan**

**gebēon:** *see* **bēon**

**beorht** *Aj* bright

**beorhtnes** *N f* brightness

**beorn** *N m* warrior, man

**bēoþ:** *see* **bēon** *V*

**beran** *V st 4* bear

**berg** *N m* pig, hog

**beroþor = brōþor**

**bescūfan** *V st 2* hurl

**bestæl:** *see* **bestelan**

**bestelan** *V st 4* move stealthily, steal

**bestēman** *V wk* make wet, drench

**bestēmed:** *see* **bestēman**

**betera, betra, betst, bettra:** *see* **gōd**

**betwix þǣm (þe)** *cj* while

**betwux þām = betwix þǣm**

**bewrēon** *V st 1* cover

**biddan** *V st 5* command, pray

**gebiddan** *V st 5* pray

**gebiddas:** *see* **gebiddan**

biddes: *see* biddan
bield(o) N *f* courage
gebield(o): *see* bield(o)
bierþ: *see* beran
bifian V *wk* tremble
bifode: *see* bifian
bīgenga N *m* inhabitant
bihald: *see* behealdan
bind: *see* bindan
gebind N *n* expanse
bindan V *st 3* bind
bindaþ, binde, binden, bindende, bindest, bindeþ: *see* bindan
binnan *pr + dat* inside, within
bint, bintst: *see* bindan
birþ: *see* beran
biscop N *m* bishop
bist: *see* bēon
bītan V *st 1* bite
biþ, biðon: *see* bēon
biwrāh: *see* bewrēon
blæd N *m* glory
blæddre N *f* bladder
blæhæwen *Aj* dark blue, dark grey (of dyes and textiles)
blæwen *Aj* dark blue (of dyes and textiles)
blind *Aj* blind
blīþe  *Aj* joyful
blīþelīce *Av* happily
blīþemōd *Aj* happy
blīþost, blīþra: *see* blīþe
blōd N *n* blood
blōde: *see* blōd
blōdig *Aj* bloody
bōc N *f* book
bōca, bōce, bōcum: *see* bōc
bōccræft N *m* literature
gebod N *n* order, command
bodian V *wk* announce
boren: *see* beran
geboren: *see* beran
brægd: *see* bregdan
brēac: *see* brūcan
brecan V *st 4* break
bregdan V *st 3* pull
brēþer: *see* brōþor
bridd N *m* chick
briddas: *see* bridd
brītt: *see* bregdan

brocen, gebrocen: *see* brūcan

brōēðer = brēþer; *see* brōþor

brogden, gebrogden: *see* bregdan

brōþor *N m* brother

brōðres: *see* brōþor

brōþur = brōþor

brūcan *V st 2* enjoy

brucon: *see* brūcan

brugdon: *see* bregdan

brycg *N f* bridge

brȳcþ: *see* brūcan

brytta *N m* one who gives, distributor

bryttan: *see* brytta

būgan *V st 2* bend, turn, bow

bunde, bunden, gebunden, gebundene, gebundenne, bundon: *see* bindan

burg *N f* city

būta(n) *Av* without, outside; *cj* except; *pr + dat* out(side) of, except

butere *N f* butter

būton = būta(n)

bycgan *V wk* buy

byfigynde: *see* bifian

bygen *N f* purchase

cann: *see* cunnan

cantere *N m* singer

caru *N f* sorrow

cāsere *N m* emperor, caesar

cealc *N m* plaster, chalk

ceald *Aj* cold

cealde: *see* ceald

cealf *N n* calf

cēas: *see* cēosan

ceaster *N f* camp

gecēgu: *see* cīegan

cēne *Aj* bold

cēnlīce *Av* boldly

cēo *N f* chough

ceorfan *V st 3* carve

ceorl *N m* peasant

cēosan *V st 2* choose

cēpan *V wk* keep

cepte, cēpte: *see* cēpan

gecerdo: *see* cierran

cīegan *V wk* call, name

cierran *V wk* make to submit, turn

cīese: *see* cȳse

cīest: *see* cēosan

gecīged: *see* cīegan

cild *N n* child
cildru: *see* cild
gecirdon: *see* cierran
cirican: *see* cirice
cirice *N f* church
ciricean = cirican; *see* cirice
clǣne *Aj* clean
clǣnsian *V wk* cleanse
geclānsa: *see* clǣnsian
clipian *V wk* speak, cry out, call (upon)
clipode, clypode: *see* clipian
cnǣwþ: *see* cnāwan
cnapa *N m* servant, boy
cnapan: *see* cnapa
cnāwan *V st 7* know
cnāwen, gecnāwen: *see* cnāwan
cnearr *N m* galley, ship
cnēoris(s) *N f* tribe, generation, nation
cnēorissa, cnēorisse: *see* cnēoris(s)
cnēow, cnēowon: *see* cnāwan
cnoll *N m* summit
cnyllan *V wk* knock, ring
cnyllas, cnyllende: *see* cnyllan
cnysað, cnysende: *see* cnyssan
cnyssan *V wk* beat, buffet, knock
cōl *Aj* cool
cōm, cōme, cōmon: *see* cuman
coren, gecoren: *see* cēosan
costnung *N f* temptation
costnunge: *see* costnung
crabba *N m* crab
cræft *N m* skill
cræftlic *Aj* skilful
cræftlīce *Av* skilfully
crēap: *see* crēopan
crēopan *V st 2* creep
crīepþ: *see* crēopan
crismlīsing *N f* removal of baptismal robes
cropen, crupon: *see* crēopan
cū *N f* cow
cudu *N n* cud
cueðestū, cuidestū: *see* cweþan
cuman *V st 4* come
cume, cumen, gecumen, gecumene: *see* cuman
cunnan *V irreg* know
cunnen, gecunnen, cunnon: *see* cunnan
curon: *see* cēosan

153

cūþe, cūþon: *see* cunnan
cwacian *V wk* quake
cwǣden: *see* cweþan
cwealde: *see* cwellan
cwellan *V wk* kill
cwēn *N f* queen
cweorn *N f* hand-mill, quern
cweoðað: *see* cweþan
cweþan *V st 5* say, speak
cwic *Aj* alive
cwica, cwice, cwicu: *see* cwic
cwicu *Aj* alive; *cf.* cwic
cwōm, cwōmon: *see* cuman
cyme *N m* arrival
cymþ: *see* cuman
cynincg = cyning
cyning *N m* king
cyninge, cyninges: *see* cyning
cyre *N m* choice
cȳse *N m* cheese
dā *N f* doe
dǣd *N f* deed
dæg *N m* day
dægas: *see* dæg
dægcandel *N f* 'day-candle' = sun
dæghwāmlic *Aj* daily
dæghwāmlican: *see* dæghwāmlic
dæglic *Aj* daily
dǣl *N m* part, share
daga, dagas, dagum: *see* dæg
dēaw *Aj* dewy, bedewed
dēd = dǣd
deg = dæg
dehter: *see* dohtor
dēma *N m* judge, ruler
dēman *V wk* judge
dēmde: *see* dēman
dēofol *N m, n* devil
dēofolcund *Aj* devilish, diabolical
dēor *N n* animal
dēþ: *see* dōn
dōēme, gedōēmed, dōēmes: *see* dēma, dēman
dōēð = dēþ; *see* don
dohtor *N f* daughter
dohtra, dohtrum: *see* dohtor
dol *Aj* foolish
dōm *N m* judgement, glory

dōmas, dōme: *see* dōm

dōmgeorn *Aj* eager for glory

dōn *V irreg* do

gedōn: *see* dōn

dorstæ, dorste: *see* durran

drēam *N m* joy

drēamlēas *Aj* joyless

drictin = dryhten

drīfan *V st 1* drive

drihten = dryhten

drihtnes: *see* dryhten

drȳ *N m* magician

dryhten *N m* ruler, lord

dryhtne: *see* dryhten

dūn *N f, m* hill

dunn *Aj* dun, dingy brown

dūnum: *see* dūn

durran *V irreg* dare, venture

duru *N f* door

dyde, dydon: *see* dōn

dyne *N m* din

dysig *Aj* foolish

ēac *Av* also

ēadig *Aj* blessed

ēadiga: *see* ēadig

ēage *N n* eye

ēagena, ēagna: *see* ēage

eahta *num* eight

eahtoþa *num* eighth

eald *Aj* old

ealda: *see* eald

ealdor *N n* life; **on aldre** = ever

eall *Aj* all

ealle: *see* eall

ēam *N m* uncle

ēare *N n* ear

earm *Aj* poor

earn *N m* eagle

eart, earun: *see* bēon

ēast *Aj* east

ēastan: *see* ēast

ēastre *N n pl* Easter

ēastron: *see* ēastre

ēce *Aj* eternal, everlasting

ecg *N f* edge

ecgbana *N m* slayer with a sword

ecgbanan: *see* ecgbana

ēci: *see* ēce
geedlēanades: *see* edlēanian
edlēanian *V wk* reward, repay
efter = æfter
ēgan: *see* ēage
ēge = ēage
ēghuelc = æghwilc
ēgo: *see* ēage
ele *N m, n* oil
ellen *N n, m* zeal
end = and
endas: *see* ende
ende *N m* end
endes: *see* ende
engel *N m* angel
engla, englas, engles: *see* engel
ēode, ēodon: *see* gān
eolh *N m* elk
eom: *see* bēon
eorlscipe *N m* manliness
eorþan: *see* eorþe
eorðan = eorþan
eorþe *N f* earth, ground
eorðe = eorþe
ēow, ēower, ēowic: *see* gē
eowu *N f* ewe
erfewordnis *N f* inheritance
erfewordnisse: *see* erfewordnis
ēsuica *N m* hypocrite
etan *V st 5* eat
gefā *N m* foe
fader = fæder
fæder *N m* father
fæderenmǣg *N m* paternal kinsman
fæderenmǣge: *see* fæderenmǣg
gefægen *Aj* joyful
gefægene: *see* gefægen
færþ: *see* faran
fæste *Av* fast, firm
fæt *N n* vessel
fāg *Aj* stained
fangen, gefangen: *see* fōn
faran *V st 6* go
faren, gefaren: *see* faran
faru *N f* journey
fatu: *see* fæt
feaht, gefeaht: *see* feohtan

feallan *V st 7* fall
feallen, gefeallen: *see* feallan
feder = fæder
fēhþ: *see* fōn
fela *Aj* many
feld *N m* field
feng *N m* grip, captivity, embrace
fēng, fēngon: *see* fōn
fēo: *see* feoh
feoh *N n* cattle, property, money
gefeoht *N n* fight, battle
feohtan *V st 3* fight
gefeohte: *see* gefeoht
fēoll, fēollon: *see* feallan
fēond *N m* enemy
fēonda: *see* fēond
feor *Aj* far
fēores: *see* feorh
feorh *N m, n* life
feorm *N f* provision, food, benefit
fēorþa *num* fourth
fēos: *see* feoh
fēower *num* four
gefēra *N m* companion
fēran *V wk* go
gefēran: *see* gefēra
gefēran *V wk* reach
fērde: *see* fēran
gefērum: *see* gefēra
fēt: *see* fōt
fieht: *see* feohtan
fielþ: *see* feallan
fiend: *see* fēond
fierd *N f* army
gefierdum: *see* fierd
fīf *num* five
fīfta *num* fifth
fīftig *num* fifty
findan *V st 3* find
fiorme: *see* feorm
fīras *N m pl* men
fīrum: *see* fīras
fisc *N m* fish
fiþre *N n* wing
fiðru: *see* fiþre
flēah: *see* flēon
flēogan *V st 2* fly

**flēon** *V st 2* flee
**flīehþ, flogen:** *see* **flēon**
**geflīeman** *V wk* put to flight
**geflīemde:** *see* **geflīeman**
**geflogen:** *see* **flēon**
**flotmann** *N m* sailor
**flugon:** *see* **flēon**
**fohten:** *see* **feohtan**
**gefohten:** *see* **feohtan**
**folc** *N n* people
**folces:** *see* **folc**
**foldan:** *see* **folde**
**folde** *N f* earth
**foldu, foldum:** *see* **folde**
**fōn** *V st 7* seize
**fōr:** *see* **faran**
**forbærnan** *V wk* burn up
**forbærned:** *see* **forbærnan**
**forcerred** *Aj* (= *participle, see* **forcyrran**) perverted
**forcerredu:** *see* **forcerred**
**forcyrran** *V wk* avoid
**foregīsl** *N m* preliminary hostage
**foregīslas:** *see* **foregīsl**
**forgefeness** *N f* forgiveness
**forgefenesse:** *see* **forgefeness**
**forgief:** *see* **forgiefan**
**forgiefan** *V st 5* forgive
**forgiefaþ:** *see* **forgiefan**
**forhergian** *V wk* ravage, plunder
**forhergod:** *see* **forhergian**
**forlǣtan** *V st 7* forget, abandon
**forlǣten:** *see* **forlǣtan**
**forlēosan** *V st 2* lose completely, abandon
**forloren:** *see* **forlēosan**
**forma** *num* first
**forniman** *V st 4* take away, destroy
**foroft** *Av* very often
**fōron:** *see* **faran**
**for þǣm (þe)** *cj* because
**for ðǣm (ðe)** = **for þǣm (þe)**
**forþǣm:** *see* **for þǣm**
**forþon** *cj* because
**forðon** = **forþon**
**fōt** *N m* foot
**fōta, fōtas, fōtes, fōtum:** *see* **fōt**
**fox** *N m* fox
**fram** *pr* from

frēa *N m* lord

frēam, frēan, frēana: *see* frēa

freme, fremed, gefremed, fremede, gefremede, fremedest, fremedon, fremmende,
    fremest: *see* fremman

fremman *V wk* perform

fremmaþ, fremme, fremmen: *see* fremman

fremðe *Aj* strange, foreign

frēond *N m* friend

frēondlēas *Aj* friendless

frēondlēasne: *see* frēondlēas

frēondum: *see* frēond

frīend: *see* frēond

frign: *see* frignan

frignan *V st 3* ask

frōd *Aj* wise

frogga *N m* frog

fuhton: *see* feohtan

fūl *Aj* foul

full *Aj* full, complete

fullian *V wk* fulfil

gefullod: *see* fullian

fulwiht *N m* baptism

fulwihte: *see* fulwiht

gefyldæ: *see* fyllan

fyll *N m* fall

fyllan *V wk* fill

fylle: *see* fyll

fylstan *V wk + dat* help

gefylste: *see* fylstan

fȳnd = fīend

fȳr *N n* fire

fyxe *N f* vixen

gā: *see* gān

gaderian *V wk* gather

gafeluc *N m* spear

gāl *Aj* proud, wicked

galan *V st 6* sing

galgu: *see* gealga

gān *V irreg* go

gegān: *see* gān

gāst *N m* spirit, soul

gāste: *see* gāst

gāt *N f* goat

gāþ: *see* gān

gǣt: *see* gāt

ge *see* ǣgðer ... ge

gē *pn* you (*pl*)

geaf, geafon: *see* giefan

geald: *see* gieldan

gealga *N m* gallows

gealgan: *see* gealga

gēar *N n* year; gēara iū: long ago

geare *Av* well

gearu *Aj* ready

gēarum: *see* gēar

gearwes: *see* gearu

gee = gē

geltas = gyltas

genga *N m* companion

gēo *Av* once

geond *pr* throughout

geong *Aj* young

georn *Aj* eager

geornful *Aj* eager

gēr = gēar

... geredæ (*damaged inscription*): *see* ongyrwan

gēs: *see* gōs

gīe = gē

giefan *V st 5* give

giefe: *see* giefu

giefen, gegiefen: *see* giefan

giefend *N m* giver

giefþ: *see* giefan

giefu *N f* gift

gieldan *V st 3* pay

gielt: *see* gieldan

giest *N m* guest, stranger

gīet *Av* yet, still

gif *cj* if

gīgant *N m* giant

gihuæs = gehwæs

gingest, gingra: *see* geong

giond = geond

gistiga: *see* gestīgan

git *pn* you two

giuias: *see* giwian

giuiendum: *see* giwiend

giwian *V wk* ask

giwias: *see* giwian

giwiend *N m* seeker

gladost: *see* glæd

glæd *Aj* glad

glædmōd *Aj* cheerful

glæsen *Aj* shiny pale grey/blue

**God, god** *N m* God, god
**gode, godes:** *see* God
**gōd** *Aj* good
**gōdan, gōde, gōdena, gōdes, gōdne, gōdo, gōdra, gōdre, gōdum:** *see* gōd
**golden, gegolden:** *see* gieldan
**goldsele** *N n* hall where gold is distributed, 'gold-hall'
**goldwine** *N m* lord
**gōs** *N f* goose
**grǣg** *Aj* grey
**grēd** *N m* grass
**grēne** *Aj* green
**grīpan** *V st 1* grip
**gripe** *N m* grip
**griþ** *N n* peace, truce
**guldon:** *see* gieldan
**guma** *N m* man
**gūþ** *N f* battle
**gūþcaru** *N f* distress of war, 'war-sorrow'
**gūþceare:** *see* gūþcaru
**gyden** *N f* goddess
**gylden** *Aj* golden
**gylt** *N m* guilt, sin
**gyltas:** *see* gylt
**gȳt = gīet**
**habban** *V wk* have
**habbað:** *see* habban
**hād** *N m* character, rank, condition
**hæfd, gehæfd, hæfde, hæfdon, hæfeth, hæfþ:** *see* habban
**hǣlan** *V wk* heal
**hælda:** *see* hyldan
**hǣlend** *N m* saviour
**hǣtt:** *see* hātan
**hāētu:** *see* hātan
**hǣþen** *Aj* heathen
**hǣþnan:** *see* hǣþen
**hǣwen** *Aj* blue (grey)
**hǣwengrēne** *Aj* blue-green (grey-green)
**hāl** *Aj* whole
**hāleg = hālig**
**hālga** *N m* saint
**hālge:** *see* hālig
**hālgian** *V wk* hallow, sanctify
**gehālgod:** *see* hālgian
**hālig** *Aj* holy
**hām** *N m* home
**hand** *N f* hand
**handgeweorc** *N n* handiwork

handgeweorces: *see* handgeweorc
hātan *V st 7* command, name
hāten, hātte: *see* hātan
gehāten: *see* hātan
hauiblauum *N n* a blue (grey) woad dye
hēafdes: *see* hēafod
hēafod *N n* head
heafunæs: *see* heofon
hēah *Aj* high
hēahmōd *Aj* proud
hēahmōdnes *N f* pride
healdan *V st 7* hold
healden, gehealden: *see* healdan
healp: *see* helpan
hēan *Aj* lowly, despised, abject
hēane, hēanne: *see* hēah
heard *Aj* hard
hearde *Av* harshly
heardlīce *Av* harshly
heardlicor, heardlicost: *see* heardlīce
heardor, heardost: *see* hearde
hebban *V st 6* lift
heben = heofon
hefænrīcæs = heofonrīces
heht: *see* hātan
helpan *V st 3* help
hēo *pn* she
hēo = hīe: *see* hīe
heofnum: *see* heofon
heofon *N m* heaven
heofona: *see* heofon
heofonrīce *N n* heavenly kingdom
heofonrīces: *see* heofonrīce
heofonum: *see* heofon
hēold, hēoldon: *see* healdan
heolstor *N n* darkness
heolstre: *see* heolstor
heom = him: *see* hīe
heonu *interjection* lo!
heora = hiera: *see* hīe
heorte *N f* heart
hēr *Av* here, in this year
here *N m* army
heres: *see* here
hergan = herian
herges: *see* here
herian *V wk* praise

herigean = herian
hēt, hēton, gehēton: *see* hātan
hī, hīa = hīe: *see* hīe
hīe *pn* they; *see also* hēo
hīehst: *see* hēah
hielt: *see* healdan
hiene = hine
hiera: *see* hīe
hīeran *V wk* hear
hiere: *see* hēo
hierde *N m* shepherd
hīerra: *see* hēah
hilpþ: *see* helpan
him: *see* hē, hit, hīe
hinæ, hine: *see* hē
hīoldon = hēoldon
hiora = heora = hiera; *see* hīe
hira = hiera: *see* hīe
hīred *N m* retinue
hīredes: *see* hīred
his: *see* hē, hit
hit *pn* it
hlǣfdīge *N f* lady
hlāf *N m* loaf
hlafard = hlāford
hlāford *N m* lord
hlāfordas, hlāfordes: *see* hlāford
hlāforddōm *N m* lordship
hlāfweard *N m* steward
hnesce *Aj* soft, delicate
hogaþ, hogde, hogdon, hogod, gehogod, hogode, hogodon: *see* hycgan
holpen, geholpen: *see* helpan
hōn *V st 7* hang
hond *N f* hand
hordgeþanc *N m* mind
hræfn *N m* raven
hrēosan *V st 2* fall
hrīpes *N ?* (*uncertain gender*) reaping, harvest
hrōf *N m* roof, dwelling
hrōfe: *see* hrōf
hrūsan: *see* hrūse
hrūse *N f* soil, earth, ground
hryre *N m* fall
hū *Av* how
huā = hwā
huæt = hwæt
hulpon: *see* helpan

163

hund *N m* dog
hund *num* hundred
hundred *num* hundred
hundtēontig *num* hundred
hundum: *see* hund N
hūs *N n* house
hūsian *V wk* house, *i.e.* put into a house
hwā *pn* who; anyone, someone
hwælweg *N m* 'whale-way' = sea
hwǣm, hwæs: *see* hwā
hwǣr *cj, Av* where
gehwǣr *Av* everywhere
gehwæs: *see* hwā
hwæt *cj, d* what
hwæt *Aj* active
hwætscipe *N m* bravery
gehwæþer *Aj* both, either, each
gehwæþere: *see* gehwæþer
hwæþre *Av* yet, nevertheless
hwatum: *see* hwæt *Aj*
hwelc *pn* which
hwīl *N f* while
gehwīl: *see* hwīl
hwon: *see* hwā; *only appears in phrase* for hwon why?
hwone, hwȳ *see* hwā
hycgan *V wk* think
hycgean: *see* hycgan
hyge *N m* thought, mind, disposition, intention; courage, pride
hygeþrymm *N m* courage
hyldan *V wk reflexive* bow
hyll *N m* hill
hyllas, hylles: *see* hyll
hyra = hiera
hȳran = hīeran
hyrde = hierde
ic *pn* I
ides *N f* lady, woman
ieldest, ieldra, ieldran: *see* eald
ilca *pn* the same
ilcan, ilco, illce: *see* ilca
inc, incer: *see* git
infindan *V st 3* discover
infindes: *see* infindan
infrōd *Aj* very wise
ingān *V irreg* enter
inngang *N m* entrance
is: *see* bēon

īuer = ēower
iugoþ *N f* youth
iugoðe: *see* iugoþ
īuh = gē
īurre = ēowre, īurum = ēowrum; *see* ēower
kyning, kyniŋ = cyning
lǽd: *see* lǽdan
lǽdan *V wk* lead
lǽfan *V wk* leave
lǽfdon: *see* lǽfan
gelǽran *V wk* teach
lǽrde, gelǽrde: *see* gelǽran
lǽssa, lǽst: *see* lȳtel
lǽstan *V wk* carry out, perform
gelǽston: *see* lǽstan
lāf *N f* remainder
lamb *N n* lamb
lambra, lambru, lambrum: *see* lamb
gelamp: *see* gelimpan
land *N n* land
lande: *see* land
lang *Aj* long
lange: *see* lang
lār *N f* teaching
lāra, lāre, lārena: *see* lār
lāþ *Aj* hostile
lāþum: *see* lāþ
gelēafa *N m* faith
gelēafan: *see* gelēafa
lecgan *V wk* place
legdon: *see* lecgan
lengost, lengra: *see* lang
lēo *N m* lion
lēode *N f pl* people
lēof *Aj* dear
leofaþ, leofod, geleofod, leofode, leofodon: *see* libban
lēofost, lēofra: *see* lēof
lēoht *N n, Aj* light
lēonan, lēonum: *see* lēo
lēosan *V st 2* lose
lēðre *Aj* wicked, base
libban *V wk* live
gelīc *Aj* similar
licgan *V st 5* lie
līchama *N m* body
līchaman: *see* līchama
gelīefan *V wk + gen, dat* believe

līehtan *V wk* give light
lifd, gelifd, lifde, lifdon: *see* libban
gelimpan *V st 3* happen
lof *N m, n* glory
lofian *V wk* praise
lond = land
lufa, lufast, lufaþ: *see* lufian
lufian *V wk* love
lufiaþ: *see* lufian
lufie = lufige
lufien = lufigen
lufiende, lufige, lufigen, lufod, lufode, lufoden, lufodest, lufodon: *see* lufian
lufu *N f* love
gelȳfed: *see* gelīefan
lȳsan *V wk* redeem
lȳtel *Aj* little
lȳtle: *see* lȳtel
lȳtlian *V wk* diminish
lȳtlum: *see* lȳtel
macian *V wk* make
mæcti = mihte
mæg: *see* magan
mǣg *N m* kinsman
mægþhād *N m* maidenhood, virginity
mǣled *Aj* adorned
mǣst *Aj* most
mǣstan: *see* mǣst
magan *V irreg* be able to
māgister *N m* master
māgum: *see* mǣg
man *pn* one
mancyn: *see* mancynn
mancynn *N n* mankind
mancynnes: *see* mancynn
manig *Aj* many
manigfaldan: *see* manigfeald
manigfeald *Aj* manifold, various
manigra: *see* manig
mann *N m* man, male human
manna: *see* mann
māra: *see* micel
mattuc *N m* spade, mattock
māþm *N m* treasure
māðma: *see* māþm
māðum = māþm
mē: *see* ic
meaht = miht

meahta: *see* meaht

meahte = mihte: *see* magan

meahton = mihton: *see* magan

mearcian *V wk* mark

gemearcod: *see* mearcian

mēares: *see* mearh

mearh *N m* horse

mec: *see* ic

medu *N m* mead

melu *N n* meal

men: *see* mann

mengeo = menigu

menigu *N f* company, multitude

menio = menigu

menn: *see* mann

mennisc *Aj* human

meoduheall *N f* mead-hall

meoduhealle: *see* meoduheall

meotodes: *see* metod

mere *N m* lake, sea

meregrot *N n* pearl

meregrotta: *see* meregrot

mergen = morgen

gemet *N n* measure

gemete: *see* gemet

mete *N m* food

metod *N m* fate; Creator

metudæs = meotodes; *see* metod

metudes = meotodes; *see* metod

micclan: *see* micel

micel *Aj* great

micelniss *N f* greatness

micelnisse: *see* micelniss

miclan, micle: *see* micel

mid *pr* with

midd *Aj* middle

middangeard *N m* world

middangearde: *see* middangeard

middungeard = middangeard

midne: *see* midd

miht *N f* power

mihte = meahte, mihton = meahton: *see* magan

mildhiortnis *N f* mercy, compassion

mildhiortnesse: *see* mildhiortnis

milts *N f* mercy

miltsa: *see* milts

mīn, mīnne, mīnum: *see* ic

mið = mid

mōd *N n* spirit, courage

gemōd, mōde: *see* mōd

mōdgeþanc *N m* conception, thought

mōdgidanc = mōdgeþanc

mōdig *Aj* bold, proud

mōdigan: *see* mōdig

mōdor *N f* mother

mōdra, mōdru: *see* mōdor

mōdsefa *N m* purpose

mōdþracu *N f* courage

mon = man

mōnaþ *N m* month

moncynnæs: *see* mancynn

monna = manna; *see* mann

monncynnes: *see* mancynn

mōrfæsten *N n* moor-fastness, fen-fastness

mōrfæstenum: *see* mōrfæsten

morgen *N m* morning

morgenne: *see* morgen

morþor *N n* murder

morþre: *see* morþor

mōste, mōston: *see* mōtan

mot *N n* mote

mōt: *see* mōtan

mōtan *V irreg* be allowed

gemunan *V irreg* be mindful, recall, remember

gemunde: *see* gemunan

munuc *N m* monk

munuclic *Aj* monastic

mūs *N f* mouse

mūþ *N m* mouth

mūðe: *see* mūþ

myhte = mihte

gemynd *N n, f* memory

myne *N m* memory, thought

mȳs: *see* mūs

nā *negative particle*

næron = ne wæron

nales *Av* not at all

nam: *see* niman

nama *N m* name

naman, namena: *see* nama

nāmon: *see* niman

namum: *see* nama

nān *pn* no-one, none

nānwiht *pn* nothing; *Av* not at all

nānwuht = nānwiht

ne *negative particle*

nēah *Aj* near

nēdrie *N f* adder

nellas, nellað: *see* nyllan

nemnan *V wk* call, name

nemnaþ: *see* nemnan

nerian *V wk* save

nest *N n* nest

ni: *see* ne

nīehst: *see* nēah

nigene: *see* nigon

nigon *num* nine

nigoþa *num* ninth

niht *N f* night

niman *V st 4* take

nimþ: *see* niman

nis = ne + is

genōg *Aj* enough

nolde = ne + wolde: *see* nyllan

noldon = ne + woldon: *see* nyllan

nōm: *see* niman

noman: *see* nama

nōmon: *see* niman

norþ *Aj* northern

nosu *N f* nose

nū *Av* now

numen, genumen: *see* niman

genyhtsumian *V wk + dat* suffice

genyhtsumiendne: *see* genyhtsumian

nyle: *see* nyllan

nyllan = ne + willan *V irreg* not wish to, not want to

.odig = mōdig

of *pr* from

ofer *pr* over, after

oferhige *N m* pride

oferhogodnes *N f* pride

oferhygdig *N n* pride; *Aj* haughty

ofermēde *N n* pride; *Aj* proud

oferwinnan *V st 3* overcome

oferwunnen: *see* oferwinnan

ofslægen, ofslagen: *see* ofslēan

ofslēan *V st 6* slay

ofslōg, ofslōgen: *see* ofslēan

oft *Av* often

oftor: *see* oft

on *pr* in, on

onbindan *V st 3* unbind

ond = and

onfēng, onfōēð: *see* onfōn

onfōn *V st 7* receive

ongēan *pr* against, opposite, toward

ongēn = ongēan

ongeotað: *see* ongietan

ongieldan *V st 3* atone for

ongierwan *V wk* strip, unclothe

ongietan *V st 5* grasp, understand

ongiotan = ongeotan = ongietan

ongyldan = ongieldan

ongyrede: *see* ongierwan

ongyrwan = ongierwan

onlīehtan *V wk* enlighten

onlūtan *V st 2* bend

onstealde: *see* onstellan

onstellan *V wk* create, establish

ōr *N n* beginning, origin

ord *N m* point, spear

oreald *Aj* very old

orgello *N f* pride

orgelnes *N f* pride

oþ (þæt) *cj* until

oð þæt = oþ þæt

ōþer *num* second

ōþres: *see* ōþer

oþþe *cj* or

oxa *N m* ox

oxna: *see* oxa

padduc *N possibly f* frog

pāpa *N m* pope

pocca *N ? (uncertain gender)* fallow deer

poccel *N ? (uncertain gender)* fawn

pohha: *see* pocca

pohhel: *see* poccel

prēost *N m* priest

prūd, prȳt *Aj* proud

prȳt(e) *N f* pride

rā *N m* roe-deer

rād, gerād: *see* rīdan

rǣcan *V wk* offer, grant

rǣces: *see* rǣcan

rǣdan *V st 7* read

rǣran *V wk* raise up

rāp *N m* rope

rāpum: *see* rāp

reahte: *see* reccan

reccan *V wk* stretch, tell, wield

regn *N m* rain

rehtwīs = rihtwīs

rēðan: *see* rēþe

rēþe *Aj* violent, fierce

rīce *N n* kingdom

rīce *Aj* powerful

rīcne: *see* rīce *Aj*

rīdan *V st 1* ride, overrun, occupy

gerīdan, riden, ridon, geridon: *see* rīdan

riht *N n* right, law

rihtlīce *Av* justly

rihtlicor: *see* rihtlīce

rihtwīs *Aj* righteous

riicnæ: *see* rīce *Aj*

rīm *N n* number

rīme: *see* rīm

rīsan *V st 1* rise

rōd *N f* cross, 'rood'

rōde: *see* rōd

rūn *N f* secret

rūnwita *N m* counsellor

sacan *V st 6* quarrel

sǣ *N f, m* sea

sægd, gesægd, sægde, sægdon, sægþ: *see* secgan

sǣlig *Aj* happy, fortunate, blessed

gesǣlig *Aj* blessed

sæt, gesǣton: *see* sittan

gesald: *see* sellan

salde = sealde; *see* sellan

samod *Av* as well, simultaneously

sanct *N m* saint

sāre *Av* grievously

sāule: *see* sāwol

savle = sāwle

sāwle: *see* sāwol

sāwol *N f* soul

scacan *V st 6* shake

scān: *see* scīnan

sceal: *see* sculan

scēame: *see* scēamu

scēamu *N f* shame

scēap *N n* sheep

scear, scēaron: *see* scieran

scēat *N m* surface

scēatum: *see* scēat

171

scēop = scōp
gesceop: *see* scieppan
sceolde = scolde: *see* sculan
sceoldon = scoldon: *see* sculan
scēotan *V st 2* shoot
scepen = scyppend
sceppend = scyppend
sciellfisc *N m* shellfish
scieppan *V st 6* create
scieran *V st 4* cut
scierþ: *see* scieran
scīnan *V st 1* shine
scinen, gescinen, scinon, scīnþ: *see* scīnan
scip *N n* ship
scipa, scipe, scipes, scipu, scipum: *see* scip
scīp: *see* scēap
sciprāp *N m* cable
scīr *N f* shire, county
scīr *Aj* bright
scīrmǣled *Aj* brightly adorned
scolde = sceolde: *see* sculan
scoldon = sceoldon: *see* sculan
scolere *N m* scholar
scōp: *see* scieppan
gescōp: *see* scieppan
scoren, gescoren: *see* scieran
Scottas *N m* Scots
scūfan *V st 2* push
sculan *V irreg* must, have to, be obliged to
sculon: *see* sculan
scūr *N m* shower
gescyldru *N pl m* shoulders
scylun = sculon
scyppend *N m* creator
se, sē *d* the, that
seah, geseah: *see* sēon
gesealla: *see* sellan
sealm *N m* psalm
sealtian *V wk* dance
sēaþ: *see* sēoþan
sēcan *V wk* seek
sēcean = sēcan
secgan *V wk* say
sefa *N m* mind
segeð: *see* secgan
seledrēorig *Aj* sad at the loss of a hall
sēlest, sēlra: *see* gōd

self *pn* self
sella: *see* sellan
sellan *V wk* give
geselleð: *see* sellan
sendan *V wk* send
sendas: *see* send
sennum: *see* synn
sēo: *see* se
seofon *num* seven
seofoþa *num* seventh
seofoðan: *see* seofoþa
sēon, gesēon *V st 5* see
sēoþan *V st 5* boil
geset *N n* seat, dwelling
settan *V wk* set, put
sette: *see* settan
sīa *N f* pupil of the eye
sīan: *see* sīa
sīe, sīen: *see* bēon
sīeþ: *see* sēoþan
siex *num* six
siexta *num* sixth
sīgan *V st 1* fall, sink
sige *N m* victory
sigon: *see* sīgan
gesihþ *N f* sight
gesiist, gesiistu: *see* sēon
sinc *N n* treasure
sinces: *see* sinc
sind, sindon: *see* bēon
singan *V st 3* sing
singende: *see* singan
sinu *N f* sinew
sinwa, sinwe, sinwum: *see* sinu
gesīon = gesēon; *see* sēon
gesiteð: *see* sittan
sittan *V st 5* sit, occupy
siþedon = sīþodon: *see* sīþian
sīþian *V wk* go, travel
sīþode: *see* sīþian
siþþan *cj* since
siþðan = siþþan
slā, geslægen: *see* slēan
slæp *N m* sleep
slæpan *V st 7* sleep
slæpe: *see* slæp
slæpen, slæpþ: *see* slæpan

geslǣpen: *see* slǣpan

slēan *V st 6* strike

slege *N m* beating, slaying

slēp, slēpon: *see* slǣpan

slīdan *V st 1* slide, fail, be transitory

sliehþ, slōg, slōgon: *see* slēan

slōh = slōg; *see* slēan

smēocan *V st 2* emit smoke

smeoru *N n* grease, fat

smīecþ: *see* smēocan

snāw *N m* snow

snāþ: *see* snīþan

snellscipe *N m* boldness

sniden, gesniden, snidon, snīþ: *see* snīþan

snīþan *V st 1* cut

snoru *N f* daughter-in-law

snotor *Aj* wise

snottur = snotor

soden, gesoden: *see* sēoþan

sōēcas, sōēcað, sōhte: *see* sēcan

sōna *Av* at once, immediately

sorg *N f* sorrow

sōþ *Aj* true

sōðe: *see* sōþ

sōþlīce *Av* truly

spor *N n* track, trail, course

spore: *see* spor

sprǣc *N f* speech

sprec, gesprec *N n* speech

sprecan *V st 5* speak

spreocu: *see* sprec

spyrian *V wk* follow

spyrigean = spyrian

gestāh: *see* stīgan

stān *N m* stone

stāna, stānas, stāne, stānes, stānum: *see* stān

standan *V st 6* stand

stānehte *Aj* stony

stelan *V st 4* steal

stīgan, gestīgan *V st 1* ascend, rise up

stīþmōd *Aj* resolute

stōd, stōdon: *see* standan

stōw *N f* place

stōwa, stōwe: *see* stōw

strǣt *N f* street, road

strang *Aj* strong

strangum: *see* strang

strē = strēaw
strēam *N m* stream
strēamas: *see* strēam
strēaw *N n* straw
strengest, strengra: *see* strang
strēt = strǣt
suā = swā
sudon: *see* sēoþan
suē = swā
sum *d* a certain
suna: *see* sunu
sunne *N f* sun
sunu *N m* son
sunum: *see* sunu
swā *Av, cj* so
swā swā *cj* just as, like
swæð *N n* footprint, track
swam: *see* swimman
swearthǣwen *Aj* dark blue
sweger *N f* mother-in-law
swelce = swilce
sweng *N m* blow
swenge: *see* sweng
sweord *N n* sword
sweostor *N f* sister
swerian *V st 6* swear
swilc *Aj* such
swilce *Av* such, in such a way, thus
swimman *V st 3* swim
swīþe *Av* very
swylt *N m* death
swȳþe = swīþe
gesyhþe: *see* gesihþ
syle: *see* sellan
sylf = self
gesȳne *Aj* visible
syngadun: *see* syngian
syngian *V wk* sin
synn *N f* sin
synnful *Aj* sinful
synnum: *see* synn
syþþan = siþþan
tā *N f* toe
tēode: *see* tēon
tēon *V st 2* pull, drag, take (violently)
teoru *N n* tar
teorwes: *see* teoru

tēoþa *num* tenth

teran *V st 4* tear

tēþ: *see* tōþ

thā = þā

thōthor = þōþor

tīd *N f* time

tīdæ, tīda: *see* tīd

tīen *num* ten

tīgle *N f* tile

til *pr* to

timbrian *V wk* build

tīð *N f* grant, share

tō *pr* to, for

tōdæg *Av* today

tōdǣlan *V wk* divide

tōdǣleð: *see* tōdǣlan

todd *N ? (uncertain gender)* fox

tō merigen *Av* tomorrow

torr *N m* rock

tōslitas: *see* tōslītan

tōslītan *V st 1* tear open, tear to bits

tōstregdan *V st 3* scatter

tōstrigdeð: *see* tōstregdan

tōþ *N m* tooth

tōþas: *see* tōþ

træd, trǣdon: *see* tredan

tredan *V st 5* tread

getrede, treden, getreden: *see* tredan

getrēowe *Aj* faithful

tritt: *see* tredan

getrymde: *see* trymman

trymman *V wk* strengthen, confirm

tū: *see* twā

tūcian *V wk* ill-treat

tūcode: *see* tūcian

tuelftan: *see* twelfta

tugon: *see* tēon

tūn *N m* settlement

tunge *N f* tongue

twā *num* two

twǣm, twēga, twēgea, twēgen, twēgra: *see* twā

twām = twǣm

twelfta *num* twelfth

twentig *num* twenty

twēo *N m* doubt

ðā = þā

þā *Av* then, *cj* when; *see also* se

176

þā þā *cj* when

þǣm: *see* se

þǣr *Av* there

þǣre, ðǣre, þǣs: *see* se

þæt *cj* that, so that; *see also* se

þætte *cj* that

þām, ðām = þǣm: *see* se

þancian *V wk* thank

þanon = þonan *Av* thence

þāra: *see* se

þās: *see* þes

þe: *see chapter 6, note 3. Can often be interpreted as* who, which, that *etc.*

þē, ðē: *see* þū

þēah *cj* (al)though

þearf: *see* þurfan

þēaw *N m* custom

þēawes: *see* þēaw

þec, ðec: *see* þū

þeccan *V wk* cover

ðeceð: *see* þeccan

þegen *N m* thane

þegnscipe *N m* valour

ðene = þone

þēod, geþēod *N f* people, nation

þēos: *see* þes

þēow *N m* servant, slave

ðēr = þǣr

þes *d* this

þider *Av* thither

ðīeda: *see* þēod

þīn, ðīn, ðīnes, ðīnra, þīnre, ðīnum: *see* þū

ðīode, geðīode *N n* language, race, people

ðīowa: *see* þēow

ðis = þis

þisne, þisse, þisses, þissum: *see* þes

ðīus: *see* sēo

þīustra *N f* darkness

þōht, geþōht *N m* thought

geðōhtas: *see* geþōht

þonan = þanon *Av* thence

þone, ðone: *see* se

þonne *cj* than

ðonne = þonne

þorfte, þorfton: *see* þurfan

þorn *N m* thorn

þōþor *N m* ball

þrāg *N f* time

þrāge: *see* þrāg
þrēo *num* three
þrēora: *see* þrēo
þridda *num* third
þrīe, þrim: *see* þrēo
þrītig *num* thirty
þrītiga: *see* þrītig
þū *pn* you (singular)
þurfan *V irreg* need
þurh, ðurh *pr* through
ðurst *N m* thirst
þuruh = þurh
þus *Av* thus
þūsend *num* thousand
þweorh *Aj* perverse
ðweoru: *see* þweorh
þȳ lǣs (þe) *cj* lest
ðȳ lǣs = þȳ lǣs
þyrs *N m* giant, demon, wizard
þysne = þisne
uard = weard
unc, uncer: *see* wit
unīeþelīce *Av* with difficulty
unmōdnes *N f* pride
unnan *V irreg* + *dat, gen* grant, allow
unrehtwīsnis *N f* wickedness, iniquity
unriht *Aj* wrong, wicked
unrihte *Av* unjustly
untȳnan *V wk* open
untȳned: *see* untȳnan
unwemme *Aj* undefiled
ūre, ūrne, ūrum, ūs, ūsic: *see* wē
ūt *Av* out
ūtlaga *N m* outlaw
uton *interjection* let us
ūðe: *see* unnan
uuldurfadur = wuldorfæder
uundra = wundra
uuoldon = woldon; *see* willan
gevvyrcan = gewyrcan
wād *N n* a blue woad dye
wadan *V st 6* go, move, journey
wæcnian *V wk* awake
wǣden *Aj* blue (possibly restricted to dyes and textiles)
wælsliht *N m* slaughter
wær *Aj* cautious, wary
wǣre, wǣren, wǣron: *see* bēon

**wærscipe** *N m* caution

**wǣrun** = wǣron

**wæs:** *see* bēon

**wæteregesa** *N m* water-terror, dreadful water

**wæteregesan:** *see* wæteregesa

**walde:** *see* willan

**Walden** = wealdend

**wammum:** *see* womm

**wannhǣwen** *Aj* dark blue

**warian** *V wk* inhabit

**warode:** *see* warian

**was** = wæs

**wāst, wāt:** *see* witan

**waþem** *N m* wave

**waþema:** *see* waþem

**wē** *pn* we

**wealdend** *N m* lord, ruler

**wealdendra:** *see* wealdend

**weallan** *V st 7* boil, rage

**weard** *N m* guardian

**wearp:** *see* weorpan

**wearþ:** *see* weorþan

**wearð** = wearþ; *see* weorþan

**weg** *N m* way

**wegan** *V st 5* weigh

**wegas, gewegen:** *see* wegan

**wel** *Av* well

**wela** *N m (often plural)* prosperity, wealth

**welan:** *see* wela

**welle:** *see* wylle

**welwillende** *Aj* benevolent

**wēnan** *V wk + gen* believe

**wendan, gewendan** *V wk* turn

**wēnde, wēndon:** *see* wēnan

**wendon:** *see* wendan

**wēop, wēopon:** *see* wēpan

**weorc, geweorc** *N n* work, labour, fortress

**geweorce:** *see* geweorc

**weorpan** *V st 3* throw

**weorþ** *Aj* worthy

**weorþan** *V st 3* become

**weorþian** *V wk* honour

**weorþode:** *see* weorþian

**weorþude** = weorþode; *see* weorþian

**weorþung** *N f* honour

**weorþuste:** *see* weorþ

**weoruda:** *see* werod

179

weorulde: *see* woruld

weotudlīce: *see* witodlīce

wēpan *V st 7* weep

wēpþ: *see* wēpan

wer *N m* man

werc: *see* weorc

werede: *see* werod

werian *V wk* defend

werod *N n* troop

werode, werodes: *see* werod

werum: *see* wer

wes: *see* bēon

wesan *V irreg* be; *see also* bēon

wesaþ, wesende: *see* bēon

weter = wæter

wīcing *N m* viking, pirate

wicum = wiecum; *see* wiece

wīd *Aj* wide

wīdcūþ *Aj* widely known

wiecan: *see* wiece

wiece = wucu

wierest, wiersa, wierst: *see* yfel

wierpþ: *see* weorpan

wīf *N n* woman

wīfman, wīfmann *N m* woman

wilde *Aj* wild

wile = wille: *see* willan

willan *V irreg* wish, want to

wille = wile: *see* willan

willende *Aj* willing

wine *N m* friend

gewinn *N n* strife, battle

winnan *V st 3* strive, fight, oppose

winnað: *see* winnan

gewinne: *see* gewinn

winnende: *see* winnan

winter *N m* winter, year

wintercearig *Aj* winter-hearted

wintra: *see* winter

wīs *Aj* wise

wīsdōm *N m* wisdom

wisse: *see* wissian

wissian *V wk* guide, know

wiste, wiston: *see* witan

wit *pn* we two

wita *N m* wise man

witan *V irreg* know

wītan *V st 1* blame

gewītan *V st 1* depart

wīte *N n* punishment

wītega *N m* prophet

witen, gewiten: *see* witan

wītgas, wītgo: *see* wītega

gewitloca *N m* mind

witodlīce *Av* certainly

witt, gewitt *N n* understanding

wiþ *pr* against

wiþsacan *Vst 6* forsake

wiðstandan *V st 6 + dat* withstand, resist

wlacu *Aj* tepid

wlæc *Aj* tepid

wlenc(o) *N f* haughtiness

wōd: *see* wadan

wōēgas: *see* wegan

wōēn *N f, m* hope, expectation

gewoendo: *see* gewendan

wōēsten(n) *N n* waste, wilderness

wōēstenne: *see* wōēsten(n)

wolde, woldon: *see* willan

womm *N m* defilement

wōpen, gewōpen: *see* wēpan

word *N n* word

geworden: *see* weorþan

worhte: *see* wyrcan

worohton = wrohton; *see* wrecan

worpe, geworpe, worpen, geworpen: *see* weorpan

woruld *N f* world

wrāh: *see* wrēon

wrāð *Aj* angry

wrecan *V st 5* avenge

wrecend *N m* avenger

wrēon *V st 1* cover

wrīehþ, wrigen, gewrigen, wrigon: *see* wrēon

wrītan *V st 1* write

gewrit *N n* writing

wrohton: *see* wrecan

wucu *N f* week

wudu *N m* wood

wudum: *see* wudu

wuldorfæder *N m* glorious father

wulf *N m* wolf

wund *N f* wound

wundor *N n* wonder

wundra: *see* wundor

wundrian *V wk* wonder (at)

wunedon: *see* wunian

wunian *V wk* dwell

wuniende: *see* wunian

gewunnon: *see* winnan

wurc = weorc

wurdon: *see* weorþan

wurpon: *see* weorpan

wurþmynt *N f, m* honour

wurðmynte: *see* wurþmynt

wutas: *see* witan

wylf *N f* she-wolf

wylla *N m* well

wylle *N f* well

wynn *N f* joy

wynnfæst *Aj* pleasant

wynnsum *Aj* delightful

wyrcan, gewyrcan *V wk* make

wyrcas: *see* wyrcan

wyrican = wyrcan

yfel *N n* evil; *Aj* evil

yfele: *see* yfel

yfelnyss *N f* wickedness

yflan: *see* yfel

yflenysse = yfelnysse: *see* yfelnyss

yflo: *see* yfel

ylda: *see* yldu

yldu *N f* age, old age

ymb = ymbe

ymbe *pr* around

ymbclyppan *V wk* embrace

ymbclypte: *see* ymbclyppan

ymblǣdan *V wk* lead around

ymblāēdde: *see* ymblǣdan

yrmþe: *see* yrmþu

yrmþu *N f* misery, crime

ȳþ *N f* wave

ȳþe: *see* ȳþ

# Glossary of Key Terms

*Ablaut (gradation)*: a regular variation of vowels in the *roots of words*, deriving from Proto-Indo-European, which seems to relate to meaning and/or grammatical function, e.g. **hot** (adjective) versus **heat** (noun), **bind** (*present tense*) versus **bound** (*preterite tense*).

*accent*: the *phonological inventory* of a particular individual or area or social group. Accent should not be confused with *idiolect*, *dialect*, or *sociolect*.

*active voice*: see *voice*.

*affixation*: a process of *lexical morphology (word-formation)*, whereby derived forms are produced through the addition of affixes (bound *morphemes*).

*agreement*: see *finiteness, headword, modifier*.

*alliteration*: a sequence of words beginning with the same sound, e.g. **round and round the rugged rocks the ragged rascals ran**. Alliteration was structural in OE verse in the same way that rhyme is structural in later poetry.

*allograph*: the realisation of a *grapheme* in writing. Replacement of one allograph by another realisation of the same grapheme does not change the meaning of the word; thus <<a, **a**, *a*, a>> are all allographs of the grapheme <a>.

*allophone*: the realisation of the *phoneme* in speech. Replacement of one allophone with another realisation of the same phoneme does not change the meaning of the word in which it occurs; thus [l] and [ł] are allophones of the phoneme /l/.

*alphabet*: the Latin-based set of graphemes commonly used in Western Europe and America, named after the first two letters in the Greek alphabet from which it was derived ('alpha', 'beta').

*analytic*: see *synthetic vs. analytic*.

*aspect*: a grammatical category to do with such things as whether the action is completed (perfect) or continuous (progressive), cf. the distinction between PDE **he was eating** (progressive aspect), **he ate** (perfect aspect), **he has been eating** (progressive aspect), **he had eaten** (perfect aspect).

*borrowing*: a process whereby a word from one language is transferred to another. Words transferred in this way are known as *loanwords*.

*bound morpheme*: see *morpheme*.

*case*: a grammatical category used to indicate relationships between and within phrases and often marked in Indo-European languages by inflexional *endings* added to nouns, pronouns and adjectives. In OE the following cases are usually distinguished: *nominative, accusative, genitive/possessive, dative*. Cases signal the function of the phrase within the clause; thus phrases marked by nominative *inflexions* prototypically function as subjects within the clause.

*clause*: a grammatical category consisting of one or more *phrases* and (in English) containing a verb phrase.

*cognate*: see *Grimm's Law*.

*cohesion*: a notion to do with a range of linguistic devices, or *cohesive ties*, which are used to connect words, phrases, clauses or sentences in a piece of discourse for stylistic effect.

*comparative reconstruction*: see *linguistic reconstruction*.

*comparison of adjectives*: sets of adjectives, semantically linked, which make up a gradable sequence, e.g. **good, better, best** or **fine, finer, finest**. Forms such as **good, fine** are referred to as absolute, forms such as **better, finer** are referred to as comparative, and forms such as **best, finest** are referred to as superlative.

*compounding*: a process of *lexical morphology (word-formation)*, whereby derived forms are produced by placing two free morphemes together.

*conjugation*: a verb-*paradigm*, i.e. the set of forms belonging to a particular verb-lexeme. Verb-paradigms can be grouped depending on the similarity of their patterns; thus we refer to the weak conjugation of the verb when referring to verbs which distinguish *present* and *preterite* forms through the addition of the suffix -(e)d, e.g. **love, loved**, and to the strong conjugation when referring to verbs which distinguish present and preterite forms through changing the vowel of the *root*, e.g. **sing, sang**.

*connotation*: *lexemes* have connotations, referring to the associated meanings a lexeme may develop; for example **beast** denotes the concept 'animate non-human' but has connotations of irrationality, brutality etc. Lexemes may have stylistic connotations; thus **commence** is more formal in style than **begin**. See also *denotation*.

*consonant*: a set of sounds made by a constriction or interruption of the airstream from the lungs. Consonants can be classified with reference to the following: *the place of articulation, the manner of articulation*, and the state of the vocal folds.

*construction*: a term in grammar used to refer to a particular phrase-, clause- or sentence-pattern.

*conversion*: a process whereby words can be transferred from one word-class to another without *affixation*. This process is common in PDE, e.g. the form **buy** remains the same whether functioning as a verb in **to buy a book** or as a noun in **a good buy**.

*declension*: prototypically a noun-*paradigm*, i.e. the set of forms belonging to a particular noun-*lexeme*. Noun-paradigms can be grouped depending on the similarity of their patterns; in PDE, most noun-paradigms are based on the OE strong declension, yielding sequences such as **stone, stone's, stones, stones'**, but there are residualisms in PDE derived from other declensions, e.g. **foot, feet** (derived from an OE irregular declension) and **child, children** (based on the OE weak declension). There are also pronoun-declensions (e.g. **she, her**); PDE no longer sustains adjective-declensions, although they existed in OE and are still to be found in *cognate* languages such as German.

*denotation*: the conceptual meaning of a *lexeme*, without reference to associated, typically stylistic meaning. Thus words such as **begin, commence** have the same conceptual meaning, i.e they are verbs signifying inception. See also *connotation*.

*diachronic*: diachronic ('through time') linguistics is an approach to the study of language which deals with the processes involved in linguistic change. See also *synchronic*.

*dialect*: the *accent*, *grammar* and *vocabulary* of a particular area.

*diatopic*: diatopic ('through space') linguistics is an approach to the study of language which deals with linguistic variation across geographical distances at a particular point in time.

*Early West Saxon*: the form of OE traditionally dated to the time of King Alfred (i.e. the ninth century AD) and located to the kingdom of Wessex. This form of the language is often adopted by scholars as a convenient point of reference, rather as Standard Southern British English or General American are adopted by students of PDE.

*feminine*: see *gender*.

*finiteness*: a grammatical category relating to the form of the verb. Finite verbs in both OE and PDE are conjugated, i.e. their form is chosen, according to the form of the subject; thus a singular subject such as **the girl** causes the finite verb governed by that subject to be given a singular ending, e.g. **loves**, as in the clause **the girl loves ponies**. This relationship is known as *agreement*. Non-finite verbs are the infinitive (base-form) and participles (present and past). The infinitive form of the verb may be regarded as the base-form from which other parts of the verb-paradigm can be derived. Participles are grammatical units somewhere between the verb and the adjective and deriving characteristics from both.

*free morpheme*: see *morpheme*.

*fuþark*: the term used to refer to the set of *runes* used widely in the early Germanic world, and slightly different from those used in Anglo-Saxon England, which are referred to as the *fuþorc*. The term 'fuþark' derives from the first six letters of the set, usually transliterated as 'f', 'u', 'þ', 'a', 'r', 'k'.

*fuþorc*: the set of runes used in OE is generally referred to as the *fuþorc*, after the first six letters in its canonical listing ('f', 'u', 'þ', 'o', 'r', 'c'). The *fuþorc* differs slightly from the *fuþark*.

*gender*: nouns and pronouns in OE belong to one of three gender-classes, and this categorisation affects the endings they have, and in turn the endings that any of their *modifiers* have. Traditionally, these three classes are known as *masculine*, *feminine* and *neuter* genders. Sometimes this *grammatical gender* corresponds to biological or *natural gender*, but sometimes it does not.

*Germanic*: the *Germanic* languages, part of the wider Indo-European family of languages, emerged in the first millennium BC in northern Europe. East, West and North Germanic groups are distinguished, all deriving ultimately from a common ancestor, Proto-Germanic.

*Gothic*: Gothic is an East Germanic variety whose written records date from several centuries before those for OE.

*gradation*: see *Ablaut*.

*grammar*: the grammar of a language is to do with how words are put together (its *morphology*) or relate to one another (its *syntax*).

*grammatical gender*: see *gender*.

*grammaticalisation*: the historical process whereby a part of speech with lexical meaning is transferred to become a part of speech whose primary function is grammatical, e.g. an adverb such as **to** starts to be used as a preposition.

*grapheme*: the written language equivalent of the phoneme, i.e. the symbolic unit being aimed at by the scribe or printer. Replacement of one grapheme by another changes the meaning of the word in which it occurs; thus <a> and <o> are distinct graphemes, illustrated by the pair <pat>, <pot>.

*Grimm's Law*: the German philologist and folklorist Jacob Grimm (1785–1863) showed that there was a predictable set of consonantal differences between the Germanic languages and the others of the Indo-European family, dating from the period of divergence of Proto-Germanic from other Indo-European dialects. The effects of Grimm's Law in Old English can be seen through comparing groups of *cognates*, i.e. words in different languages with a presumed common ancestor.

*half-line*: the basic metrical unit of the OE poem; half-lines were linked together in pairs by alliterating syllables.

*headword*: the principal element of phrases. Thus, in the noun phrase **the big boy**, **boy** is the headword, while in the verb phrase **was singing**, **singing** is the headword. See also *modifier*. Headwords and modifiers *agree* in many languages, e.g. French, OE, but not for the most part in PDE.

*idiolect*: the accent, grammar and vocabulary of a particular individual.

*imperative mood*: see *mood*.

*indicative*: see *mood*.

*inflexion*: bound morpheme added to the stem of the word and signifying the word's grammatical function. See *endings*.

*inflexional morphology*: see *morphology*.

*insular script*: a manner of writing, developed largely in Ireland and first employed in Britain in Christian Northumbria, and commonly appearing in late Anglo-Saxon manuscripts.

*internal reconstruction*: see *linguistic reconstruction*.

*kennings*: compound words which are a particular feature of OE verse, e.g. **dægcandel** 'day-candle' (i.e. the sun), **hwælweg** 'whale-way' (i.e. the sea).

*Late West Saxon*: a *dialect* of OE found in many Anglo-Saxon manuscripts dating from the late tenth and eleventh centuries.

*lexeme*: the overall term for words which are related in *paradigmatic* terms, that is, which vary inflexionally; thus **love, loves, loved** are members of one lexeme, **pony, ponies** are members of another, and so on.

*lexical morphology*: see *morphology*.

*lexicography*: =making of dictionaries.

*lexicology*: the study of the lexicon, not to be confused with *lexicography*.

*lexicon*: =vocabulary. The lexicon of a language is the set of *lexemes* found in a given language.

*linguistic reconstruction*: past states of a language, and relationships between daughter and sister languages, may be determined by linguistic reconstruction, involving two procedures: *comparative* and *internal* reconstruction. Comparative reconstruction involves comparing distinct languages, or varieties of the same language, in order to work out the structure of the common ancestor language or variety. Internal reconstruction involves analysing *paradigmatic* variation within a single language or variety.

*loanword*: see *borrowing*.

*logographic*: see *phonographic vs. logographic*.

*manner of articulation*: the manner in which the airstream is emitted from the lungs, used in defining *consonants*.

*masculine*: see *gender*.

*Middle English*: =ME, the form of the English language spoken and written after *c.* 1100 and before *c.* 1500.

*Modern English*: =ModE, the form of the English language spoken and written since *c.* 1500, including *Present-Day English* (PDE).

*modifier*: those elements within a given phrase other than the *headword*. Thus, in the noun phrase **the big boy**, **the big** are modifiers, while in the verb phrase **was singing**, **was** is the modifier.

*mood*: a verbal category to do with different degrees of possibility. Three moods are traditionally distinguished: *indicative*, *subjunctive* and *imperative*. Indicative mood forms are those where the form chosen indicates that the action referred to is a real action, as in **I** ate **my breakfast**. Subjunctive mood is used to suggest hypothesis, conjecture or volition, e.g. **I may eat my breakfast**, while imperative mood is used for commands, e.g. **Eat your breakfast!**

*mora*: a unit of sound used for measuring lexical length. V = one mora, VV = two morae, VCC = three morae, and so on.

*morpheme*: the minimal unit of grammatical analysis. Morphemes can be *free*, i.e. they can appear as independent *words*, e.g. **love**, or they can be *bound*, i.e. they are always affixed to free morphemes, e.g. **-ing**.

*morphology*: the part of *grammar* concerned with word-form, such as the kinds of ending which the form **love** can adopt, for example **loves** as opposed to **loved** (=*inflexional morphology*); it is also concerned with how words can be put together from other words, such as **blackbird** (from **black + bird**) or **undo** (from **un + do**) (=*lexical morphology*, *word-formation*).

*natural gender*: see *gender*.

*negation*: the expression of negativity through grammar and the lexicon.

*neuter*: see *gender*.

*Norse*: the traditional term used for all the North Germanic languages, viz. Swedish, Danish, Norwegian, Faroese, Icelandic.

*number*: a grammatical category to do with whether a word refers to one or more than one entity. In PDE, a distinction is made between *singular* and *plural*, but other numbers are recorded in languages around the world, e.g. *dual* (=2), trial (=3). OE distinguished singular, plural and dual numbers.

*Old English*: =OE, the language of the Anglo-Saxons, as spoken and written before *c.* 1100.

*Old High German*: a variety of German contemporary with OE.

*onomastics*: the study of names (personal, place) and naming-practices.

*palaeography*: the study of older forms of handwriting.

*paradigm*: the set of words which can be grouped together to form a *lexeme*.

*parts of speech*: words are traditionally classified into *parts of speech*. Parts of speech fall into two classes: *open* and *closed*. Open-class words are: nouns, lexical verbs, adjectives, adverbs, interjections. Closed-class words are: pronouns, auxiliary verbs, prepositions, determiners.

*passive voice*: see *voice*.

*phoneme*: either the smallest speech-unit that distinguishes one word from another in terms of meaning, or the prototypical sound being aimed at by speakers within a speech community. Replacement of one phoneme by another changes the meaning of the word in which it occurs; thus /a/ and /ɒ/ are distinct phonemes, illustrated by the pair /pat, pɒt/ 'pat, pot'.

*phonemic inventory*: the set of phonemes in a given variety of language. See also *accent*.

*phonographic vs. logographic*: in phonographic languages, there is a mapping (however conventional) between grapheme and phoneme, while in logographic languages there is a mapping between a conventional symbol and a word or morpheme.

*phrase*: a grammatical construction consisting of a *headword* and optional *modifiers*.

*place of articulation*: the location of the articulation of consonants, with reference to the lips, teeth, alveolar ridge (the ridge of cartilage behind the top teeth), the hard palate ('roof of the mouth') and the soft palate or velum.

*plural number*: see *number*.

*polysemy*: *lexemes* can have more than one meaning, i.e. they can be polysemous. Polysemy is exemplified by words such as **star**, which can refer to a gaseous body at the centre of a solar system or a Hollywood actor.

*pre-language*: a period of divergence between varieties of an ancestor language resulting in the appearance of a distinct language. Thus pre-English is the period when the variety which ultimately became English was diverging from the other varieties of West Germanic.

*present*: see *tense*.

*Present-Day English*: =PDE, i.e. English used in speech and writing at the present day.

*preterite*: see *tense*.

*principal parts*: those forms in a verb paradigm from which all other forms in the paradigm may be generated according to rule.

*proto-language*: presumed common ancestor language, thus Proto-Germanic is the presumed common ancestor of all the Germanic languages.

*root*: the basic lexical element in open-class Indo-European words, carrying the primary semantic content of the word.

*runes*: a distinctive Germanic writing-system. See also *fuþark, fuþorc*.

*semantic field*: an area of the lexicon dealing with associated notions, as classified in (e.g.) *Roget's Thesaurus*.

*semantics*: =meaning, as expressed through the lexicon and grammar of a language.

*singular*: see *number*.

*sociolect*: the accent, grammar and vocabulary of a particular social group.

*sound-change*: a phenomenon whereby speakers adjust their phonologies, or sound-systems. Outcomes of sound-change include mergers of previously distinct phonemes, the phonemicisation of allophones (splits) and the addition of new phonemes to a language's inventory, and the redistribution of phonemes within the lexicon (shifts).

*stem*: the *root* and *theme* make up the *stem* of a word, to which an *ending* may, or may not, be added.

*stress*: stress is to do with the assignment of prominence to a particular syllable. A prominent, or stressed, syllable, may be louder, or more heavy, or distinct in pitch, or may manifest any combination of these features.

*subjunctive mood*: see *mood*.

*suppletion*: a process whereby two older *paradigms* are blended to form a new paradigm.

*syllable*: in English, a syllable prototypically consists of a vowel, sometimes referred to as the *peak* of the syllable, which may be preceded and/or followed by consonants; a consonant which precedes the vowel is known as the *onset*, while a following consonant is the coda.

*synchronic*: synchronic ('with time') linguistics is concerned with the systemic features (or 'rules') of the language at a particular point in time and space.

*syncretism*: a process whereby *inflexional* distinctiveness is lost.

*syntax*: an aspect of grammar which deals with the ways in which words combine to form phrases, clauses and sentences, i.e. *constructions*.

*synthetic vs. analytic languages*: a synthetic language expresses the relationships between constructions primarily by means of inflexional endings. An analytic language expresses the relationships between words primarily by means of element-order and the use of special 'grammar words'.

*tense*: a category to do with time (from Old French **tens** 'time', cf. Latin **tempus**, PD French **temps**). Finite verbs in PDE (as in OE) have special forms depending on whether they are in the *present* or *preterite* tense, e.g. **I bind, I love** (present), **I bound, I loved** (preterite).

*theme*: in open-class Indo-European words, the primary semantic content of the word is carried by the *root*, which is generally followed by the theme, to which an *ending* may be affixed.

*transitivity*: verbs which govern an object, e.g. **love, bind**, are transitive; verbs which do not govern an object, e.g. **come, go**, are intransitive.

*transmission*: the grammar and lexicon of a language are transmitted from speaker to speaker primarily through speech, and secondarily through writing. Transmission is therefore the level of language to do with speech and writing.

*Verner's Law*: the Danish philologist Karl Verner (1846–1896) accounted for some apparently anomalous deviations from Grimm's Law by formulating a rule from which they could be generated.

*vocabulary*: see *lexicon*.

*voice*: a grammatical category which indicates whether the subject governing the form of the finite verb is the agent of the action, i.e. *active*, or the target, i.e. *passive*.

*vowel*: vowels may be defined as those segments of sound where the airstream from the lungs does not give rise to audible friction, or is not prevented from escaping through the mouth; all other sound-segments are consonants. *Vowels* may be defined as either *monophthongs* or *diphthongs*. Diphthongs are vowel-clusters with a glide from one vowel to another; monophthongs are so-called 'pure' vowels without any change in that vowel's quality in its duration.

**word:** a stable, uninterruptible grammatical unit, made up from a *free morpheme* and (optional) *bound morphemes*. See also *lexeme*.

**word-endings:** bound morphemes added to the stem of a word. See *inflexion*.

**word-formation:** = *lexical morphology*.

# References

*ASPR* = Krapp, G. and Dobbie, E. (eds.) 1931–1942. *Anglo-Saxon Poetic Records* (New York: Columbia University Press).

*CHEL* = Hogg, R. (gen. ed.) 1992–2001. *Cambridge History of the English Language* (Cambridge: Cambridge University Press).

EETS = Early English Text Society.

*OED* = *Oxford English Dictionary* (www.oed.com).

*TOE* = *Thesaurus of Old English* (http://libra.englang.arts.gla.ac.uk/ oethesaurus/). Print version = Roberts, J. and Kay, C. 1995. *A Thesaurus of Old English* (London: CLAMS London).

Aitchison, J. 1991 (and subsequent editions). *Language Change: Progress or Decay?* (Cambridge: Cambridge University Press).

Aitken, A. J. 1981. 'The Scottish Vowel-Length Rule', in M. Benskin and M. L. Samuels (eds.), *So meny people longages and tonges: Philological Essays in Scots and Mediaeval English presented to Angus McIntosh* (Edinburgh: the editors), 131–57.

Alexander, M. 1966. *The Earliest English Poems* (Harmondsworth: Penguin).

Baldinger, K. 1980. *Semantic Theory* (Oxford: Blackwell).

Ball, C. 1968. 'The Germanic dental preterite', *Transactions of the Philological Society*, 162–88.

Barber, C. 1993. *The English Language: A Historical Introduction* (Cambridge: Cambridge University Press).

Baugh, A. C. and Cable, T. 2002. *A History of the English Language* (London: Routledge).

Bennett, J. A. W. and Smithers, G. V. (eds.) 1974. *Early Middle English Verse and Prose* (Oxford: Clarendon Press).

Biggam, C. P. 1995. 'Sociolinguistic aspects of Old English colour lexemes', *Anglo-Saxon England* 24, 51–65.

Biggam, C. P. 1997. *Blue in Old English* (Amsterdam: Rodopi).

Biggam, C. P. 1998. *Grey in Old English* (London: Runetree).

Bosworth, J. and Toller, T. N. 1898–1921. *An Anglo-Saxon Dictionary* (Oxford: Oxford: University Press).

Campbell, A. 1959. *Old English Grammar* (Oxford: Clarendon Press).

Campbell, A. 1972. *An Anglo-Saxon Dictionary: supplement* (Oxford: Clarendon Press).

Chambers, W. and Wilkie, J. 1970. *A Short History of the German Language* (London: Methuen).

Clark, C. (ed.) 1970. *The Peterborough Chronicle 1070–1154* (Oxford: Clarendon Press).

Clark-Hall, J. 1960 (fourth edn). *Concise Anglo-Saxon Dictionary* (Cambridge: Cambridge University Press).

Collinge, N. 1992. *The Laws of Indo-European* (Amsterdam: Benjamins).

Dance, R. 2004. *Words Derived from Old Norse in Early Middle English* (Tempe: MRTS).

Daunt, M. 1939. 'Old English sound changes reconsidered in relation to scribal tradition and practice', *Transactions of the Philological Society*, 108–37.

Denison, D. 1993. *English Historical Syntax* (London: Longman).

Dickins, B. 1932. 'A system of transliteration for Old English runic inscriptions', *Leeds Studies in English* I, 15–19.

Dunning, T. P. and Bliss, A. J. (eds.) 1969. *The Wanderer* (London: Methuen).

Elliott, R. 1959. *Runes* (Manchester: Manchester University Press).

Fennell, B. 2001. *A History of English: A Sociolinguistic Approach* (Oxford: Blackwell).

Fischer, O., van Kemanade, A., Koopman, W. and van der Wurff, W. 2000. *The Syntax of Early English* (Cambridge: Cambridge University Press).

Fox, A. 1995. *Linguistic Reconstruction* (Oxford: Oxford University Press).

Gordon, E.V., rev. Taylor, A. R. 1957. *An Introduction to Old Norse* (Oxford: Clarendon Press).

Halliday, M. A. K. and Hasan, R. 1976. *Cohesion in English* (London: Longman).

Hamer, R. 1967. *Old English Sound-Changes for Beginners* (Oxford: Blackwell).

Haugen, E. (ed.) 1972. *First Grammatical Treatise: The Earliest Germanic Phonology/an edition*. 2nd edn (Harlow: Longman).

Haugen, E. 1976. *The Scandinavian Languages* (London: Faber).

Hogg, R. 1992. *A Grammar of Old English: Phonology* (Oxford: Blackwell).

Hogg, R. 2002. *An Introduction to Old English* (Edinburgh: Edinburgh University Press).

Hogg, R. and Denison, D. (eds.) 2006. *A History of the English Language* (Cambridge: Cambridge University Press).

Horobin, S. and Smith, J. J. 2003. *An Introduction to Middle English* (Edinburgh: Edinburgh University Press).

Hough, C. 2001. 'Place-name evidence for an Anglo-Saxon animal name: OE *\*pohha /\*pocca* "fallow deer" ', *Anglo-Saxon England* 30, 1–14.

Hough, C. and Corbett, J. 2006. *Beginning Old English* (Basingstoke: Palgrave Macmillan).

Hualde, J. and Prieto, M. 2002. 'On the diphthong/hiatus contrast in Spanish', *Linguistics*, 40, 217–34.

Jack, G. (ed.) 1994. *Beowulf: A Student Edition* (Oxford: Clarendon Press).

Jackson, K. 1953. *Language and History in Early Britain* (Edinburgh: Edinburgh University Press).

Jones, C. 1989. *A History of English Phonology* (London: Longman).

Kastovsky, D. and Bauer, G. with Fisiak, J. 1988. *Luick Revisited* (Tübingen: Narr).

Keller, R. 1978. *The German Language* (London: Faber).

Ker, N. R. 1957. *Catalogue of Manuscripts Containing Anglo-Saxon* (Oxford: Clarendon Press).

Ker, N. R. 1976. 'A supplement to *Catalogue of Manuscripts Containing Anglo-Saxon*', *Anglo-Saxon England* 5, 121–31.

Klaeber, F. (ed.) 1950. *Beowulf* (Lexington: Heath).

Lass, R. 1994. *Old English* (Cambridge: Cambridge University Press).

Lass, R. 1997. *Historical Linguistics and Language Change* (Cambridge: Cambridge University Press).

Laver, J. 1994. *Principles of Phonetics* (Cambridge: Cambridge University Press).

Lehmann, E. 1992. *Historical Linguistics* (London: Routledge).

Lockwood, W. 1969. *Indo-European Philology* (London: Hutchinson).

Lowe, K. 1993. 'Never say *nefa* again: problems of translation in Old English charters', *Neuphilologische Mitteilungen* 94, 27–35.

McCully, C. and Hilles, S. 2005. *The Earliest English* (Harlow: Pearson Longman).

McMahon, A. 1994. *Understanding Language Change* (Cambridge: Cambridge University Press).

Marsden, R. 2004. *The Cambridge Old English Reader* (Cambridge: Cambridge University Press).

Millward, C. 1989. *A Biography of the English Language* (Holt, Rinehart and Winston: Forth Worth).

Mitchell, B. 1985a. *Old English Syntax, Volume I* (Oxford: Oxford University Press).

Mitchell, B. 1985b. *Old English Syntax, Volume II* (Oxford: Oxford University Press).

Mitchell, B. and Robinson, F. 1992 (and subsequent editions). *A Guide to Old English* (Oxford: Blackwell).

Mitchell, B. and Robinson, F. (eds.) 1998. *Beowulf* (Oxford: Blackwell).

Mugglestone, L. 2007. *The Oxford History of English* (Oxford: Oxford University Press).

Myres, J. N. L. 1986. *The English Settlements (The Oxford History of England, Volume 1B)* (Oxford: Oxford University Press).

Nielsen, H. F. 1981. *Old English and the Continental Germanic Languages* (Innsbruck: Institut für Sprachwissenschaft).

Nielsen, H. F. 1989. *The Germanic Languages: Origins and Early Dialectal Interrelations* (Tuscaloosa: University of Alabama Press).

Okasha, E. 1971. *Handlist of Anglo-Saxon Non-runic Inscriptions* (Cambridge: Cambridge University Press).

Page, R. 1999. *An Introduction to English Runes* (Woodbridge: Boydell).

Pheifer, J. D. 1974. *Old English Glosses in the Epinal-Erfurt Glossary* (Oxford: Clarendon Press).

Prins, A. A. 1972. *A History of English Phonemes* (Leiden: Leiden University Press).

Prokosch, E. 1938. *A Comparative Germanic Grammar* (Chicago: Linguistic Association of America).

Pyles, T. and Algeo, J. 1982. *The Origins and Development of the English Language* (New York: Harcourt Brace Jovanovich).

Quirk, R. and Wrenn, C. L. 1955. *An Old English Grammar* (London: Methuen).

Renfrew, C. 1987. *Archaeology and Language* (London: Cape).

Roberts, J. 2005. *Guide to Scripts Used in English Writings up to 1500* (London: British Library).

Robinson, O. 1992. *Old English and its Closest Relatives* (London: Routledge).

Samuels, M. L. 1972. *Linguistic Evolution* (Cambridge: Cambridge University Press).

Smith, J. J. 1996. *An Historical Study of English* (London: Routledge).

Smith, J. J. 1999 (later edition 2005). *Essentials of Early English* (London: Routledge).

Smith, J. J. 2007. *Sound Change and the History of English* (Oxford: Oxford University Press).

Stenton, F. 1971. *Anglo-Saxon England (The Oxford History of England, Volume 2)* (Oxford: Clarendon Press).

Stockwell, R. and Barritt, C. 1951. 'Some Old English Graphemic–Phonemic Correspondences', *Studies in Linguistics: Occasional Papers* IV.

Strang, B. 1970. *A History of English* (London: Methuen).

Sweet, H. 1885. *The Oldest English Texts* (London: EETS).

Sweet, H. rev. Davis, N. 1953. *Sweet's Anglo-Saxon Primer* (Oxford: Clarendon Press).

Sweet, H. rev. Whitelock, D. 1967. *Sweet's Anglo-Saxon Reader* (Oxford: Clarendon Press).

Sweet, H. rev. Hoad, T. 1978. *Sweet's Second Anglo-Saxon Reader: Archaic and Dialectal* (Oxford: Clarendon Press).

Szemerenyi, O. 1996. *Introduction to Indo-European Linguistics* (Oxford: Oxford University Press).

Townend, M. 2002. *Language and History in Viking Age England* (Turnhout: Brepols).

Ullmann, S. 1962. *Semantics* (Oxford: Blackwell).

Van Coetsem, F. and Kufner, H. 1972. *Towards a Grammar of Proto-Germanic* (Tübingen: Niemeyer).

Waldron, R. A. 1979. *Sense and Sense Development* (London: Deutsch).

Welna, J. 1996. *English Historical Morphology* (Warsaw: Warsaw University Press).

White, D. 2004. 'Why we should not believe in short diphthongs', in A. Curzan and B. Emmons (eds.), *Studies in the History of the English Language II: Unfolding Conversations* (Berlin: Mouton de Gruyter), 57–84.

Wilson, D. 1981. *The Anglo-Saxons* (Harmondsworth: Penguin).

Wright, J., supplemented by O. Sayce, 1954. *Grammar of the Gothic Language* (Oxford: Oxford University Press).

# Index